ADVANCE PRAISE FOR

# GOVERNING THE *Self*

"In *Governing the Self*, Patrick Fitzsimons lays bare the intellectual and human shortcomings of human capital theory and managerialism. Delighting in the contradictions of ideas which both demand the independence of individuals and at the same time constrain them to an extent never known before, Fitzsimons exposes the powerful ways in which managerialism changes the ways we think and act, in accordance with a rationality which is itself irrational, but seldom questioned. He has a masterly control over the complexity of the ideas he explains and a vivid understanding of the way they work in the lived world."

Nesta Devine,
Associate Professor, AUT University, Auckland

"Patrick Fitzsimons presents a masterly grasp of Foucault's historical method in order to understand the effects of managerialism on education since the later part of the twentieth century. This book demonstrates poignantly how neoliberal managerialism undermines the public purposes of education. It constitutes an invaluable resource for those working with Foucault's ideas in education and also for those seeking to understand how education has been transformed by the neoliberal agenda. A rich book, warmly to be welcomed."

Mark Olssen, AcSS,
Professor of Political Theory and Education Policy,
Faculty of Arts and Human Sciences,
University of Surrey, United Kingdom

"This book provides an insightful reading of Foucault and a thoughtful critique of managerialism in education. *Governing the Self* raises questions of ongoing significance for all educationists in a neoliberal, globalised world."

Peter Roberts,
Professor of Education,
University of Canterbury, New Zealand

# GOVERNING
# THE *Self*

This book is part of the Peter Lang Education list.
Every volume is peer reviewed and meets
the highest quality standards for content and production.

**PETER LANG**
New York • Washington, D.C./Baltimore • Bern
Frankfurt • Berlin • Brussels • Vienna • Oxford

Patrick Fitzsimons

# GOVERNING THE *Self*

A Foucauldian Critique
of Managerialism
in Education

PETER LANG
New York • Washington, D.C./Baltimore • Bern
Frankfurt • Berlin • Brussels • Vienna • Oxford

**Library of Congress Cataloging-in-Publication Data**

Fitzsimons, Patrick.
Governing the self: a foucauldian critique of
managerialism in education / Patrick Fitzsimons.
p. cm.
Includes bibliographical references and index.
1. Education—Economic aspects. 2. Critical pedagogy.
3. Self-management (Psychology) 4. Neoliberalism.
5. Foucault, Michel, 1926–1984. I. Title.
LC65.F535   370—dc22   2011007679
ISBN 978-1-4331-1002-3 (paperback)
ISBN 978-1-4331-1001-6 (hardcover)


Bibliographic information published by **Die Deutsche Nationalbibliothek**.
**Die Deutsche Nationalbibliothek** lists this publication in the "Deutsche
Nationalbibliografie"; detailed bibliographic data is available
on the Internet at http://dnb.d-nb.de/.


The paper in this book meets the guidelines for permanence and durability
of the Committee on Production Guidelines for Book Longevity
of the Council of Library Resources.

© 2011 Peter Lang Publishing, Inc., New York
29 Broadway, 18th floor, New York, NY 10006
www.peterlang.com

All rights reserved.
Reprint or reproduction, even partially, in all forms such as microfilm,
xerography, microfiche, microcard, and offset strictly prohibited.

Printed in the United States of America

# Contents

*Acknowledgments* ............................................................................................. *vii*
*Foreword* ......................................................................................................... *ix*
*Preface* ............................................................................................................ *xi*

**Chapter One: Introduction** ........................................................................ 1
    Managerialism ............................................................................................ 4
    Public sector management .......................................................................... 7
    Managerialism in education ....................................................................... 8
    Chapter overview ..................................................................................... 10
    Why Foucault? ........................................................................................ 14

**Chapter Two: The Rationale for Reform** ............................................... 19
    The dominant discourse .......................................................................... 19
    Technologies of domination .................................................................... 22
    Oppositional discourse ........................................................................... 24
    Changes to the self through the mode of information ............................ 27

**Chapter Three: Metaphysical Sources of the Self** .................................. 31
    The Platonic self ..................................................................................... 31
    The Renaissance self .............................................................................. 32
    The modern self ...................................................................................... 34
    The dialectic and the rise of individual conscience ................................ 38
    The mediation of the self through language .......................................... 40

**Chapter Four: The Enlightenment Self** ................................................... 43
    What is Enlightenment? .......................................................................... 43
    Challenges to the Enlightenment self ..................................................... 46
    Heidegger's notion of self (Dasein) ........................................................ 49
    A sense of futility ................................................................................... 50

**Chapter Five: Technologies of Domination** ............................................ 51
    Power ....................................................................................................... 51
    Foucault and the epistemes .................................................................... 53
    Sovereign power ..................................................................................... 56
    From the monarchy to the modern state ................................................ 58
    From public spectacle to confinement .................................................... 59
    Normalization and disciplinary knowledge ............................................ 62

**Chapter Six: Technologies of Self** ............................................................ 67
    Knowing vs. caring for oneself ............................................................... 68
    The rational autonomous self ................................................................. 71
    Foucault's way out ................................................................................. 76
    An ethic of self ....................................................................................... 80

**Chapter Seven: Governmentality** ............................................................ 85
    The arts of government .......................................................................... 85
    Theories of State .................................................................................... 92

Liberalism and neoliberalism .................................................................................... 93
Governmentality ........................................................................................................ 101
Governance and discipline ........................................................................................ 102

**Chapter Eight: A Genealogy of Managerialism ........................................... 107**
The context of capitalism ........................................................................................ 107
The discourses .......................................................................................................... 110
Principles of managerialism .................................................................................... 120
Illusions of freedom ................................................................................................. 123

**Chapter Nine: The Management of Human Capital ................................... 125**
Human capital theory ............................................................................................... 126
Bio-power .................................................................................................................. 129
The management of busno-power .......................................................................... 131
The management of education ................................................................................ 134
The management of growth ..................................................................................... 139
The management of the State .................................................................................. 145

**Chapter Ten: A Poststructuralist Critique of Managerialism ................... 149**
The rational subject of managerialism ................................................................... 149
An analytics of preference ....................................................................................... 152
Rationality, choice and autonomy .......................................................................... 156
The subject of consumption .................................................................................... 159
The subject of work .................................................................................................. 163

**Chapter Eleven: A Poststructuralist Critique of the Subject .................... 165**
Poststructuralism ...................................................................................................... 165
The mode of information ........................................................................................ 166
The management of autonomy ............................................................................... 170
Construction of self through language as practice ............................................... 171
Managing oneself ..................................................................................................... 174
Implications for education ...................................................................................... 179

**Chapter Twelve: Futures ................................................................................... 185**
Poststructuralist possibilities ................................................................................... 192

**References ............................................................................................................ 197**
**Index ....................................................................................................................... 205**

# Acknowledgments

It all started with the writing of a PhD proposal in Christchurch one very cold winter's day not long after I had met Eleanor and while I was visiting fellow at the Teacher Development Centre at the Christchurch Polytechnic. The proposal was the result of discussions with Dr. Michael Peters of the University of Auckland who was then at Canterbury University. I did not however, realize where the investigation would take me. The work continued at conferences and other sites throughout New Zealand, London, New York, Bangkok (thanks to you Peter Fox for the opportunity to test some of the ideas in the multinational corporations), Melbourne, Sydney, and Brisbane. Most of it—thousands of hours in fact—was done in Auckland. As I approach winter yet again, the book is now completed.

First, I would like to thank Professors Jim Marshall and Michael Peters. Both of you are deeply implicated in the discourse within which this work is situated and you still have the courage to continue to explore new pathways. Both of you have stimulated my thinking, provided guide posts for me to follow in the early days, and helped me find my voice as my research progressed. From you both I have gained a whole new direction. Jim, I found your knowledge of the works of Michel Foucault to be first rate. And Michael, the papers we published together gave me the confidence to continue. To Professor Roger Dale thank you for your help on some aspects of Human Capital Theory. To my friend and colleague Stephanie Mackie: With your encouragement I developed the material in Chapter Eight which formed the teaching material for Curriculum Design which we both taught for four years during the time the government was changing the 'rules'. I would also like to thank Dr. Joce Jesson for reading an early draft, for helping bring the discussion down to at least some local issues, and helping me see that I might actually get the thesis completed.

To Peter, my brother, I also owe you a lot for the work we have done together throughout the time this book was coming together. Your capacity to think things through with me as well as assist me with my computer skills made it more probable that the thesis would be completed. Your proof reading and formatting at the end enabled this presentation. The errors however, as they say, are still mine. Finally, to my partner and co-author of other work, Eleanor, you have encouraged and challenged me in so many ways. And, although the book is completed, the relationship, thankfully, is not. Maybe it is now the winter of my content.

# Foreword

In his Acknowledgments to this work Patrick Fitzsimons alludes to the first day we met in Christchurch one day in 1991 when he suggested the topic of a PhD that he wanted to study. He was engaging and his enthusiasm was infectious. He clearly knew what he was about. A PhD in the New Zealand system of higher education is different from the U.S. system—there are no courses and generally there are only a couple of supervisors rather than a full committee and advisor. A prospective PhD candidate in New Zealand is expected to formulate a topic or question and to develop a full proposal including research questions and bibliography which is circulated among relevant faculty. Institutional acceptance is dependent on the perceived viability of the research topic and the demonstrated expertise of the candidate. Patrick had some ideas about what he wanted to study. He was a mature student who had worked in several schools as a teacher. He was already highly motivated, well organized, and a successful professional. He knew how to conduct research. He had written academic papers previously. He also had a range of different life experiences including recent and ongoing experience in business. He chaired a medical trust. He had lived in therapeutic commune for a while. He was great at communicating his ideas and he had a forceful personality. He was by all accounts an excellent teacher. What impressed me most was a sort of rebellious spirit he possessed and his experimentalism: if something didn't work he would quickly change tack and try something else. Patrick was also one of my first PhD students and the fact that we were of similar age cemented an immediate friendship that turned into an easy two-way learning relationship during his PhD years which quickly morphed into a close collegial relationship after he graduated. He was one of the most successful learners I have come across. He had a voracious appetite for learning and read even the most difficult texts with ease. What impressed me most was his personal confidence in himself and his own direction. He was the very definition of a scholar who loved his work. Patrick loved nothing more than immersing himself in a newly acquired text. He quickly became an expert on any topic or form of research and he read widely across the humanities.

When Patrick discovered Foucault it was as though the engagement was made in heaven. Foucault immediately spoke to him. The excitement in reading Foucault for the first time was clearly evident and Patrick didn't need much encouragement after being introduced to Foucault's thought. I know the response because Foucault had the same effect on me. Patrick read Foucault at white heat; he read everything he could lay his hands on; he read

Foucault's biography and all the secondary material that was emerging in English in the early nineties. He explored the influences on Foucault's thought and soon read Heidegger and Nietzsche as well as many of Foucault's contemporaries. The gusto and enthusiasm with which Patrick approached his subject matter was impressive. Within a short time Patrick had reformulated his topic as a Foucauldian critique of neoliberal managerialism in education. It wasn't long before he became a colleague presenting with me and with other colleagues at conferences in New Zealand, the US, Australia and Britain. His confidence and skill enabled him to make remarkable progress very quickly and soon he was publishing in the best journals.

It may seem a strange thing to say but it was a pleasure to watch him learn and also to learn with him. In short, Patrick was an excellent scholar on a mission and he soon won himself a position as researcher for New Zealand Council of Educational Research and later as an associate professor at James Cook University. Patrick is a close friend, a great colleague and someone I enjoyed hanging out with. This work is essentially his PhD thesis reworked and edited. I am really pleased that it has found the light of day and has finally been published. I think there is much that we can learn from it but I shall let the reader judge for herself.

*Michael A. Peters*
*University of Illinois at Urbana-Champaign, USA*

# Preface

'Full of mischief!' his mother used to say, 'Got the devil in him!' As his brother, I remember Patrick being trouble: for his mother, for his teachers, for church folk, and for those who tried to govern him throughout his educational career. Now, he is trouble for the prevailing dogma in education—managerialism.

True to his long-held view that education is a site of contest, Patrick uses this book to engage with the function of managerialism in the constitution of the self. Within the prevailing neoliberal meta-narrative, the self is construed as a *rational autonomous chooser*, with managerialism providing the imperative for individuals to redefine themselves in terms of human capital, and *homo economicus* as the archetype. Foucault's analysis of power, in particular the relationship between governmentality and subjectivity, explains the way self-regulation and control accompany normalization. The problem for education and for the self so-constituted is the way this relationship is firmly rooted within the rationality of government and unreservedly economic in both its focus and its outcomes.

Patrick's choice of Foucault to inform this critique is apt, and led him on a journey that I was fortunate to share with him over the years. We spent many an evening, over a red wine or two, discussing the relative merits of Foucault and Nietzsche in making sense of the rather strange world both of us were embroiled in as teachers in New Zealand. Considering the increasingly instrumental role education was being asked to play in economic development, we saw educational institutions reframed as production factories for the human capital required by business. Both of us had been brought up in a religious household, rather too severe in many respects, but one in which personal worth was more than economic productivity. Qualities such as honesty, integrity and self-reflection were valued, and one's neighbor was more than a competitor or a customer. Neoliberalism has no such values.

Patrick sought inspiration in the work of Foucault, while I went the way of Nietzsche. I'm not sure yet whether either of us can claim to have made sense out of the political milieu we call education, but we both agree that economic considerations have become paramount in driving the production of modern subjectivity, and that philosophical critique is useful in exposing the rhetoric that underpins recent education policy. Nietzsche and Foucault were invaluable in providing a basis for such critique.

Although Foucault was quick to avoid being associated with any particular intellectual tradition or philosophical category, there are clear similarities in many themes that emerge in Nietzsche and Foucault, and in fact, Foucault acknowledges Nietzsche as a significant intellectual influence. Both thinkers share a radical skepticism in which power, truth and knowledge are strongly linked. Both use genealogy to create new perspectives on the present and the past. Both embrace the fluid nature of subjectivity as a function of discursive rules. And both philosophers profoundly reject any totalizing or normalizing trend in favor of difference. Both can be seen, then, as espousing a perspective on human *becoming* (as opposed to *being*) in the development of subjectivity. In the case of the subject of managerialism, there is much to be done in exposing the economic and political role occupied by what Foucault calls a *regime of truth*, as part of a political discourse linked to systems of power, and understood as a system of ordered procedures for the production of statements. For Foucault, there is no universal truth and no totalizing theory, but rather, a set of mechanisms for the production of truth, a process for legitimating certain claims to truth, and techniques for identifying those charged with saying what counts as true.

The book concludes that the 'truth' of managerialism in education is inadequate for self governance on the basis that its subject, *homo economicus*, cannot adequately account for the *other* in the educational relation. In true Nietzschean/Foucauldian style, Patrick does not nihilistically leave the subject in tatters. Instead, he advocates ethical pedagogical relationships that explore open networks of obligation, decentering the teacher, the referent, and the self and its knowledge. Nor does he reject managerialism outright, calling instead for its disciplinary force to be delimited and some attention paid to the *other* in the pedagogic relationship. Such a direction is itself a *strategic reversal* of power relationships, and includes a de-emphasis on privatization in education policy—anathema to the neoliberal ideology of managerialism.

Nietzsche talked about 'untimely men', i.e., those prepared to stand outside the homogenizing influence of the State: those not caught up in the political rhetoric of the day. Patrick's perspective on the insertion of managerialism into education may not go far enough to qualify him as untimely, but as far as neoliberal policy makers are concerned, and in his preparedness to consider the possibility of a subject outside the disciplinary managerial mode of neoliberal governance, he would definitely fall into the 'full of mischief' category that his mother reserved for him years ago.

*Peter Fitzsimons*

# Chapter One: Introduction

*Governing the Self: A Foucauldian Critique of Managerialism in Education* is about the constitution of the self. Self-constitution is a discursive formation, taking place within a neoliberal discourse that is problematic as a mode of governance. Through self-constitution, the subject is also implicated in its own governance, presenting a problem for managerialism. Michel Foucault's (1991b) notion of governmentality is employed to expose self-management as a neoliberal disciplinary mode of self-constitution.

As a result of the introduction of neoliberalism, the State can be seen as minimized. But, at the same time, it has become more powerful and pervasive in terms of its construction of both the public sector and what might be called the regulatory civil society—a broad sphere of activity that encompasses the education sector. The insertion of a set of neoliberal practices (like managerialism) into education, then, makes for a problematic account of State reason.

In arguing that the subject of managerialism is implicated in its own governance, the book undertakes an historical investigation into the problem of the self, identifying a particular notion of the self implied by the discourse of neoliberal reforms in education. This self is said by Marshall (1995b) to have acquired a necessary faculty of self-production and consumption. That acquisition arises from an entrepreneurial imperative for neoliberalism to demand continuous production. Managerialism is the mode of discipline and the meta-narrative for this continuous self-production. Since the self is subject to neoliberal reforms, the management of self is a matter for education.

Managerialism is not rejected outright here, but its disciplinary force needs to be delimited and some wind taken out of its meta-narrative sails, allowing for what Readings (1996) calls *infinite attention to the other* in the pedagogic relation. Without that ethic, education is a commodity with no inherent ethical foundation despite its pretensions to enlightenment.

Four interrelated questions are addressed in order to provide a structure for this investigation:
1. What is managerialism?
2. What role has it played in the public sector reforms and in education policy?
3. What is the Foucauldian critique of managerialism and how does it relate to governing the self?
4. What follows from this critique for an analysis of managerialism in education?

These questions are addressed through an archaeological investigation within the philosophy of the Enlightenment to establish a genealogy of the modern managerial self. This self is ahistorical, standing apart from society, featuring characteristics of the European Enlightenment subject: humanism, rationalism, essentialism, individualism, universalism, and the self as sole source of agency, signification and moral authority.

The modern self arises from erroneous liberal and neoliberal claims that the process of self-development is free and politically neutral. Under a neoliberal regime of self-management, autonomy implies both freedom to choose and freedom from power, and even though managerial discourse presents the self as rationally autonomous, that self is trapped: it neither sees the effect of power on itself, nor admits that power is integral to its own functioning. Within managerialism, power issues are reframed as issues of authority. When this authority is problematised, it becomes contestable, especially when, as Foucault (1982: 221) points out, power relations allow for power to be characterized as "strategically reversible".

Within a neoliberal entrepreneurial market, individuals are required to experience themselves as acting rationally, autonomously, and maximizing their own self-interest. A neoliberal ethos makes the individual *seem* free, supporting popular belief about the so-called freedom of individualism. To critique this kind of freedom, the book engages with Marshall's (1995b) argument about the implausibility of the notion of the *rational autonomous chooser*.

In neoliberal culture, as in any other, the individual is subjectivized within the prevailing political rationality. But individuals still have agency and some will seek spaces within which to critique prevailing values. For managerialism to deny such agency constitutes a problem, since the neoliberal subject needs that agency for its ongoing reform. Reform to the economy, society, education, and hence the self, is frequently justified in terms of progress, although such reform may be more about reshaping than improving. Under conditions of reform, the self becomes unstable, forming and reforming *ad infinitum* to meet the challenges of neoliberal enterprise culture. Whatever form the self takes at any particular moment is just an interim stage in a process of continuous reform.

In neoliberalism, many influences shape the realm within which a 'knowing' subject can govern itself. The implication is that the subject is 'free' only insofar as it is constituted within the current dominant political rationality of neoliberalism, a rationality that entails a fundamental shift in the relationship between the individual and the State. Neoliberalism has been adopted as both the theoretical and the political basis of the reforms and provides a context for altered subject positions. As Peters (1993: 49) puts it, "even those theorists who are favorably disposed to the ideology of the New Right detect the common theme of those various standpoints critical of statism as a form of individualism".

The driving force behind managerialization of the self is the insertion of economic rationalism into institutions, locating the subject as part of a wider historical and political story. Recent structural adjustments to many facets of life in New Zealand, and to education in particular, limit the modes of existence available to the self. The country has been described as an experimental laboratory where neoliberal economic theory has been applied since 1984, and where a central state authority has revolutionized New Zealand's economy and its people's lives (Kelsey, 1995). A key point is the willing and voluntary nature of the reception of these ideas, achieved by neutralizing potential sources of criticism, and instilling a neoliberal ethos in the minds of the future generation that would become known as the *children of the market*. Education, construed as a set of governmental practices, is heavily implicated in such reform.

Within neoliberal reform, the individual as a self-managing citizen is redefined as *human capital* (OECD, 1993). The State has an economic interest in this human capital which it wants to 'upgrade' to a viable human resource, the value of which depends on an economic theory of supply and demand in the market. Under market conditions, the self must manage itself for the economic good of both itself and the State. A problem with the market is that the self is inevitably involved in its own self-management under the erroneous belief that the self is the sole and original source of signification and authority. Under market conditions of supply and demand, education presents the individual with an apparent freedom for self-management.

Education and training have been recently promoted as national human resource determinants of competitive advantage in the global competitive economy, redefining education as an economic activity, and personal achievements as appreciating human capital. One commentary suggests that the goals of education should focus more strongly on the economic and less on the social (Crocombe et al., 1991). The irony is that the reforms employ a notion of societal values within a neoliberal world whose very reason of state denies that there is such thing as society.

The idea of a national human resource development strategy aligns with the global economy that the New Zealand Qualifications Authority (NZQA) espouses as important for New Zealand, in its role as a signatory to several international economic accords. In one of these agreements, an extended role for international agencies is advocated in the development of human resources (Lythe, 1995).

Neoliberalism offers a limited account of subjectivity through its conception of rational man (*homo economicus*), an account promoted through the discourse of managerialism. Clearly, many new values, attitudes, skills, behaviors and particular ethics are required to be instilled in the individual for successful human resource development. Amid the neoliberal rhetoric of minimizing the State, State security requires more intensely self-governed subjects. Governance is to be deployed within institutions and in other spaces through managerialism. An important matter for governance, then, is what the new subject positions are to consist of.

## Managerialism

Managerialism can be explained in various ways. In management literature, it legitimates the control of individuals, their organizations and whole societies. Managerialism is a set of neoliberal practices investigated throughout this book as both a normalizing force and a form of disciplinary knowledge. Managerialism arises from an historical set of discourses under which managers are constituted as having certain organizational leadership expertise. It is the attribution of this very expertise that allows them to constitute their subordinates as objects in need of a disciplinary technology. At the same time, these subordinates come to constitute themselves as subject to the same discourse, a mechanistic relationship in which

> power is not totally entrusted to someone who would exercise it alone, over others, in an absolute fashion; rather, this machine is one in which everyone is caught, those who exercise power as well as those who are subjected to it (Foucault, 1977b: 156).

Managerialism renders discussion of other organizational possibilities mute, and presents itself as an antidote or rational organizational mode in an assumed irrational world of chaos. In its assumed superior rationality, managerialism presents itself as a moral technology, setting itself against social disorder via a set of discursively constituted oppositions. These counterpoised, dialectical nodes of thesis and antithesis locate managerialism as a modernist notion within the Enlightenment tradition.

The management *self*, then, is the rational, autonomous being of the Enlightenment world. Managerialism, through its valiant struggle against the forces of darkness, irrationality and disorder, attempts to fulfill the Enlightenment hope of an orderly, rational and progressive world. Its individualism is manifest in the responsibility that the individual self has for its own destiny. Its universalism is demonstrated in the legislative commitment of managerialism to ensure that all others within its discourse come to adopt the same view.

Managerialism is a form of economic rationalism. Applied to the public sector, it seeks to legitimate limited notions of allocative efficiency and policy effectiveness. In education, it stresses the need for *transparent budgeting, definable results*, and *value for money,* shifting the emphasis of education away from long term individual and societal benefits towards short term efficiency and profit (Marginson, 1993).

Originating in the private sector around the late 19$^{th}$ century, managerialism is a discourse that claims to be able to solve almost any problem, especially if we accept the managerial 'Great Man' theories which promote managers as being 'in authority'. However, the application of managerialism to education is problematic. Problems are 'addressed' rather than solved, and are often merely exposed or even ignored. Managerialism cannot politicize the public sphere; it merely makes efficient that which has already been decided. It may function adequately in relation to a commodified, economic view of education, but is unsuitable for theorizing the ethical engagement that educators aspire to. In this regard, managerialism has been criticized as a "fiction, but a serious and persistent one because of the widespread fascination with theories of management and the status of managers" (Rees and Rodley, 1995: 15).

Management is usually seen as a distinct function within organizations, promoting itself as universal, rational and individualistic. The values of managerialism thus resemble the key features of the subject of the Enlightenment project. In this sense, managerialism presents itself as neutral and scientific, restricting its sphere of activity to areas where rational agreement is possible—the realm of facts, measurability, and efficiency. Inherent in these positivist notions are values which depict a certain view of order in the world, and, consequently, life within organizations.

Because it claims to be neutral and scientific, managerialism is unable to engage in a debate about the value of its own objectives. Through its focus on rationality, efficiency and neutrality, it stands beyond debates on political and moral issues. Managerial calculations about economic efficiency set limits for the self, limiting the cultural and political context within which the self is situated. Unlike liberalism, neoliberalism has no internal spaces within which to contest values.

In a democracy, successful governance through managerialism requires the active cooperation of its 'knowing' subjects. Managerialism has deployed the notion of self-management for this purpose. The most recent wave of managerialism, culture management, allows for the introduction into organizational culture of psychoanalytic, self-referential technologies of self as integral to self-management. For its management of, and by, itself, the self can be viewed like a business enterprise—Self Inc. In this analogy, the self is construed as an autonomous enterprise which invests in its own human capital development with the aim of improving its position in the market. It has a 'Head Office' governed by reason and organizational power, which it exercises over its other internal, irrational departments such as the 'department of passion', the 'department of excess', the 'department of desire', etc. The inherent contradiction in this architecture of self is that the irrational (passion, desire, excess) are by definition, not under rational control. Such contradictions are simply ignored in the practices of neoliberalism. They are, however, explained in Foucault's notion of governmentality.

Governmentality allows for an analysis of the intersection of what Foucault (1988b) calls technologies of self and technologies of domination. Managerialism is not just about individuals having things done to them—individuals are also implicated in their own governance. That is why we need an account of the individual in the context of culture, politics and desire, not merely the limited account provided by *homo economicus*.

Governmentality allows for an account of social life that incorporates the ways in which individuals are multifaceted and complex beyond any economic theory. This flexibility is crucial because on the basis of the documented social costs of managerialism, there is a need to contest managerialism and reject its modernist explanations. Since education has been managerialised, any rejection of managerialism as a form of governance would be counter-productive to the advance of neoliberalism and would have implications for education.

Perhaps the most problematic managerialist fiction is the rejoinder from its supporters that if the managerialist prescription does not work, it is because workers and organizations have not 'properly' understood the prescriptions or have not implemented them fully enough. If the logic of the supporters were to be prosecuted, there would then be a more intense application of managerialist practices, including an increase in surveillance. This illustrates the problem with the incapacity of managerialism to account for the politics inherent in everyday practices. From a politicized perspective, the reason that managerialism is unable to implement public policy may be that public concern and political debate cannot be subsumed under a limited set of disciplinary practices. That is simply not the nature of public policy under a democracy.

Under *busnocratic rationality* (Marshall, 1995b), there are no internal spaces within which to contest the purposes, values, or even the disciplinary practices of neoliberalism, so it may be some time yet before it becomes generally accepted that managerialism is so limited in its explanations. When that time comes, there may be what Foucault (1982: 221) calls a "strategic reversibility of power relations", in which spaces might be opened up for critique, and managerialism as a mode of governance put under threat. That time, however, has not yet arrived.

Managerialism, as a modernist approach to governance, is problematic when its values, practices and theories are exposed. This is a serious issue for liberal education—one that underlies the purpose of this book. Education is potentially a site of contest over values about self-management, because education has traditionally involved the idea of self-improvement, an idea firmly grounded in the Enlightenment project. Under managerialism, the subject has been redefined through the application of human capital theory, to be managed through education for self-improvement. The subject is to be managed by itself, in the interests of the economy. The legacy of the Enlightenment is that this explanation of self-management is made to appear as solely for the benefit of the self and under its executive control. The irony is, however, the way that personal autonomy is unwittingly (for the most part) harnessed through education as a mode of discipline.

## Public sector management

One of the features of managerialist discourse in contemporary Western society is the tendency to define social, economic, and political issues as problems to be resolved through management. This is clearly the case in New Zealand, where since 1987 and with little debate, managerialism has been inserted into the public sector as a key element in dealing with complex social, economic and political issues of governance. Managerialism has been driven primarily by practitioners and private sector consultants rather than academics or theoreticians, and has had a significant impact on public administration, not only in New Zealand, but also in many OECD countries (Boston et al., 1996). Since managerialism was 'given' to education through the reforms, and since education is integral to governance in the modern state, it seems important to problematise the nature of this 'gift' by investigating its genealogy, its status and its implications for education.

Private sector managerialism may not be applicable across all sectors of the public service. Nor can it be assumed a priori that private sector organizations are managed any better than public ones, since the criteria for judging the value of the private sector arise from within the private sector itself. On the other hand, it would be churlish to argue that the private sector has nothing to offer public organizations. Nevertheless, there remain important differences between the two sectors, especially in relation to their operating environments, governance structures and accountability relationships.

Despite inherent differences, private sector managerialist practices are held up as models for the public sector to emulate and have been structured into the reforms to education. Private sector managerialist practices are considered by policy makers applicable to public education, and debates about privatization of education can, to some extent, be understood in terms of managerialism. Entities such as Private Training Establishments and ideas like user pays, contestable funding, direct resourcing, self-management, and state subsidy, are all dependent for their conceptual bases and for their implementation on managerialism.

Hood's (1991) theory of *New Public Management* (NPM) reveals the way, he argues, that the managerial role is privileged in organizations over the service provision role, through the elaboration of explicit standards and specific performance targets for personnel, measured in quantitative terms. Management emphasizes the value of private sector practices which demand greater labor flexibility, as well as relying on public relations to change the ways people think about the organization. In NPM rhetoric, there is a new emphasis on vocabulary that reflects enterprise and action, rather than professional tradition and service. According to its apologists, managerialism is bringing about a cultural revolution in the way public sector services are thought about and designed (Hood, 1991).

## Managerialism in education

Managerialism has had a significant role in the recent reforms to education in New Zealand. The Treasury Reports, *Economic Management* (1984) and *Government Management* (1987), introduced managerialism to public education, and are indicative of this discourse. The former publication asserts that the "aim of management should be the implementation of systems in the public system that can perform broadly the same role for the public service as the price system does in the private sector" (Treasury, 1984: 287). The report limits its discussion of education to issues of pricing and efficiency, arguing that the tertiary sector offers the greatest prospect for immediate improvement. Tertiary education institutions were targeted for corporate style restructuring of their governance and management along business lines. The value of the public system is now calculated on, and limited to, its economic role. Under Public Choice Theory, the remaining role for the public service is functional management, which, although still relevant, indicates the extent of the changes to the public sector.

The 1987 Treasury publication devoted one of its two volumes completely to an economic view of education in which improved performance was the focus. The report asserts that "micro-economic analysis of management issues ... can be applied ... to educational institutions in order to improve levels of performance" (Treasury, 1987: 18). The Government publication, *Performance Indicators For Tertiary Institutions* (Ministry of Education, 1989), outlines some of the ways in which the managerialist policy implications of *Learning For Life* (Department of Education, 1989a; 1989b) can be implemented.

The delivery structures of the NZQA are managerialist. Simon Upton, the (then) Associate Minister of Finance and Minister of Research, Science and Technology, remarked that "the concept of self-managing institutions remains a useful one" (Upton, 1993: 13) in the face of the Government's uncertainty about the role of the universities. According to the Ministry of Education (1991: 5), direct resourcing is one of the means of achieving "improved learning opportunities" through a "devolution of decision making to schools" where managerialism is imbued with what Boston (1991: 9) calls the "new institutional economics" of agency theory and transaction cost analysis. The important questions about which decisions to devolve, and which decisions not to devolve, have not been open for debate.

Against this, it might be argued that much of this change is rhetorical rather than substantive and that teachers will learn to clothe their actions in new sets of words while continuing to do the same old things. I do not think so. Rhetoric has its own discursive force in that it encourages people to see and define the world differently. The problem is illustrated in Hall's (1993) observations of institutional transformation within the Open University:

> The Open University is (was) filled with good social democrats. Everybody there believes in the redistribution of educational opportunities and seeks to remedy the exclusiveness of British education. And yet in the past ten years, these good social democratic souls, without changing for a minute what is in their hearts and minds, have learned to speak a brand of metallic new entrepreneurialism, a new managerialism of a horrendously closed nature. They believe what they have always believed, but what they do, how they write their mission statements, how they do appraisal forms, how they talk to students, how they calculate the cost—that is what they are really interested in now. The result is the institutions are transformed (Hall, 1993: 15).

It is tempting for teachers to think that resistance to (re)form, through specific protests such as campaigns by teachers against the direct resourcing of schools, will enhance professionalism through the maintenance of autonomy. But under managerialism, there are no spaces within which these issues can be contested legitimately. Those who do not desire quality, efficiency, improved productivity or self-management are simply defined as absurd, since these notions are represented as self-evidently good. Any resistance is seen as negative, and is likely to strengthen the resolve of those supporting the reforms. It might even be that threats to professional dominance in education will actually increase if alternative sources of education provision in the private sector were made available. This may already be happening through the establishment of closer links between formal education and the needs of business for specific skills and knowledge.

**Chapter overview**

This current chapter provides a brief introduction to the function of managerialism in the constitution of the self, some preliminary ideas about why this is an issue for education, and a rationale for drawing on the work of Michel Foucault to critique managerialism. Some quite complex ideas are touched upon, but in the interests of readability, detailed explanations are left to later chapters, where such matters can be analyzed in terms of the theoretical basis and related to their philosophical underpinnings. The chapter is, then, a brief overview of the argument and direction of the book.

Chapter two, *The Rationale for Reform*, presents the rationale for the book: a desire to critique the problem of the political, social and cultural experiment which New Zealand has undergone since 1984—an experiment characterized as a technology of domination. Commentators (e.g., James, 1992) have even called these economic reforms a revolution. This revolution involves the insertion of economic rationalism into the restructuring of the economy, the *core* public sector and the *residual* public sector. As part of the reform of the residual public sector, New Zealand's education system has undergone a series of rapid reforms which focused initially upon changes to educational administration. The reforms have been driven by a particular mix of neoliberal philosophy, including public choice theory, human capital theory, managerialism and so-called new public management.

Chapter three, *Metaphysical Sources of the Self*, outlines some sources of European notions of the self, culminating in what is termed the *Enlightenment Self*, located in its historical context through an account of the from which it emerged. The chapter starts with an outline of a Platonic notion of self through reference to the philosophy of Plato and Augustine. Second, is an account of the Renaissance Self, reflecting the writings of Descartes, that show how the self became interiorized and disengaged from the Platonic world of Forms and Ideas. Third, is a discussion of the modern self of the Enlightenment project, as developed by Kant and Locke, is discussed. Fourth, is the development of the dialectic and individual conscience, with reference to Hegel. Finally, there is some consideration of the way in which traditional analytic philosophy characterizes the relationship between body and mind through the mediation of language.

Chapter four, *The Rise and Fall of Enlightenment Notions of Self*, considers some factors that influenced the development of the Enlightenment self. The Enlightenment self is described as a transcendent self that describes itself in its own terms and within its own discourses. Three key elements of this self (rationalism, humanism, and individualism) are used to explain some key resemblances to the self of managerialism. Finally, challenges to Enlightenment notions of self are presented with reference to Hume, Nietzsche and Heidegger. Since Foucault acknowledges Nietzsche and Heidegger as his intellectual antecedents, this provides a background for chapters five and six, where Foucault's attack on the Enlightenment self is elaborated.

Chapter five, *Technologies of Domination*, explains part of Foucault's attack on Enlightenment notions of the self, focusing on his contention that there never was such a thing as the essential, rational, humanist subject of Enlightenment proportions. In his account of domination, the subject is shown to be merely an artifact of the discourses of a disciplinary society. Because of the force of counter-arguments against Enlightenment notions of the self, managerial constructions of the self based on such Enlightenment notions of self are problematic for governance.

Chapter six, *Technologies of Self*, presents the other part of Foucault's criticism of the Enlightenment, considering the way in which individuals act upon themselves to produce their subjectivity. It examines Poster's (1993) account of three historical shifts in Foucault's thinking about the constitution of the self. Foucault's focus on ethics involves a hermeneutics of the self using a strategy of historicism, the emphasis being on the activity of self-constitution in discursive practices. Foucault's distinction between *knowing* oneself and *caring for* oneself is discussed, leading to consideration of an individualized ethics of self as one of the problems generated by the spread of neoliberalism.

Chapter seven, *Governmentality*, focuses on practices such as the infinite and strategically reversible relations of power not able to be subsumed by neoclassical economics. Since it cannot be accounted for within neoliberal explanations, governmentality offers a critique of the *homo economicus* of managerialism. The chapter locates Foucault's genealogy of the arts of government as a rupture with sovereign power. Theories of State are rejected as they attend too much to institutions and too little to practices. Following Foucault, liberalism provides a rational basis for governmental practices, not as a type of society but as a formula of rule. The challenge of neoliberalism is then outlined, with the notion of governmentality allowing for the possibility of explanations of the self that go beyond the economic. In this respect, governmentality provides a more satisfactory account than neoliberalism of the way in which subjectivities are developed. Managerialism, and therefore self-management, are identified as problematic modes of discipline.

The theme of chapter eight, *A Genealogy of Managerialism*, is the managerial discourse introduced into the reform of tertiary education in New Zealand through the restructuring of the State sector. It is human capital that is managed under the Government's Industry Training Strategy, under the rubric of increased participation in tertiary education within a *seamless* education policy. There has not, however, been much public debate about managerialism—its genealogy, its legitimating rhetoric (apart from an account of *homo economicus*), or even its role in governance. The chapter outlines the discernible historical discourses of managerialism and discusses the way in which managerialism functions as a meta-narrative in various attempts to legitimate the governance of individuals, their organizations and their societies. Such a meta-narrative has been discredited following Lyotard's (1984) account of knowledge in the post modern condition.

Chapter nine, *The Management of Human Capital*, deals with the way education has been redefined to manage the development of human capital. Drawing on Marshall's (1995b) notions of *busno-power* and *busnocratic rationality*, the chapter critiques the way one neoliberal form of governmentality (Human Capital Theory) produces education as an economic device for New Zealand's new national economic enterprise. Marshall's ideas are used to critique the inadequacies of neoliberal aspects of governmentality that have been recently legislated into the education discourse.

Chapter ten, *A Poststructuralist Critique of Managerialism*, illustrates the way in which managerialism as a neoliberal doctrine provides an account of its subject of economics (*homo economicus*). The chapter points out some key resemblances of the managerial self to the Enlightenment notions of self, viz.: rationality, choice, collective rationality and autonomy. The conclusion is that the subject of managerialism is the liberal subject, but with the important addition of an almost mandatory faculty of choice that, within its compulsion towards entrepreneurialism, facilitates the development of an enterprise culture and an enterprising self.

Chapter eleven, *A Poststructuralist Critique of the Subject,* provides a general poststructuralist approach to the decentering of the subject, going beyond Foucault's critique of Enlightenment notions of the self. One of the more notable consequences of the introduction of managerialism into education is the inevitability of new explanations for subject positions, and hence for governance. These explanations demand new modalities of self, and so are necessarily political, although within official discourses there are some who find it in their interests to deny that this is so. Accordingly, the chapter investigates the possible changes to the self as a result of the mode of information. Some consideration is given to the way in which the self is constituted under modern electronic technology which has become integral to managerialism. The idea of metaphor as a technology of self is examined as an example of the way in which the self implicates itself. The chapter also exposes the social roots of psychoanalytic culture—a culture that admits to the possibility of technologies of self, paving the way for the development of 'culture management'. Within a psychoanalytic cultural context, managerialism is viewed as an element of governmentality.

The final chapter, *Futures*, supports the idea that social and cultural conditions determine identities. The chapter also advances the proposition that there is a significant degree of indeterminacy in the construction of identities and in possible interpretations of the life-world generally, allowing for alternative constructions of the self and for multiple notions of governance in education. Foucault's (1984) *attitude of permanent critique* allows for multiple and changing subjectivities, negating the notion of fixed identity.

Multiple or unstable subjectivities have traditionally been seen as a problem in terms of Enlightenment notions of universality, rationality, autonomy, authenticity, transparency, and the idea of a self with a unified, stable core. The argument is that discontinuities, ambiguities, tensions, and even chaos, are actually ways of characterizing the postmodern world. These ideas feature in the exercise of *power/knowledge* (Gordon, 1980) in constituting the self. If this self is to be involved in its own governance, it will require more than an executive theory of managerialism. This issue is addressed through a consideration of the ethics involved in the pedagogic relation, regarded as fundamental to education.

## Why Foucault?

The question of the self has been problematised by various intellectual movements this century. Psychoanalysis, surrealism, existentialism, structuralism and post-structuralism have all called the self into question as too centered, too unified or too rationalist. In Foucault's case, "the issue of the decentered self becomes very complicated" (Poster, 1993: 64). His work on the self spans three periods or, as Poster puts it, positions. Position 1, the period of Foucault's archaeology in the 1960s, was a critique of the rationalist self, involving reversal, by pitting, for example, madness against sanity. In this strategy, the authenticity of madness was interpreted as a form of decentering and thus challenged rationalist claims. Position 2, the period of genealogy in the 1970s, was a critique of the self as a centered core. In this strategy, the focus shifted from subject to structure. Position 3, the period of ethics of the 1980s, was a critique of the hermeneutics of self through historical studies of self-constitution as discursive practices.

Foucault's critiques were a challenge to philosophies that totalize human experience: philosophies such as existentialism, Marxism and Critical Theory. For Foucault, the issue of universalism goes back beyond Hegel to the Enlightenment. Foucault argued that the thread connecting us with the Enlightenment is not faithfulness to doctrinal elements, but rather the permanent reactivation of an attitude, a philosophical ethos he describes as a "permanent critique of our historical era" (1984: 42). Accepting our heritage of this attitude is what Foucault calls maturity, and provides the basis of this current volume to offer educational research a new framework for enquiry into the management of education under a neoliberal regime. Foucault's commitment to ongoing critique as an ethic of self is not an ultra-relativist orthodoxy or a private whimsy. Rather, Foucault provides us with a distinctive view of history and historical method, emphasizing "multiple perspectives from which truth and the real can be grasped and the view that our attempt to understand the real is always mediated through the prevailing discourses of an epoch" (Olssen, 1996: 102).

Self constitution has changed radically over the history of Western discourse. In Foucault's theme of self-constitution, language is prominent, and self is constituted through discursive practices. This theme is developed further by Poster's (1993) observation that we now constitute ourselves as the object of our own knowledge through electronically mediated language in what he calls the mode of information.

Any inquiry into self-constitution must take into account how the self is implicated in the "strategic reversibility of power relations" (Foucault, 1982: 221). What is required is an analysis of power focused on education to show the possibility of the governance of the self through the construction of a variety of subjectivities. Foucault (1982: 223) argues that an analysis of power relations should be conducted under five main headings, presented here in abridged form:

1. The systems of differentiations which permits one to act upon the actions of others: differentiations determined by law, traditions, economic conditions, and so forth, which give some prima facie position for power relationships to be brought into play.
2. The types of objectives pursued intentionally by those who act upon the actions of others when power relations are brought into existence.
3. The means of bringing power relations into play, by force, compliance, consent, surveillance, or economic reward.
4. The forms of institutionalization. These may be a mixture of legal, traditional, hierarchical structures such as the family, the military, or the State.
5. The degree of rationalization that, depending upon the situation, endows, elaborates, and legitimates processes for the exercise of power.

According to Foucault (1982: 18), any relationship between individuals or groups designates the presence of power where "certain actions modify the actions of others". These powers include the political, economic, institutional, expert, technical and cognitive. Through such exercises of power, the self is constituted and constitutes itself and its relations. Political rationality is thus involved in notions of *self-development* in education.

Capturing this sense of power is what Foucault (1988a; 1991b) calls governmentality, an interpretation of governance, not as an application of sovereign power, but as an unstable state of the subject resulting from an interactive effect of the subject and the discourse. Governmentality is the interaction of technologies of domination with technologies of self. Technologies of domination are concerned with defining and controlling the conduct of individuals, submitting them through the exercise of power to certain ends so as to lead useful, docile and practical lives. Technologies of self permit individuals to effect certain operations on their bodies, souls, thoughts, conduct and ways of being, so as to reconstruct and transform their selves to attain certain states of wisdom, perfection, purity and even happiness.

Foucault's productive notion of power gives some force to the idea that, in a knowledge-based economy, those who name the world exercise power. To the extent that naming is unproblematically accepted as representing the real, the acceptance of the dominant narrative becomes a mode of self-governance. The adoption of Foucault's notion of governmentality argues for an explanation where the interactive functioning of both the technologies of domination and technologies of self, refers to governance. The current approach is not dialectical, but rather, focuses on practices which "possess up to a point their own specific regularities, logic, strategy, self-evidence and 'reason'" (Foucault, 1991a: 75). This focus is a Nietzschean genealogical approach, developed further by Foucault, in his argument that genealogy

> must record the singularity of events outside of any monotonous finality; it must seek them in the most unpromising places, in what we tend to feel is without history—in sentiments, love, conscience, instincts; it must be sensitive to their recurrence, not in order to trace the gradual curve of their evolution, but to isolate the different scenes where they engaged in different roles. Finally, genealogy must define even those instances where they are absent, the moment when they remained unrealized (Foucault, 1977c: 139).

Since neoliberalism can be regarded as an aspect of governmentality, and since neoliberalism has been established as the underpinning doctrine of the recent reforms to education, governmentality has relevance as a form of critique. In terms of Foucault's technologies of *domination*, we might expect such restructuring to result in the development of subject positions that reflect neoliberal doctrine. In terms of Foucault's technologies of *self*, however, the development of neoliberal subject positions are also partly dependent on the way in which structural changes are represented to the self, by the self. The rationality of the characterization of self represented in the neoliberal discourse of managerialism, is therefore of major importance for research.

In an economic system which regards its human capital as its last untapped resource (OECD, 1993; 1994), a re-problematisation of managerialist doctrines, philosophies and techniques is vital. The Foucauldian 'historian of the present' has a research focus on evaluating what is happening. With regard to the rationality of managerialism, a Foucauldian critique might ask: What is the condition of the subject? the economy? the system? What accounts for the problems and what would lead to their improvement? What effects have managerialism produced in the past? What can be done and should be done? By whom? A Foucauldian analysis does not preclude that at some times and in some places, there are progressive practices. The point is, however, that progress is not inevitable.

The subject of governance in education needs to be re-theorized and taken beyond the discourse of executive management. If management requires new conceptualizations and ethical positions, how can education be restrained within a tradition of management that is already under-theorized? Foucault's notion of governmentality highlights the absurdity of the present trap of reform to education within neoliberal philosophy. That philosophy is simply too limited to account for the self in an ethical sense.

Alternative constructions are unlikely to be welcomed within the metanarrative of neoliberalism. This is especially so when the poststructural subject exhibits and acknowledges all the discontinuities, ambiguities, tensions, and chaos for which neoliberalism cannot account and which managerialism cannot discipline, but which all feature in relations of power. By opening up spaces for self-governance through alternative subjectivities, poststructuralism contributes to the very play of differences that underpins the poststructuralist subject. Such a move may even take the subject outside the disciplinary managerial mode of neoliberal governance.

Foucault's position has been described as nominalist, in that even the ways we describe ourselves emanate from reflections on knowledge and language—history made it so. As Ian Hacking (1986) argues, we may have been led along this route by reflections on knowledge and language, but we should drop the metaphors that they suggest. Instead, he suggests, we should turn to power, and metaphors of war and battle.

> The history which bears and determines us has the form of a war rather than that of a language: relations of power, not relations of meaning. Every new way in which to think of a person—and hence a way in which people can think of themselves, find their roles, and choose their actions—'is the pursuit of war by other means' (Hacking, 1986: 37).

Foucault's notion of productive power entails an immanent capacity for reversal. If Hacking is right, that new ways of thinking about our selves constitute the pursuit of war, then let battle commence!

## Chapter Two: The Rationale for Reform

Since 1984, explanations about New Zealand economic and social life have been dominated by neoliberal philosophy. The book argues, however, that there are problems with neoliberal explanations about its subject, *homo economicus*. One major problem for governance is the possibility of subject positions other than the *homo economicus* subject of neoliberalism, positions for which neoliberalism cannot account. In order to provide a context for critique of this problem, chapter two focuses particularly on education an overview of the rationale for what Foucault (1988b) calls technologies of domination that are implicated in the construction of alternative subject positions.

**The dominant discourse**

When social systems experience a structural crisis brought about by internal contradictions or unacceptable historical events, they have to be adapted to deal with that crisis. Capitalism was in such a crisis in the 1970s and so was restructured. The essential features of the restructuring have been described as the appropriation by capital of a significantly higher share of surplus from the production process; a substantial change in the pattern of state intervention, with the emphasis shifted from political legitimation and social redistribution to political domination and capital accumulation; and, the accelerated internationalism of all economic processes, to increase profitability and to open up markets through the expansion of the system (Castells, 1989).

These features of the global restructuring of capital have resonated in the New Zealand discourse since 1984. One commentator (James, 1992: 343) considers that the New Zealand experience can almost be regarded as a cold revolution in that *hot* revolutions may be increasingly replaced with *cold* (or *cultural*) revolutions in the age of urban, information-based, bureaucratic authority. With respect to the reforms to education policy, Lauder (1990) speaks of the *New Right revolution*.

Neoliberal philosophy, as the basis for monetarism, human capital theory, managerialism, public choice theory and the rhetoric about the minimization of the State, occupies the dominant position in New Zealand discourse—it is regarded as the only game in town. Neoliberalism presents notions of a 'hollowed out' State, mirroring the world scene where traditional international conceptions of sovereign nation States gives way to global visions, and where individual nation states are seen as economic accounting units in a global economy. From this conceptualization we are now able to refer to New Zealand as the national enterprise of New Zealand (Inc).

In this view, New Zealand is reduced to structurally adjusting its national economic capacity to adapt to, and/or contribute to, a global economy within world markets, where the nation and its people are said to have a place insofar as they have, or develop, economic value. According to the American Secretary of State in the time of the Clinton administration, the national State is now subordinate to the world economy (Reich, 1992). Under this rationale of globalization, a centralized model of State would indeed find difficulty in governing.

Neoliberal discourse undermines New Zealand's traditional trading arrangements. The theory is that after a long period of colonial dependency, New Zealand had lost its secure market in Britain for its primary products when Britain joined the European Economic Community. Expensive transportation to world markets generates the need to improve efficiency. World terms of trade are "largely determined by terms of trade fluctuations which are beyond the control of government" (Bayliss, 1994: 5). Foreign debt has risen as Governments during the 1970s borrowed to make up the difference. Rising unemployment is attributed to a lack of capital accumulation, a compounding situation which puts pressure on national budgets. This has put New Zealand, by comparison, among the lower groups within the OECD.

The drift towards consumerism in Western societies has raised expectations about consumption within New Zealand. The ability of individuals and corporations to transfer knowledge and financial capital from one country to another independent of governments now means that the sovereignty of a nation state such as New Zealand is greatly diminished (Reich, 1992). Modern electronic technology, like videos, internet and computers, have added to this effect through the provision of previously prohibited or largely unavailable information. As the information is made available, the effect on the subject multiplies.

New possibilities for governmentality from disciplining the knowing self arise from these influences. A self that constitutes its subjectivity in the face of technologies of domination can be regarded as a self-disciplined subject. Human Capital Theory is characterized in this book as a neoliberal technology of domination which is implicated in the development of disciplined subjects. Since Human Capital Theory is the dominant explanation for education in Western countries since 1960 (OECD, 1993), a recurring theme for this book is the critique of Human Capital Theory and its technology of domination through notions of self-management.

If the State withdraws to create space for the market, State security requires subject positions that are self-disciplined. If the reason of state is not convincing, the consequent subject positions may not be self-disciplined, and so they may not be governable within that particular political rationality. We would be left with *unruly practices* (Fraser, 1989), or even worse, unruly subjects. This lack of discipline may defeat neoliberalism as a reason of state which will have failed to produce intelligible subject positions for the self to inhabit. Individuals might not then trance themselves into becoming human capital, management subjects, entrepreneurs of themselves in their own enterprise of self-development, globally competitive *homo economicus*.

Monetarism abandons all controls in the economy except control over the money supply:

> The essence of monetarism can be conveyed in five assumptions or propositions; (1) that the quantity of money in the economy can be defined; (2) that the demand for money is stable and therefore its velocity of circulation is nearly constant; (3) that its supply can be controlled and (4) that there is a causal link between money supply and demand, and, as in the Friedmanite view, (5) a reduction in the money supply will be followed (about two years later) by a fall in inflation (Gilmour, 1992: 15).

The experiment in monetarist economics and the introduction of neoliberal philosophy have resulted in massive changes to the social fabric of New Zealand society where the experiment has been argued for on the basis of radical changes that have taken place in the economies of advanced countries. The literature used to justify the revolution in the New Zealand economy argued that there have been shifts in the global system of production and consumption which have changed the mode of growth in these countries and that, following overseas examples, State intervention must be minimized.

The monetarist policies of Great Britain and USA were underpinned by the idea that so long as the market and private business are left to their own devices, the *unseen hand* will provide guidance. This, according to Chandler (1977) has legitimated the introduction of managerialism into organizations, with the owners of capital as the *visible hand*. Individuals in this view are seen primarily as consumers not citizens. The task of economic redistribution is to provide consumers with money and then construct a market that will be a competitive mechanism to decide which services should be provided.

The value of State intervention is supported by O'Brien and Wilkes (1993) who argue that many successful economies, such as Japan, Sweden, Germany, Korea, Austria and Singapore, have demonstrated that the State can and does contribute to successful economic outcomes. In 1987 the fourth

Labor Government continued with the technologies of domination with three key passions—"to reduce inflation, to stimulate economic growth and to cut government expenditure" (O'Brien and Wilkes 1993: 26) with monetarism as the economic rationality. The primary features of monetarism under the Labor administration were explained as

> a major emphasis towards deregulating the economy; a move towards privatizing the state sector; a move towards introducing a business logic of commercialism into what remained of the state sector after privatization; a move to open the economy to external investors; a move to break with the old working class alliances traditionally tied to labor; an attempt to influence the field of social culture by altering the shape of public opinion; and, an alteration in the way we think about the state from a notion of welfare to a notion of individualism (O'Brien and Wilkes, 1993: 26).

**Technologies of domination**

Technologies of domination are the dividing practices that make an object of the subject. These practices are "concerned with how the self, or personal identity, is constructed by others, by 'official' discourses, and by what Foucault calls power/knowledge" (Marshall, 1995a: 24). To the degree that educators are affected by these technologies of domination, they are constituted subject to the prevailing rationality. This creates a demand for new subject positions within education which stem from a variety of sources.

I will now distinguish between three sets of technologies of domination within the context so far outlined. The first and most obvious mode of domination is the introduction of Government legislation in the New Zealand democracy without an electoral mandate (e.g., Sharp, 1994). The imposition of legislation on education sets up new possibilities for practices. Such structural and material changes have a bearing on the way educators act—new practices arise out of politics. The *State Sector Act 1988*, for example, removed the long standing assumption of consensus in relations between education workers and the State in New Zealand since the enactment of the *Arbitration and Conciliation Act of 1894*. Consensus was replaced by an assumption of conflict in the political sphere.

The second way the practice of domination is exercised is through the process used in a democracy to exclude certain groups selectively either from the conception or implementation of legislation. Reforms to education which separate policy conception from implementation, are but manifestations of this exercise of domination. One commentary by a diverse group of educators on the reforms points out that, "the educational sectors, institutions, unions and associations, at all levels, did not seem able to obtain

## The Rationale for Reform 23

'seats' at the agenda tables, especially when policy began to be implemented" (Coxon et al., 1994: 9). The undemocratic manner of the conception and execution of the reforms is an intellectual activity which results in the decline of democracy, especially when such changes are implemented with no debate and little study of the issues.

The New Zealand Qualifications Authority (NZQA) has a structural approach to exclusion. What counts as evidence of quality is now to be found as traces of individuals on paper through accreditation and appraisal systems. Educators are being asked to change the way they view themselves and their colleagues. Individualism, competition, measured performance, contractualism and entrepreneurialism are new, and the traditional professional collegial review system is no longer accepted as a suitable mechanism for indicating quality.

The criteria for 'success' of the reforms—the deliberate speed of the policy initiatives and the exclusory nature of the two Labor Government administrations—has now been admitted, even lauded. Roger Douglas, the architect of the economic changes in their present form in New Zealand, addressed the Australian Educational Council Conference in Adelaide on the 6th December, 1990. In that address he issued some advice for those considering implementing reforms:

> Implement reform by quantum leaps. Moving step by step lets vested interests mobilize. Big packages neutralize them. Speed is essential. It is impossible to move too fast. Delay will drag you down before you can achieve your success. Once you start the momentum rolling never let it stop. Set your own goals and deadlines. Within that framework consult in the community to improve detailed implementation (Lauder, 1991: 8).

The third means of the exercise of domination is the demand for subject positions through the unproblematic acceptance of the rationale of the reforms. The subject position under neoliberalism is that of *homo economicus*, characterized by a faculty of continuous choice in an enterprise culture. The performance of continuous choice is required for this subject to be fully human, in the sense of enterprising in a neoliberal world of competition and contract. The insertion of busnocratic rationality into the reforms to education suggests there is neither reason nor space to contest the rationality of the required subject positions. Under busnocratic rationality, the requirements of the dominant discourse are self evidently *how things are*.

There are then, pressures for changes to subject positions in tertiary education in New Zealand, with the reforms implicated in their construction as technologies of domination. These pressures have the opposite value system to that which underlies Barnett's (1990) account of the Western liberal professional heritage, which he claims, underpins tertiary education over the last two thousand years. Both positions, however, are still well within the Enlightenment frame of reference for the possibility of progress.

**Oppositional discourse**

Foucault's (1982: 221) notion of the strategic reversibility of power relations alerts us to the idea that the application of power implies an equal and opposite set of resistances since "freedom must exist for power to be exerted". There has been a range of oppositional discourses, but so far the neoliberal grip has not loosened. One idea is that New Zealand ought, at least to some degree, close its borders to the economic controls of the global economy.

Neoliberal discourse promotes the idea that 1984 was the beginning of economic rationalism in New Zealand, celebrating policy implemented after 1984 as the solution to the problems of policy before 1984. One supporter of W. B. Sutch (one of the architects of the welfare state in New Zealand), the New Zealand economist Rosenberg (1993), argues for a return to history when he disputes this type of analysis. When New Zealand was a welfare state (i.e., not liberalized) from 1938–1975, it had, he suggests, the best welfare system in the world. A notion of the basic social wage was the fundamental determinant of the State in this Keynesian economic system of governance. Rosenberg's data show that the overseas debt in 1938 in today's terms was $523 million and the overseas debt in 1974 was $465 million, whereas by the early 1990s it stood at $62000 million. This, he argues, illustrates that there was a change of direction in Government policy.

Rosenberg suggests that the liberalization began in 1975 when overseas borrowing began in earnest. If liberalism had been introduced since 1975, then it is wrong, he suggests, to claim that 1984 was the beginning of the changes. From an analysis of the growth of New Zealand foreign debt, Rosenberg (1993) argues that the problem was not the lack of competition in a deregulated world economy, but rather, lack of controls over the domestic economy, a problem that arises through the adoption of monetarism as economic policy.

The problems of 1984 were caused by liberalization back in 1975 and exacerbated in 1984 with the beginning of the restructuring. Rosenberg argues, therefore, that the current characterization of New Zealand as needing to compete in the global economy is a construction that is designed to suit transnational corporations. Under this rhetoric, New Zealand is no longer a nation State among many nations, but is rather, at the mercy of transnational corporations. New Zealand may even be now as insignificant as a minor stock market. He criticizes the use of language such as *global* instead of *transnational*, because it has the effect of masking the capital accumulation agenda of these corporations. One further important effect is to legitimate the rationale of economic determinist government policies that typically exhort the need for a new competitive individual morality that fits with an enterprise culture (Keat and Abercrombie, 1991) in order to market our products and thereby improve our terms of trade.

As a response, Rosenberg wants to see an import substitution orientation to the economy instead of an export oriented one. Import substitution and other controls would reduce the reliance on the transnational corporations. In this way New Zealand would not need to be dominated by competition which is masked as a drive for efficiencies throughout domestic organizations.

There is, in Rosenberg's account, a sense of nostalgia for the protection of the neo-Keynesian economy, which denies many of the radical developments that now define our social and economic world. Such nostalgia was evident in the political scene in New Zealand, with the move from the old two-party 'first past the post' electoral system to the German-style Mixed Member Proportional representation (MMP) system in which each party's share of parliamentary seats reflected more closely its share of the overall vote. This, of course, allowed for the rise of a number of minor parties, including the Alliance party with ideas about a protected economy.

Prior to 1984, world environmental politics had affected New Zealand as political pressure was put on economic decisions. New political parties emerged: New Zealand for example, paid a large social cost through the decision to stage the South African Rugby tour in 1981. Maori also were making demands under the rubric of the Treaty of Waitangi. A national Hui at Ngaruawahia in 1984 focused on the gap between Maori educational attainments and retention in the system. The gap between Maori and the rest of the population was widening with Maori registering towards the lower end of the socio-economic scale. Ironically, it was this latter type of equity argument that the Treasury (1987), among others, used to articulate the need for reform of education. Such reform was rather abrupt, with the introduction of Rogernomics—New Zealand's own version of neoliberal economic theory named after its them Minister of Finance, Roger Douglas.

The idea that neoliberal philosophy provides the subject positions necessary for democratic self-governance has been hotly contested (e.g., Marshall, 1993; Snook, 1994; Sharp, 1994; Haworth, 1994; Rosenberg, 1993; Kelsey 1993; 1995). There is opposition to the idea that the restructuring has produced the neoliberal dream of New Zealand as a competitive, highly skilled competitor on the world markets. Using empirical data, Peters (1996), Kelsey (1995) and, even more widely, *The Economist* (1994) asked us to rethink what the reported success of the neoliberal experiment means to most New Zealanders. And, under managerialism, even democracy itself is questionable (Enteman, 1993). Pure neoliberalism, as laid out in *Unfinished Business* (Douglas, 1993), devolved into a pragmatic form. There is clearly a question concerning the constitutional legitimacy of the reforms, since the State's assets were sold without express permission of the electorate, and by a government acting contrary to its traditional manifesto, the one under which it was elected. Several informed commentators claimed that there was no mandate for the reforms (Sharp, 1994; Dale, 1994)—a level of uncertainty which might suggest why Sharp (1994) entitled his book about the reforms *A Leap in the Dark*.

In defense of the reforms, it could be argued that there were certain negative features within the neo-Keynesian welfare tradition that had been built up in New Zealand since around 1938. Until 1984, government intervention had been taken for granted in providing for the good life: a prominent role for the welfare state; state-led education, health and social services; an interventionist strategy in relation to prices, incomes and employment; and government control of the exchange rate and interest rates.

There were, however, contradictions and tensions. Anomalies for example, appeared between welfare unemployment payments and wages for low paid work. By 1980, welfare payments had never been so generous (or perhaps it was just that work was poorly remunerated) but individuals were paying high taxes to support that welfare and were consequently getting less perceived value for their labor. Contradictions had been articulated by various commentators, but not enough to justify the introduction of neoliberalism by claiming (as Margaret Thatcher had done) that *there is no alternative* (TINA). According to both Kelsey (1995) and Waring (1988), there were alternatives, but both argue that these had been largely kept out of the discourse.

On one account, the reforms have failed, even on their own terms. Peters and Marshall (1996) argue that it was the Treasury's 1984 policy agenda that dominated the reforms. After an empirical review of data on the benefit system, national superannuation, social services, unemployment, income distribution, housing and education, their conclusion is damning:

> It is bewildering for these outsider groups living in the conditions of 'institutionalized poverty', to hear the government insist on a set of moral values stressing self-reliance, individual effort, and freedom from dependence on the State,

when the State itself, paradoxically, has been responsible for deepening a 'culture of dependency' it was officially committed to combating (Peters and Marshall, 1996: 16).

## Changes to the self through the mode of information

If we are constituted by discourses (and this includes knowledge about our self), then to that extent, the way in which we know ourselves is contingent; so too are the ways in which we are constituted. We need, then, to account for the discursive effects on the subject within what Poster (1994) calls the "mode of information", i.e., through the mechanism of interactivity. New information technologies have given New Zealanders access to new views of the world and themselves and put them in touch with the idea of the knowledge-based economy. Castells (1989) argues that the cities and regions of the world are being transformed under the combined impact of restructuring and a technological revolution. Postman (1993) asserts that *technopoly* (totalizing technology) has transformed our world and as a result we are also controlled by it. Poster (1990) argues that the flexibility of language allowed by the computer makes the written word less certain and less concrete with the result that we are faced with a new kind of communication experience. We now have new kinds of expectations. Watts (1994) refers to distanciated, disembodied, social exchanges which take place through computerized technologies. He says this mode of information does not have a pre-modern or modern cultural proximity with face to face contextual communication clues, and has thereby become an abstract enterprise for a small select group of knowledge workers who are implicated in the very idea of the State.

Lyotard (1984) reports on the condition of knowledge in computerized societies, a condition he calls postmodern. The status of knowledge is altered as societies enter into what is known as the post-industrial age and cultures enter the postmodern age. Lyotard (1984) says that scientific knowledge is a discourse that defines the object of study. He notes that science is in conflict with narratives and that the playing field is not level:

> Science has always been in conflict with narratives. Judged by the yardstick of science, the majority of them prove to be fables. But to the extent that science does not restrict itself to stating useful regularities and seeks the truth, it is obliged to legitimate the rules of its own game (Lyotard, 1984: xxiii).

Further on, he argues:

> It is fair to say that for the last forty years the "leading" sciences and technologies have had to do with language: phonology and theories of linguistics, problems of communication and cybernetics, modern theories of algebra and informatics, computers and their languages, problems of translation and the search for areas of compatibility among computer languages, problems of information storage and data banks, perfection of intelligent terminals, paradoxology. The facts speak for themselves (and this list is not exhaustive) (Lyotard, 1984: 3).

Such technological transformations can be expected to have an impact on knowledge. Research and transmission of acquired learning are two important functions of knowledge and are already feeling the impact. Cybernetics, for example, aids research by giving genetics its theoretical paradigm. In terms of transmission of knowledge, miniaturization and commercialization of machines "is already changing the way in which learning is acquired, classified, made available, and exploited" (Lyotard, 1984: 4).

Lyotard points out that the nature of knowledge will not survive unchanged in the face of these developments. Knowledge can fit into the new channels, and become operational, only if learning is translated into quantities of information. "Along with the hegemony of computers comes a certain logic, and therefore a certain set of prescriptions determining which statements are accepted as 'knowledge' statements" (Lyotard, 1984: 4). This knowledge is exteriorized with respect to the knower and becomes a commodity: it is produced in order to be sold—it has exchange value. Knowledge that has become an informational commodity ceases to be an end in itself; it loses its *use value*. Knowledge in this respect has become the principal force of production and has affected the composition of the work force. There are those who have 'knowledge' and those who do not. It is conceivable that knowledge will become the major stake in world competition for power. The mercantilization of knowledge affects the privilege that nation states enjoy with respect to the production and distribution of learning.

> The notion that learning falls within the purview of the State, as the brain or mind of society, will become more and more outdated with the increasing strength of the opposing principle, according to which society exists and progresses only as the messages circulating within it are rich in information and easy to decode. The ideology of communicational 'transparency', which goes hand in hand with the commercialization of knowledge, will begin to perceive the State as a factor of opacity and 'noise'. It is from this point of view that the problem of the relationship

between economic and State powers threatens to arise with a new urgency (Lyotard, 1984: 5).

Multinational corporations already have cross national access to storage and control of channels of data. Such corporations also have a hand in defining what counts as knowledge. The State must therefore reconsider its relationship to civil society as well as to the large corporations. The idea that the State can control or even guide investments needs re-examining, with implications for the restructuring of the State in New Zealand. Lyotard can visualize learning circulating along the same lines as money, where the pertinent distinction would no longer be made between knowledge and ignorance, but rather, as is the case with money, between *payment knowledge* and *investment knowledge*.

> If this were the case, communicational transparency would be similar to liberalism. Liberalism does not preclude an organization of the flow of money in which some channels are used in decision making while others are only good for the repayment of debts. One could similarly imagine flows of knowledge travelling along identical channels of identical nature, some of which would be reserved for the 'decision makers', while the others could be used to repay each person's perpetual debt with respect to the social bond (Lyotard, 1984: 6).

Lyotard refers to the above position as his working hypobook that defines the field within which he considers the question of the status of knowledge.

The examples in this chapter of official explanations for the need for reform, are technologies of domination that have functioned since 1984 to link global economic difficulties with the need for the reconstruction of self within a neoliberal State apparatus. Following Foucault's notion of governmentality, a few questions arise: What are the origins of the technologies? Of what do the technologies consist? How have the technologies become legitimated? What is the nature of the subject positions that are required to engage with these discourses? By what practices do subject positions become constructed? What are the poststructural subject possibilities? What are the policy implications for education? What are the implications for management of the self? Before these questions can be addressed, the next chapter will investigate the dominant notion of self that underpins Western society—that notion of self arising from what Hampson (1968) calls the Enlightenment.

## Chapter Three: Metaphysical Sources of the Self

Chapter three discusses the sources of a range of European metaphysical notions of the self, culminating in what is termed the Enlightenment Self. The Enlightenment self is a transcendent self that describes itself on its own terms within available discourses, rendering that notion of self tautologous. To understand this self, it is necessary to locate its historical context through an account of the discourses within which it was situated. The chapter starts with an outline of a Platonic notion of self through reference to the philosophy of Plato and Augustine. Second, is an account of the Renaissance Self, reflecting the writings of Descartes, that show how the self became interiorized and disengaged from the Platonic world of Forms and Ideas. Third, is a discussion of the modern self of the Enlightenment project, as developed by Kant and Locke, is discussed. Fourth, is the development of the dialectic and individual conscience, with reference to Hegel. Finally, there is some consideration of the way in which traditional analytic philosophy characterizes the relationship between body and mind through the mediation of language.

The chapter argues that in order to accept the conclusions of Enlightenment arguments about the self, their basic metaphysical suppositions need to be accepted. Otherwise, the establishment of the identity (essentiality) of the self is a false hope. As we approach what is increasingly being described as the postmodern world, metaphysical, intellectual meta-narratives are discredited. If fundamental suppositions about the self made by Enlightenment philosophers are shown to be metaphysical, there seems to be no logically binding position concerning the identity of the self emanating from the universalistic suppositions of their arguments.

**The Platonic self**

Sometimes the self is simply identified with Plato's concept of *soul*. Plato's philosophy was founded on an objective theory of reason which stood outside individual capacities which, in turn, were to be measured against such reason. Reason, as a mental activity based on a transcendent set of values, was seen as superior to experience as a way of knowing. Plato altered the pre-Socratic Greek ontology of the world-as-physis to one of discrete Forms and Ideas. This new conception of the world then led to a need for a new conception of the self as part of that world. Plato argued that the self is an essential, rational subject. In this view the body and mind are separated. Because experience was seen as inferior to reasoning, subsequent conceptions of self arising from experience must be evaluated as inferior. In Plato's scheme, reasoning might arise from experience insofar as thought is the theory of the Forms or Ideas. These eternal transcendent realities, which are directly apprehended by thought, are contrasted with the transient, contingent phenomena of our empirical existence.

The self in Plato's philosophy was to develop from the learner's discovery of rationality through Socratic questioning. Presumably the self would then be a rational being. But this self may not be rationally autonomous, as reasoning was based on a process that was to uncover an absolutely true set of transcendent values. Such values were assumed to be *within the self* from birth and rulers had, by definition, superior access to such systematic knowledge. Unproblematic acceptance of such an explanation of the order of things comes from an individual's life position where they are dominated by the rulers who know the 'correct' values.

Arguably, Plato's notion of self is thus politically dominated by the rationality of one philosophical thought system. Plato's view of self can be represented graphically as the inner circle of three concentric circles. The other two in outward order being the body and the physical world. Such a view, locating the self as the center and controller of the universe has prevailed in Western philosophy since Plato. This central position, possibly the necessary location of the self needed to construct empirical philosophy and later the social sciences, was exposed by Foucault as illusory.

**The Renaissance self**

Descartes wanted to reconstruct philosophy using mathematical reasoning as the paradigm for his new system of knowledge. The self was deduced as existing because the mind could think about its own thoughts: it was able to reason, and mathematics was the most precise and logical method. The mind was identified with consciousness. Descartes' notion of the self is intensely individualistic. Reasoning, in contrast to its position in the Platonic schema, is seen as a private mental exercise.

Descartes invoked three radical theses: first, his method of doubt, the insistence that every belief be considered false until proven true; second, his treatment of the mind as a distinctive realm, with the consequent question about how we know that we know about the world outside of our experience; third, his emphasis on the first person standpoint, on experience from one's own point of view, with an eye to establishing the objectivity of that knowledge and thus solving the problems raised in the first two points.

Experience as a way of knowing is shown by Descartes in the *First Meditation* to be suspect because it is possible that the self may be dreaming.

## Metaphysical Sources of the Self

He argued this with his dictum of *ergo dubito sum*. Arguing from this existential doubt, Descartes posits the existential truth that the self exists: *cogito ergo sum*—'I think, therefore I am'. To arrive at such a truth, the self had to rid itself of all previous pre-conceptions and accept Descartes' version of the analogy of self as a mathematical reasoner. The self is constructed through an a priori assumption of its own reasoning which depends for its validity upon an acceptance of the idea that it is self-evident that the individual thinks about their thoughts in the first place. This implies a notion of a *thinking thing*.

Modern philosophy, since Descartes, has been committed to the philosophy of the self as subject. It has been said that modern individualism was first articulated by Descartes because his theory requires the individual thinker to build an order of thought for himself, although within some universal criteria. The Cartesian quest is for clear and distinct knowledge, involving a "radical disengagement from ordinary experience" (Taylor, 1989: 182).

This radical disengagement from ordinary experience began prior to Descartes with the Augustinian internalization that has gone into making a modern identity.

> We 'have' selves as we have heads. But the very idea that we have or are 'a self', that human agency is essentially defined as 'the self', is a linguistic reflection of our modern understanding and the radical reflexivity it involves. Being deeply embedded in this understanding, we cannot but reach for this language, but it was not always so (Taylor, 1989: 177).

We go inward in secularized ways not to discover the God within, but in order to discover or impart order, meaning and justification to our lives. Taylor argues that Descartes, as part of a late Renaissance Augustinian revival, emphasized radical reflexivity, the importance of the cogito and the central role of a proof of God's existence which starts from *within*: from features of the individual's ideas, instead of starting, as in the past, from an external being. For Taylor, reflexivity refers to the idea of a continual monitoring of behavior and its contexts in modern society so that humans keep in touch with the *grounded* aspects of what they do, as an integral part of what they do—a thinking about *thinking*. Reflexivity is the antithesis of the role of the ritual in traditional societies through which individuals can commune directly with the sacred.

To the extent that this form of self-exploration becomes central to our culture, radical reflexivity becomes crucially important to us alongside our facility for disengagement. Radical reflexivity is different and in some ways antithetical to disengagement. Rather than objectifying our own nature and hence classing it as irrelevant to our identity, it consists in exploring what we are in order to re-establish this identity, because the assumption behind modern self-exploration is that we don't already know who we are. We lose our understanding of our self-experience through the disengagement from the world.

For Augustine, there was a cosmic order of things, but to know the good we had to be healed of sin in order to be able to love as we should. Sin was what stopped us from knowing God. Although the healing comes to us from within, the power of healing was outside us. Unlike Descartes, Augustine did not think that the moral sources were situated within us. So Descartes' source of moral strength of the self was a twist on Augustine's thinking. Augustine saw God as the ultimate source of moral strength and cosmic order: mastery over self was not possible, but the route to the higher order of the *Good* passes within. In his *Confessions*, Augustine refers to God as "the power which weds my mind to my inmost thoughts" (Taylor, 1989: 140). The search for inner thoughts as the origin of the self is the beginning of the rational self.

> The light Augustine finds inside is the light of reason, but in more general terms it is the light of the soul, which God created in His own image. This brings us very close to the Cartesian cogito. (Touraine, 1995: 36).

Augustine is the originator of that strand of Western spirituality which has sought the certainty of God within the subject. Descartes changed Augustine's theory to envisage gaining mastery over oneself. Reason for Descartes was the a priori source of the self. Augustine's understanding of thinking as an inner assembly of an order we construct, was the basis of Descartes' cogito—thinking is a kind of bringing together of the order of things. The moral sources are placed within us in Descartes' thinking and an important power (a priori reasoning as a source of self) has been internalized.

## The modern self

In the *Critique of Pure Reason,* Kant critiqued Descartes' empirical notion of self. Kant was interested in the question, Under what conditions is experience of an objective world possible? The argument that Kant employs to legitimate his conditions for knowledge, he called the Transcendental Deduction of the Categories. In Kant's philosophy there are two sources of human knowledge. The first is empirical, using incoming sense data from the sensory world. The second source is thinking, which is understanding through the imposition of transcendental form in the mind. For Kant, the forms are innate, i.e., a priori and biological. Unlike Descartes, Kant acknowledged the empirical world of space and time in the construction of knowledge.

Through transcendental analysis, Kant suggests we can uncover the universal and necessary conditions imposed on all experience and judgment. But these conditions provide no means for gaining knowledge either about the contents of experience (as opposed to its form) or about what transcends experience, a supposedly real world, a self and a God. The contents of experience can be learned only empirically and inductively, and such information is only probable. Metaphysical knowledge cannot be attained through empirical means since there is no way of telling if the conditions of experience apply beyond the limits of all possible experience, and no way of telling what to apply to them.

For Kant, knowledge is in part constituted by a priori or transcendental factors which are contributed by the mind itself and which the mind imposes upon the data of experience. Knowledge for Kant, is the 'product' (i.e., a priori structured product) of the knowing subject and not a description of an external reality. When the data are those of sense experience, the transcendental (mental) apparatus constitutes the subject's experience. These transcendental mental elements are of three different orders. At the lowest level are forms of space and time. At the second level above time and space are categories and principles of a person's intelligence among which are substance, causality, and necessity. At the third level of abstraction are reason, the transcendental "I", the world as a whole, and God.

It is through encounter between the forms of a person's sensory intuition of space and time and his or her perception, that phenomena are formed. Perception focuses on phenomena that are within the physics of space and time. For Kant, it is only through thinking that sense experience comes to be ordered and classified. So phenomena are wholly created within the transcendental apparatus.

But in limiting his frames of reference to internal reasoning, he was, like Descartes, disengaging the self from the external world. Although Kant admits to a real world (noumena), he says that the construction of knowledge (phenomena) cannot fully know what is out there. The self that 'knows', constitutes, to a considerable extent, the object of its knowledge (i.e., the phenomena). The transcendent apparatus of the mind structures experience. Such an explanation implies a notion of an all powerful, capable, universal, self: a human essence that is the center of the 'known' (i.e., in the mind through perception of the noumena) universe.

In Kant's theory, the self that is the fundamental source of concepts and experience is called self-consciousness—the transcendental ego. Principles that are basic to the various realms of experience are called the transcendental principles. Demonstrations that establish universal validity of these principles are called transcendental arguments. *Transcendental* refers to necessary and universal in contrast to the merely personal and physiological. For Kant, the transcendental self which structures the world for the individual, is the center of the universe.

Kant began with the view that human reason was universal and objective. The self for Kant was a metaphysical entity to be demonstrated through calculations of deductive logic. He used a combination of logic and scientific methodology. Universality and objectivity are tenets of empirical science. New historical developments in science added to metaphysics and logic. If logic and metaphysics were philosophical constructions, Kant's self then is not essential but historically constructed, despite his metaphysical analysis. Kant used rationalist means of mental calculations (i.e., deductive logic) to reach his conclusions about the nature of self.

Kant also applied reasoning to morality. For Kant, a rational agent is one who follows rules and principles of his or her own choosing. Initially, this seems to allow rules and principles that are merely subjective, but justification for holding moral concepts must not resort to factors outside morality, such as *inducements* of one kind or another—the realm of morality must be autonomous. Kant identifies the good will with the self-ruled, or autonomous will. The question becomes one of how the rational will, from which emanates all desires and feelings, can be translated into a principle of action.

The subservient relationship of practical reason (i.e., Kant's will) to desire is what Kant calls *heteronomy of the will*. A heteronomous morality is one which locates the supreme moral good in something outside the rational will itself. Insofar as a rational agent is compelled to act, through heteronomy, rationality is missing. Compulsion is not indicative of rational initiation. In order for the choice to be moral in Kant's view, it must be based on duty and not on something extraneous. It cannot simply be a matter of taste or preference.

The noumena are the real *things-in-themselves* which are not fully knowable. Through phenomena, they are at best a guess. Nevertheless, the element of incomprehensibility, or the sublime, plays, for Kant, an essential role, because without it moral actions would be explicable only in heteronomous ways; i.e., ways which fail to account for their distinctively moral aspect. The incomprehensibility of the world seems to provide the knowledge-construction structures of Kant's mind with a function. The choice between certain forms of knowledge gives that mind an exercise in judgment of morality inherent in the Categorical Imperative—*the* fundamental moral principle or law to guide all moral action, expressed typically as the prescription: "Act according to a maxim which can at the same time make itself a universal law". (Kant, 1988: 66). Compulsion (irrational impulse) then is not moral. But if freedom of the will is a condition that exists to enable the will to choose the moral law, then that, given the nature of the sublime, is not a choice but a programmed reaction to the causality of nature. Prior to Kant, it was assumed that our knowledge must conform to objects, but Kant incorporates the noumenal world in the process of knowledge formation.

If we accept Kant's distinction between noumena and phenomena we are able to discern the noumenal self. This self Kant calls *the* (the definite article) not *a* (the indefinite article) transcendental ego—'consciousness in general'. This noumenal self is a rich source of a priori knowledge, being timeless, and, since it is universal, not being *mine* at all but belonging to *all of us*. The noumenal self is the *thing in itself* which cannot be known. From its a priori categories, the mind constructs the empirical phenomena (appearance) of the noumenal self.

A second self apparent in Kant's work is the transcendental self that can choose between autonomy and heteronomy. Autonomy is the basis of freedom and heteronomy is the basis of determination. According to Kant, the noumenal self comes into relation with objects, and brings those objects under concepts, according to certain innate forms which lie ready in the mind and are imposed on experiences. The active imposition of these a priori forms is called synthesis, and the locus of the activity of synthesis is the transcendental unity of apperception, i.e., the transcendental self. The entire world order, including both objects of nature and the empirical self that perceives them, is produced by the activity of synthesis. The active knowing mind, or transcendental self, knows things as they appear, not as they are in themselves, including of course itself, which also it knows only as phenomena.

In Kant's theory of self-consciousness, consequences of our actions are reduced to secondary status. What counts is what one intends, the maxim or principle upon which one acts, the act of rational will, and not actual results. But when the social is reduced to secondary status, and the individual will and universal principles take priority, we lose what would seem to be the primary ground of ethics—our membership in a community and interaction with others. The historical promotion of humanist assumptions in this sense denies the human need for others and consideration of others. Instead of morality we have cosmic self-righteousness—the transcendental pretence.

Empiricists, such as Locke, believed that the self, although initially a blank slate, was built up through absorbing raw data in the form of experience. This empirical process constructs the self as a 'victim' of uncontrolled data sensations, a view which is to be contrasted with Kant's view of the self as an agent in its own selection. For Locke, the mind categorized and stored the data through a structuring process called reasoning which was attributed to the self as a biological given. Locke questioned the view that a self is only a material substance, and argued that consciousness makes personal identity. "Rightly or wrongly, Locke has been taken as the founder of the view that the identity over time of a person consists in facts about memory and the capacity to remember" (Shoemaker and Swinburne, 1984: 35).

## The dialectic and the rise of individual conscience

In contrast to previous philosophers, Hegel looked historically at important concepts about the human condition. On Kant's view of human nature, human beings are eternally divided between reason and desires and we will always be torn between these two aspects of our nature. But Hegel denied that this was immutable, suggesting that our concepts are embedded in ways of life, and thus in societies; and when societies change, concepts change. He argued that there was a development in the way history occurred, that it was always moving forward in what he termed the *dialectic process*.

Hegel asserted that, in Ancient Greece, human nature was more harmonious. People were not so conscious of any conflict between their desires and their reason. So the division that Kant saw must have been something that occurred historically, with, as Hegel argued, the development of individual conscience in Protestant Europe. And, because it was an historical development, it need not be a permanent feature. The conflict between will and desire could, in some other historical period, again be overcome and harmony restored. The dialectic is then the engine of progress.

Hegel's nostalgic view of Greek society envisaged a simple harmony between reason and desire because individuals had not considered themselves as separate from their city state, and able to make their own judgments about right and wrong—such was the thesis. Then, into that simple harmony came Socrates, whom Hegel considers a world historical figure because it was he who introduced the idea of questioning everything. When people tried to answer questions such as What is justice? or What is virtue? they realized that they had accepted conventional assumptions about these things. Socrates had no trouble in showing that their assumptions could not be sustained.

Under this assault, the simple harmony of Greek society broke down. Hegel considered that the Athenians were justified in putting Socrates to death because he was corrupting and subverting their society. Hegel argued, however, that Socrates was an essential part of the historical process which ultimately led to the rise of individual conscience. This was the second necessary element of historical development—the antithesis. It was the very opposite of the governing principle of Greek society.

We have moved now in history from what Hegel calls the *thesis* of simple harmony to the *antithesis* of individual conscience, risen to its height in Protestant Europe. But that, too, turns out to be unstable. It leads to the destruction carried out by the French Revolution, and the terror that followed; and so that too must give way to a *synthesis*. This is a third stage which combines harmony and individual conscience. Very often, in this process, the synthesis serves yet again as the new thesis from which a further antithesis will arise; and so the process will continue cyclically. Once people in a society question the simple harmony, individual conscience begins to rise and destroys the naive harmony on which the society is based.

The innumerable random conflicts of history might suggest that the direction of the dialectical process would be indeterminate. Hegel's explanation of the direction of dialectical change, on the contrary, shows it to have a direction. The goal for Hegel is greater development of mind towards freedom, and of increasing knowledge of ourselves. Hegel believes that history is purposively moving forward these principles of freedom and knowledge. Conflict and confrontation of opposed ideas, concepts, and forms provokes new ideas, concepts, and forms, improved by the dialectical process until a single idea emerges that satisfies the demands of all participants. This implies for Hegel the idea of an all embracing identity—the spirit. When this is reached we will have reached the end of history.

The underlying image of the dialectic is hardly universal and essential to human existence. The sense of self developed from Hegel is the projection of one's own 'enlightened' attributes of humanism, rationalism and individualism, onto the whole of humanity and the universe. His model of freedom as the goal of human history is to diminish the importance placed on other goals by non-European societies. History for Descartes and Kant was separate from the logic and reasoning of the self. Hegel's notion of freedom, however, is the reconciliation between mutually dependent reason and history.

With Hegel's concept of the dialectic, private structures of the self are a shared, communal reality; the *other* is needed in order to establish oneself as separate. A person had to objectify the self in order to see themselves from the outside and this was a source of alienation. Hegel had transcended the dualism of Descartes and Kant but alienation implies a residual duality (Poster, 1975: 26). Hegel's notion of truth requires a perspective that leads to complete comprehension. His account of reason is, then, closely linked to a narrow conception of rationality. The idea that there are no individuals in nature—that knowledge, self, and everything else is a product not of nature but of culture—is an idea that comes mainly from Hegel.

## The mediation of the self through language

The notions of self described in this chapter assume the existence of some a priori description (called *the self*) prior to its subsequent discussion and construction through language.

> The idea that the word 'I' stands for or refers to something—an idea that is presupposed by the question 'What am I?'—has its basis, not primarily in the fact that the word 'I' functions grammatically as a subject, but in the fact that corresponding to any first person statement there are third person statements that are in a certain sense equivalent to it and certainly 'about something'—what he (sic) is essentially (Shoemaker, 1963: 13).

An alternative way to investigate the nature or essence of the self is by considering how the self can be known. The traditional and popular concept of the mind and its attributed powers has mystified human discourse for centuries. Ryle (1949) who describes such an empirical picture as the *Ghost in the Machine*, says there is a human propensity for treating certain forms of linguistic expression as literally descriptive when in fact they serve as abbreviated references to things and relationships that are often very complex. Much of the language of description is metaphorical.

According to Ryle (1949) the official doctrine is the dualist view that a person is generally supposed to be able to exercise an inner perception or introspection. Persons are supposed to be able to view non-optically what is passing through their mind, without illusion, confusion or doubt. But at best, one person can only make problematic inferences about the inner life of another based on observed behavior. Thus the idea that others *have* minds is not directly knowable—only bodies can meet. Ryle (1949) says that the traditional doctrine of the mind/body split is a category mistake. He attributes the origin of the category mistake to Descartes. Descartes' religious beliefs conflicted with 16th century scientific discoveries about the mechanical workings of the body. To keep his theories intact he invented a mechanical theory of mind which is typical of what Ryle calls polarized, categorical thinking.

What is argued philosophically about the mind is, according to Ryle, at odds with what we know in the common sense world of knowledge. How, for example, apart from telepathy, can there be any causal connection between mind and body or indeed the minds of any two people? We commonly use language to convey concepts from our consciousness but with no way of knowing if they are descriptions of other people's minds.

Identity entails the idea that every person remains identically one and the same person throughout his/her lifetime. This idea fits with our common sense understanding that we know that we are not several people during our lifetime.

> This raises the idea that a person is not identical with their physical body which undergoes almost complete renewal in the course of a lifetime. The crucial question, then, is whether first person, past tense statements can be memory statements, of whether they must always be conclusions from what is remembered, conclusions that require justification in terms of criteria of identity (Shoemaker, 1963:136).

There is a question then, about whether we are is also identical with our own memories or states of consciousness which also change from moment to moment. If memory is our only or chief source of self-knowledge and the reliability of constructed memory is, as Hacking (1995) suggests, in question, then in this sense, we may not know who we really are. Even if we do, that knowledge is transitory, and so to say who we are is merely to note another moment in history. An implication of this is that a person is a substance, distinct from its own human body and from its own thought. As such, a person is capable of surviving the death of the body and of enjoying a conscious future state. Many religions have been founded on this belief.

The notion of identity entails the view that the apparently private mental states that each person is conscious of, are literally identical with certain states of the brain and nervous system. The brain and nervous system are accessible in principle to public, scientific observation. Identity is also held to be contingent or empirical and not a logical necessity. This latter theory of identity provides a materialist account of mind and conscious mental life. The identity theory of mind relates being in such a state of consciousness with some corresponding neuro-physiological state. It maintains that the modes of consciousness involved in the occurrence of thoughts, feelings or wishes cannot be considered as constituting a separate class of entities or happenings. This substance account of identity does not deny self-consciousness and nor, since modern theories of artificial intelligence accept this type of account of the self, does it assert an entirely implausible synonym of mental and neural terms.

Shoemaker (1963) argues that statements of personal identity are not capable of analysis. A succession of different events through time is not identical with the self. It is something else, a set of statements of events or statements of memories of events. Language is used as criteria but is not evidence of identity. In this way language is used to create the illusion of identity.

Considering the variety of sources of the self, there are many historical acts of faith as well as analyses of language, but no metaphysical argument concerning the identity of the self that is logically binding. The self is presented as a priori, but with many competing descriptions from both the rational-deductive and empirical approaches.

# Chapter Four: The Enlightenment Self

Chapter four begins by asking, what is Enlightenment? Key elements of the self are outlined within the philosophical movement commonly known as *the Enlightenment*. That notion of self is then seriously challenged with reference to the work of Hume, Nietzsche and Heidegger.

## What is Enlightenment?

When Kant asked in a German periodical in 1784, what is Enlightenment? he was not dealing with the question of his contemporary reality alone; rather, he was asking, "What difference does today introduce with respect to yesterday?" (Foucault, 1984: 34). Kant saw Enlightenment as a process that releases us from the status of *immaturity*, meaning a certain state of our will that makes us accept someone else's authority to lead us in areas where the use of reason is called for. We are defined, a priori, as immature and in need of the 'progress' offered by science. Foucault sees things differently:

> Enlightenment must be considered both as a process in which man participates collectively i.e., a political act, and as an act of courage to be accomplished personally. Men (sic) are at once elements and agents of a single process. They may be actors in the process to the extent that they participate in it; and the process occurs to the extent that men decide to be its voluntary actors (Foucault, 1984: 35).

There are two elements here: (1) the process through which the Enlightened state is to be attained; and, (2) the period of history to which it refers. The *way out* of our immature status, as Foucault has suggested, is characterized in an ambiguous manner. On the one hand, it is a phenomenon and a process; on the other hand, a task and an obligation. Man himself is responsible for his immature status. Thus he will be able to escape from it only by a change that he himself will bring about in himself. Kant assumes that it takes rational courage to face up to a difficult path out of immaturity. It could be argued (against Kant), that insofar as man is immature he would make immature decisions about the way out thereby negating 'escape' from immaturity. In terms of the period in which man participates collectively, the Enlightenment refers to European history from about 1700–1820.

Foucault suggests that modernity may be envisaged more as an attitude than as a period in history:

> By attitude, I mean a mode of relating to contemporary reality; a voluntary choice made by certain people; in the end, a way of thinking and feeling; a way too, of acting and behaving that at one and the same time marks a relation of belonging and presents itself as a task (Foucault, 1984:39).

During the advance towards Enlightenment, humanism, rationality and universalism were interiorized as essential to the self. The basic conviction of Enlightenment was that, through reason, mankind could find knowledge and happiness, as human reason gradually took shape through the 'natural progress' of civilization. The development of science, technology, the discovery of new lands, the improvement in European economies and the consequent lengthening of life spans gave the impression that civilization (as Europeans knew it) was synonymous with making enlightened progress.

The Enlightenment stressed tolerance, reasonableness and common sense as essential values inherent in what might now be called the rational, autonomous conception of the self. The Enlightenment period saw a "decline in religious persecution, judicial torture, murderous popular superstition, the humanizing of the laws of war and the growing outcry against the slave trade" (Hampson, 1968: 233). Rousseau 'discovered' a new inner self of considerable moral substance. Whereas Descartes' self appealed to logic, Rousseau emphasized feeling rather than reason as the key to the self, "and the private sense of goodness rather than the logic of self reference was its justification" (Solomon, 1988: 17). Locke's self was introspective, accounting for memory and, therefore, for personal identity over time; but it lacked the personal persuasiveness of Rousseau's moral inner self.

In examining Rousseau's confessions, Gutman (1988: 115) argues that "by abandoning himself entirely to his reverie, to the imaginary, the imagining self is annihilated, and the self and nature, me and not me, are merged into an undifferentiated and undivided unity". In other words, the individual differentiated self must merge with the world in order to create happiness. Rousseau's notion of self is by implication an essence, because to *lose oneself* by (acting as an agent) by becoming undifferentiated with the totality of the universe, one must *have* a self to lose in the first place.

The romantic thought of the Enlightenment was such that transgressive individuals—through their subjectivity—became the target for punishment (in the hope of enlightenment) rather than their crime. Enlightenment thinkers, however, did not see how this enlightenment could lead to other forms of oppression resulting from trying to enlighten indigenous peoples through colonization. The new scientific discoveries enabled technology to provide capacity for exploration, categorization and scientizing of other peoples. The methods of science were mimicked to enable social science that resulted in governance through the development of certain forms of knowledge. Because they were different (and universality did not allow for difference), conquered peoples did not, by and large, appear to scientists to be enlightened. The *other* became the object of scientific investigation.

Colonization of nations radiates the effects of subjection to Enlightenment, perhaps better termed *Endarkenment*, in that the effects of subjugation did not, in general, bring progress for colonized peoples.

As scientific rationality came to be applied to human nature, the hope was that

> experiment and reflection could expose wrong association of ideas, and chains of reasoning formed converging subjective paths towards an ultimate reality. In fact, both Berkeley and Locke, as Christians, assumed that individual sense impressions had an objective content that was guaranteed by God (Hampson, 1968: 98).

Human beings 'experience' God within themselves. Experience, in this sense, is empirical. In *Émile*, Rousseau portrayed a set of conditions where the essential human nature of Émile (the child) would be discovered and developed if kept away from the contamination of the world outside the garden wall. Demonstrating the primitive nature of Émile would show that man, apart from environmental influences, is essentially scientifically rational.

### Humanism

'Humanism' signifies theories that take human experience as the starting point for knowledge of humankind about itself and about the natural world. Systematic application produced a secular humanism which was directed against the claims of orthodox Christianity. Positivism and scientism are expressions of a belief known as scientific humanism which, assuming that scientific method is the sole source of knowledge, provides a rationale for the idea that the natural and human sciences in time will yield a comprehensive, rational explanation of human life. Previous superstitions and myths would then be replaced with a scientific model of the self which would be improved as scientific methodologies and knowledge progress.

In a different strand, humanism broadly embraces very different views not held together by a unified structure but by certain shared assumptions. First, there is a belief that human beings have a potential value in themselves: respect for this is the source of all other human values and rights. Second, the rejection of any system of thought about other human beings which is reductionist in terms of human consciousness, denies any meaning to human life, or at least regards people as having only instrumental value.

Humanism opposed authoritarian, religious, one-world views and promoted learning from empirical data. Its notion of self was not prominent prior to the development of science. When scientific rationality replaced more traditional religious explanations about physical phenomena, God was seen to reside within man. Hence, inherent in humanism was the *God space* of the all knowing, rational self.

According to Peters (1991) we might summarize the features of humanist construction of the subject as the fount of all knowledge, signification and moral authority, in universal and ahistorical terms, often standing prior and separate to society; as an origin and a unity of consciousness (a self presence), as the source of agency in history; and as the *hero* of knowledge, progress and emancipation. The humanist notion of the rational autonomous self is an historical, social construction, arising from the development of scientific thinking. It would, I conjecture, be difficult for an individual to maintain a presence in this construction of self for any sustained period.

*Rationalism*

The term *rationalism* is often used rather loosely. The rationalistic outlook presumes an optimistic view of the power of scientific enquiry and education to increase happiness and to provide foundations for a free but harmonious social order. In most cases, this view did not naively underestimate the importance of non-rational factors such as tradition and faith in the human economy. Reason was praised in contrast with faith, traditional authority, fanaticism and superstition. It chiefly represented an opposition to traditional Christianity.

Rationality can be identified as that property that satisfies two conditions: consistency and fulfillment of certain aims. The key to the Enlightenment self was its inherent rationality or its ability to represent the world through pure reason. Human nature was now thought to have an inborn faculty of reason. Reason was seen as basic to human nature, because reason enabled universal agreement on questions about the world and about mathematics. Confidence in reason and rationality was extended to social life, where the broader values of humanism, such as the pursuit of happiness, were seen as subject to the organization of reason according to nature.

## Challenges to the Enlightenment self

Hampson (1968: 119) considers that "the most telling blows against the self assurance of the Enlightenment were those struck by Hume". Hume argues that our concept of causation rests merely on the habitual observation of the same sequence of events in time. In other words we develop laws based on habitual observations.

Hume is a critic of the *substance* theory of self, seeing a person as nothing but a collection of different perceptions.

> Hume set himself to analyze the relation of cause and effect, and what emerged from his analysis was that the idea of force, or of causal activity, in its ordinary interpretation, was myth. There could be no necessary connection between distinct events. All that remains, then, is a series of fleeting 'perceptions' with no external object, no enduring subject to whom they could belong, and not themselves even bound to one another (Ayer, 1980: 17).

Denying the material nature of the self challenges the idea of the self as substance, or as thinking, perceiving or feeling pain. The logic runs, since I am not thought or I am not pleasure, there must be an *I* that knows and feels these things.

Hume argued against unqualified faith in Enlightenment powers of reason and experience. Reason and experience could not justify a basic belief about the world, that such a world exists outside of our experience. He denied that we ever actually experience the necessary connections between events that we call *causes*, so that there is no way that we can rationally or empirically justify even the most common causal explanations. For Hume, the mind was a blank slate that received the data as a bundle of sensations. The weakness of this notion of the self in the empiricist tradition is that the self is seen to be built unproblematically upon the reception of sense data. Hume attempts a serial account where the self has no substance or boundaries—a serial self. The trouble with Hume's account, though, is that if the self does not already exist, the data has nowhere to imprint.

Nietzsche observed the phenomenon of cultural relativism, presenting his critique of the notion of absolute truth through a parody of Christianity in his novel *Thus Spake Zarathustra*. There are an immense number of value systems in the world and it was not yet clear whether values are what distinguishes one group from another. There are other potential criteria for making such discriminations, e.g., history, language or biology. We need not interpret values only in moralistic terms either; there are non-moral values that tell us that we belong to a group, e.g., the proximity of another person in social conversation, dialects or clothing. People also identify with their history and their geography. Customs are observable behaviors from which we can interpret or infer values.

For Nietzsche, humanity *creates* values, but his assertion that "you can guess their table of values once you know their land, sky and neighbors" (Kaufmann, 1982: 170) implies a basis for the creation of values. Values are created by esteeming certain things to which the environment sets the limits. The individual of modern times is itself a recent creation, and since values existed prior to the historical development of the notion of the individual, it cannot be the modern individual who creates the value. According to

Nietzsche, conditions that supported previous beliefs no longer exist, and there is now no rationality for a belief in a deistic being.

In Plato's transcendent philosophy, the philosophical precursor to Christianity, the physical was bad and all we could ever know was the shadow of the forms. But for Nietzsche, the world of forms can actually be known (as Zarathustra's parable of the Cave demonstrates), and there is therefore, no rationality now for transcendent explanations. Since transcendence is now without value, Nietzsche proclaimed God dead, Plato wrong, and Christianity an illusion. Man, he contends, is all there is left to value. Therefore, for Nietzsche, the way that man (sic) conducts his life is of the utmost importance—he must become what he is. Nietzsche's imperative throughout his writings to *become who you are* is not about the emergence of an existing a priori essence, nor to achieving a finite potential, but about the ongoing process of creation and re-creation of one's existence.

Heidegger developed Nietzsche's individualistic self that *becomes what he is* into a social Being. Dasein is Heidegger's notion of existence. Dasein is constituted by set of existentials. Authenticity is an *existential* of Dasein. Dasein, the 'who', can be authentic or inauthentic. Heidegger (1962) gives two reasons for questioning what constitutes the 'who'. Merely stating that it is 'I' who is Dasein is ontologically misleading. This 'I' can be ambiguous. On the one hand, it can be seen as 'I' as a birthright or origin, and on the other hand, it can be seen as a task and therefore not ontologically guaranteed. The *who* of Dasein is not (most of the time), a self that conducts everyday existence. If this were the case, Dasein would be limited to what was currently the case and no other possibility could be entertained.

Authentic Dasein is self-determined and moving forward, but with death in focus. Although Dasein is not overcome by this knowing, it provides a sense of resoluteness (Heidegger, 1962). Dasein draws its possibility for existence from its *thrownness* into the world (*Gerworfenheit*). Thrownness, as an existential, denotes Dasein thrown into the world of its own culture, family and political life. This necessarily limits the existential possibilities of the *for-the-sake-of-whichs*, that in themselves contain values and allow certain things to be possible. So, for Heidegger, the choices available to Dasein are not culturally relative—they are delimited within what is possible in that culture.

What enables Dasein to be authentic is learning the cultural heritage, not pursuits like psychoanalysis, or a reductionist leaping-ahead by information services in our age of technology and artificially stimulated consumerism.

> The more authentically Dasein resolves ... Once one has grasped the finitude of one's existence, it snatches one back from the endless multiplicity of possibilities

which offer themselves as closest to one—those of comfortableness, shirking and taking things lightly—and brings Dasein into the simplicity of its fate (Heidegger, 1962: 384).

The authenticity of Dasein stands in critique of today, from a perspective of the cultural heritage into which Dasein is born. It is not possible to speak outside of a language community so we need a place from which to examine modernity. Without this heritage, there is nowhere to stand apart from conformity. Inauthentic Dasein, i.e., *das Man*, exerts pressure for conformity because it has no other option—it does not belong to any other speech or cultural community except for the one it presently exists within and from which it has no vantage point to critique itself. Authentic Dasein can access the past to anticipate the future and critique the present.

### Heidegger's notion of self (Dasein)

Heidegger's Being-in-the-World is based on his (1962) notion of authentic Dasein, engaging with the world to create itself with *absorbed concern*. This contrasts with two traditional, influential accounts of self: the Cartesian self, the disengaged dualistic rational Being discussed by Taylor (1989); and the Kantian rational a priori self with its universal categories.

Heidegger argues that philosophy must return to the question of Being which has been obscured by the preoccupation of Western thought with epistemology. This preoccupation has manifested itself in accounts that have begun both from the subject and from the object. Thus the Cartesian cogito did not enquire into the *am* of the *I am*, taken for granted as a background to the thinking subject. On the other hand, philosophies that have concerned themselves with the nature of *objects* or *things* have remained, in Heidegger's terms, at the relatively shallow level of the 'ontic', rather than permeating to the ontological. For Heidegger, we have to rediscover Being through the *primordial horizon* of time which is the means whereby both the subject and object *exist in time*.

> If Being is to be conceived in terms of time, and if, indeed, its various modes and derivations are to be intelligible in their respective modifications and derivations by taking time into consideration, then Being itself (and not merely entities, let us say, as entities 'in time') is thus made in its 'temporal' character (Heidegger, 1962: 40).

For Heidegger, the point is that time is not a derivative of space and Being is not a passing sequence of *nows*. Being exists in the coming-to-be of presence, which replaces both the idea of the *present* and the *point in space*. Heidegger resists the traditional Western tendency to spatialize time and the notion that the measurement of time-space gives us the clue to its true nature. He argues that measurable time-space is derived from (i.e., imposed on) time-space relations in Western culture. Dasein (the human being), then, has no essence except existence and is a product of its circumscribed choices. As Heidegger (1962: 53) puts it, "while Being-in-the-World cannot be broken up into discrete contents which may be pieced together, this does not prevent it from having several constitutive items in its structure". Such a Being is finite, its agency transcends the immediacy of sensory experience. This Being is historical in the sense that it has an awareness of the passing of time incorporated into the nature of social institutions. It has a memory incorporated into personality of the passing of events, and exists in time/space relations where "different processes of presencing and absencing are achieved in the human body, its media of sensory interchange with the world and others, and the extensions of those media made possible by varying forms of technology" (Giddens, 1995: 37).

Giddens further argues that such a view is a necessary corrective to both Anglo-American philosophy of action and Heideggerian hermeneutic phenomenology, neither of which emphasizes the body as the focus of presence. This lack of emphasis on the body is significant, but as I argue later in the book, absence of the body does not necessarily constitute a problem for managerialism.

**A sense of futility**

There is a sense of futility around the optimism of the Enlightenment. The spiritual collapse of hopes for progress, peace and human happiness in the course of the 20$^{th}$ century has led us to be skeptical about our ability to know either our self or the world, and about the merits of the ideals we have been striving for. This collapse has led to the collapse of belief in meta-narratives about the self, to a focus on intensive examination of ordinary practices, and to our personal involvement in what sometimes seem to be absurd, meaningless, situations.

From Nietzsche, we can take the self as having no transcendent value; life is all there is, and therefore what we do is actually what we are. Heidegger argues that modernity is essentially nihilistic as it suffers from *forgetfulness of being*. Both Nietzsche's and Heidegger's accounts of the self are a direct assault on Enlightenment.

## Chapter Five: Technologies of Domination

Foucault (1988b) identifies four techniques that human beings employ to interpret, control, and turn themselves into subjects: technologies of domination, technologies of self, technologies of production and technologies of sign systems. The first two were the most important for Foucault, and so form the subject matter of this chapter and the next. The current chapter will focus on technologies of domination.

Foucault's 1970 study, *The Order of Things*, has been described as "a mode of inquiry about the practices that create the self as a subject and which try to give themselves the status of a science" (Dreyfus and Rabinow, 1982: 208). Foucault's project was to "create a history of the different modes by which, in our culture, human beings are made subjects" (ibid.).

A later set of studies focus on the dividing practices that make an object of the subject. These practices are "concerned with how the self, or personal identity, is constructed by others, by 'official' discourses, and by what Foucault calls 'power/knowledge'" (Marshall, 1995a: 24). "The subject is either divided inside himself or divided from others. ... Examples are the mad and the sane, the sick and the healthy, the criminals and the 'good boys'" (Dreyfus and Rabinow, 1982: 208). In *Discipline and Punish*, for example, Foucault (1979) illustrates the dividing practices that set up a division between the body and the soul of the offender. In the early part of that text, Foucault describes the application of sovereign power to the body of the offender, Damiens. There is, in the later parts of the book, a shift to the application of discipline to the body of the offender, but with the subjugation of the soul as the object of power. Foucault appropriated Jeremy Bentham's idea of the panopticon to illustrate an ideal model of subjugation, although Marshall (1995a) notes Foucault's later focus on how we subjugate ourselves.

**Power**

Foucault was interested only in how power was exercised, arguing that modern power operates through relations within discourse—producing rather than repressing. The modern state can operate only "on the basis of other, already existing power relations ... (which are) a whole series of power networks that invest the body, sexuality, the family, kinship, knowledge, technology and so forth" (Foucault, 1977b: 122). But, as Marshall (1995a: 24) argues, this poses considerable problems for Foucault, since "it is the state which establishes the frameworks that permit the existence of many of the power relations with which Foucault is concerned".

> According to Foucault's strict nominalist position, power only exists when power relationships come into play. Power is not something which I can own or claim: only when a relation of power exists, when it is 'exercised' does power exist. Power in this sense is to be distinguished from power/knowledge which involves only certain relations of power and a certain kind of knowledge (Marshall, 1995a: 24).

In his earlier writings, Foucault targets the soul as the object and subject of power. Technologies of domination are applied to the soul through the body inside disciplinary blocks (prisons, schools, hospitals, etc). Foucault (1979: 29) argues in relation to the soul that "rather than seeing this soul as the reactivated remnants of an ideology, one would see it as the present correlative of a certain technology of power over the body".

By the time he wrote *The History of Sexuality, vol. 1* and *Afterword: The subject and power* Foucault had moved to a concept of power as productive rather than repressive. Unlike the sovereign power of his earlier periods, Foucault now elaborates the invisibility and pervasiveness of power in modern society. "The eighteenth century invented, so to speak, a synaptic regime of power, a regime of its exercise within the social body rather than from above it" (Foucault, 1980a: 39). The key features of this form of power are: power is productive rather than merely repressive; power circulates rather than being possessed; power exists in action; power functions at the level of the body; and, often, power operates through governmentality. Foucault's conception of power governs actions while nonetheless leaving individuals free.

> Power is exercised only over free subjects, and only insofar as they are free. By this we mean individual or collective subjects who are faced with a field of possibilities in which several ways of behaving, several reactions and diverse comportments may be realized (Foucault, 1982: 221).

Herein lies a strategic reversibility of power relations. In later writings, Foucault was able to examine the micro-physics of power from the ways in which we ourselves construct a self. He calls these *technologies of the self* which he argues, permit individuals "to effect certain operations on their own bodies, souls, thoughts, conduct and ways of being" (Foucault, 1988b: 18). Each technology implies certain modes of training and modification of individuals, not only in the obvious sense of acquiring certain skills, but also in the sense of acquiring certain attitudes.

Foucault (1988b: 1991b) was interested in the rationality of this governmental reason, developing the idea of "governmentality" (a neologism, for governmental reason) to explain that self-governance is produced by the interaction of technologies of domination and technologies of self. Governmentality, among other things, is implicated in domination under political discourses. Accordingly, this chapter is concerned with four interrelated questions about the politically dominated subject: What is the self (the subject)? How is the self constituted? What is Foucault's objection to the notion of the rationally autonomous self? What is Foucault's way out of the problems inherent to the humanist notion of the rationally autonomous essential self?

The conclusion is that although, in the modern state, a rhetoric of freedom is needed to service such notions as justice, reform, liberation, education, correction and progress, the outcome is *subjectivization*, a process Foucault sees as a neoliberal form of governmental rationality that is at the same time, "individualizing and totalizing" (Gordon, 1991: 36).

## Foucault and the epistemes

Foucault insists that *man* is a peculiarity of modern thought, arguing that before the end of the 18$^{th}$ century, man did not exist, and that he will disappear with the (apparently imminent) collapse of the modern episteme. According to Dreyfus and Rabinow (1982), *The Order of Things* is about that practice which creates the self as a subject. It is the mode of inquiry which tries to give itself the status of a science. In order to investigate this problem, we now need to explore Foucault's (1970) notion of the modern episteme.

The modern conception of order, signs and language, along with the conception of knowledge they entail, constitutes what Foucault calls the *episteme* of a period. Since an episteme is not an invariant cultural absolute, it needs to be understood against the background of previous epistemes. An episteme in this sense could be seen as a discourse framework that gives clues about what is possible—a fundamental ontological understanding.

The episteme of our Modern Age needs to be understood against the Classical Age which it followed. The dominant philosophical tradition in the Western world is descended from European thought. Two of the fundamental philosophers in this classical modern European tradition, Descartes and Kant, were essentially proposing a science of humanism where the rational power was a priori in the self and where the Enlightenment project was to be predicated on individual rationality. Descartes and Kant proposed a notion of self that took into account the scientific explanations of the time. But in order to understand the status of the human sciences which are weakly modeled on science, Foucault maintains that we need to understand the place of human sciences in the overall epistemological field of human knowledge (Gutting, 1989: 139). This requires a grasp of what knowledge means in modern culture, what forms it takes, and where, among these forms, the human sciences are situated.

In *The Order of Things*, Foucault (1970) bases his effort to understand what knowledge means in modern culture, on four fundamental propositions. The first proposition is that what knowledge is has varied from one historical period to another. To demonstrate this variation, Foucault analyzes three historical periods in Western culture: the Renaissance period which runs from 1500–1600; the Classical Age which runs from 1650–1800, and the Modern Age which runs from about 1800–1960. The second proposition is that any given epoch's conception of knowledge is ultimately grounded in its *experience of order*—that is the fundamental way in which it sees things connected to one another. The third proposition is that, since knowledge is always a matter of somehow formulating truths about things, its nature in a given period will depend on the period's construal of the nature of the signs used to formulate truths. The fourth is that since the signs most important for formulating knowledge claims are linguistic ones, the nature of knowledge depends on an epoch's conception of language.

Accordingly, in order to understand the cognitive status of the human sciences, we need to understand the modern conception of order, signs and language. Such a set of conceptions, along with the conception of knowledge they entail, constitutes what Foucault calls the episteme of a period.

## The modern episteme

When representation lost its central place, there was a fundamental break with the Classical episteme. In Foucault's view, this occurred around the end of the 18$^{th}$ century.

> As the archaeology of our thought easily shows, man is an invention of recent date. And one perhaps nearing its end. ... If those arrangements were to disappear as they appeared, if some event ... were to cause them to crumble, as the ground of Classical thought did, at the end of the eighteenth century, then one can certainly wager that man would be erased, like a face in sand at the edge of the sea (Foucault, 1970: 387).

According to Foucault, the modern age involved a fundamental reordering of reality. The modern age is a new way of regarding things and their interrelations. The basic realities are no longer related to one another by identities and differences. Foucault presents them as rather *organic* structures, connected to one another by analogies between their structures and hence between their functions. The essential reality of things is found in their existence as discrete structures. Their similarities of structure are not similar by virtue of "their adjacency in a classificatory table (or) due to the fact that they are close to one another in a temporal succession" (Foucault, 1970: 218). A thing is what it is, not because of its place in an ideal classification system, but because of its place in real history. The order of concretely existing things is from now on determined not by ideal essences outside themselves, but by virtue of the historical forces buried within them. Genealogy is one means of uncovering this sedimentation of history.

Corresponding to this new conception of order, there is, Foucault (1970) maintains, a new conception of the sign, one that displaces the central role that the Classical Age gave to representation. Modernity is closely tied to a decline or failure of representation in the Classical episteme. Although representation is still a feature in the modern conception of signs, language and of knowledge, it is no longer accepted as a function identical to thought itself. Since representation was no longer the unquestionable form of thought and knowledge, there was a need for a new sort of reflective inquiry that probes the origins and basis of the mind's powers of representing objects.

Representation is essentially a relation between a subject and the objects that it thinks about and what it experiences. Kant's approach to the philosophical account of representation begins from the side of the experiencing subject. He seeks in his transcendental philosophy of the subject, the conditions for the possibility of objects of representation. Here the idea is that the mind is a transcendental reality that constitutes the objects of representative knowledge.

But Foucault (1970) notes that it is also possible to approach the question from the side of the object. The idea is to find in the object the conditions of the possibility of the subject's representational experience, thereby developing a transcendental philosophy of the object. Such philosophies focus on life, labor and language which are introduced in the empirical sciences as non-representational sources of representational systems. Thus life, labor and language define fields of what we might term *transcendental objectivity*, opposite poles to Kant's field of transcendental subjectivity. Foucault argues that, in fact, they are simply another way of taking the transcendental turn introduced by Kant. We can look for the world in the world of discourse rather than in the *human-ness* of us.

With the decline of representation and the fragmentation of knowledge, language lost the central place it had held in the Classical episteme. The structure of language is no longer that of knowledge as such (i.e., the ordering of representations); nor is all scientific knowing just a refinement of the knowledge implicit in ordinary language. Foucault maintains that verbal roots do not represent objects; rather, they express the actions and volitions of a subject. In order to illustrate this idea, he suggests that we perceive language as a "product of will and energy, rather than of the memory that duplicates representation" (Foucault, 1970: 290). In this way, language manifests and translates the will of people who use it and is thus not merely a representation. Language can be seen as arising from what people desire, not as the knowledge that has been learned by elites. Creating knowledge in this sense is an exercise in freedom. Language is now itself "just one object of knowledge among others" (Foucault, 1970: 296). Even so, it is not entirely reduced to an object, as it is still present in a person's efforts to express what he or she knows.

Technologies of domination are concerned with defining and controlling the conduct of individuals, submitting them through the exercise of power to certain ends so as to lead useful, docile and practical lives. This section aims to illustrate the shift from the rationality of sovereign power, to the rationality of knowledge/power through disciplinary techniques, and finally to the rationality of the historical techniques of self which permeate modern society at the micro-level of power.

**Sovereign power**

Foucault conducts his discussion of the art of government through a reading of Machiavelli's *The Prince* (Bull, 1961), describing how a technique of government that he terms *governmentality* arose in explicit opposition to the conception of sovereign power proposed by Machiavelli. Throughout the Middle Ages and Classical Antiquity, there were many publications addressing the issue of sovereign power. Machiavelli gave advice to the Prince about such topics as proper conduct, the exercise of power, the means of securing the acceptance and respect of his subjects, the love of God and obedience to him, and the application of divine law to the cities of men. These are all issues of sovereign power, of which the Prince is the symbol. The prevailing discourse was that the prince ruled by divine right. The prince, in many cases assisted by the clergy of the Roman Catholic Church, was the temporal ruler of the church militant on earth. The clergy, as the Pope's representatives, were the spiritual arm of Christendom. The biblical story of the division of heaven and earth was the only admissible explanation of the ultimate order of things since the time of Christ. In a world of pre-scientific rationality, the theory about the divine right covered all aspects of life. The fact that some of the subjects of the monarchy traditionally and predictably had more power than others was explained away as a divine mystery, an explanation which itself provided further evidence of the rightness of things. The celebration of the mysteries were the mechanisms for preserving the explanations for the mysteries themselves. The hierarchies inherent in the system were thus sustained.

Sovereign power gradually became irrational due to pressures from the many political, social and cultural changes. The development of the modern state and the Reformation and Counter-Reformation were transformations that destabilized feudal social structures. From these forces there were tendencies towards state centralization on the one hand, and religious dissidence on the other. Government became problematic between these two inexorable forces.

The problem of government was posed in terms of a "language of persons" (Gordon, 1991: 12). To obey meant not a mere abnegation or servitude of the will, but an active form of life conduct. This neo-Stoic rationality of the individual was an easy fit with the notion of enterprise at the level of the State. There were problems around the government of children to which the development of pedagogy was a response, and questions about how the Prince should govern the State when sovereign power was no longer rational. The problems for the Prince in particular have been identified by Foucault (1991b) as being twofold: by whom the people will accept being governed; and how it is possible to become the best governor.

Foucault (1979) illustrates how the law was used by the sovereign to impose his power on the bodies of selected subjects. The punishments described in the early parts of the book *Discipline and Punish* were public displays of power by the sovereign on the body of the offender. In Foucault's (1979) account, this display was given with excessive force. Technologies of domination were employed by the sovereign in order to sustain a situation within which subjects could construct themselves subject to his power. One such technology was the manner in which an attack on the King's body was dealt with. The King's body was interpreted as the whole monarchy, including attributes like the demesne, servants, messengers and privileges. Any affront to the sovereignty of the King was taken to be an affront against the King's body and was dealt with publicly by a massive show of force. Torture and execution on the scaffold were the techniques of power. The executioner was the representative of the King and the whole display was of the King's power and its reassertion. Severe penalties for treason and perjury today are remnants of this tradition.

In the period just pre-dating the French Revolution, things began to change. Increasingly, as humanitarian philosophies became popular, the public displays of power were regarded as barbarous. There were also practical problems with these confrontations. If "power is war, a war continued by other means" (Foucault, 1977a: 90), then the public physical confrontations described in *Discipline and Punish* (1979) were too dangerous for the maintenance of the power of the sovereign in that they invited challenge to the King's representative and possible identification with the condemned from the observers of the 'war'. The process was contestable in that the person on display or the watching crowds could, and sometimes did, resist the proceedings. In a psychological sense, the observing subjects often identified with the underdog. If the condemned person resisted and prolonged struggles ensued, as sometimes happened, the executioner had to apply more force. If the condemned person was the object of too much force, the crowds sometimes changed their sympathies towards the condemned prisoner. Occasionally, riots broke out, scaffolds were overturned, and the condemned prisoner sometimes escaped. More importantly, such disruptions called into question the power of the sovereign.

In the interests of the art of sovereign propaganda, it was important that the power of the King be seen as the strongest power available. If punishment for the crime by death was the sole intention, it would have been more efficient and less troublesome to kill the condemned person quietly in some private place. The effect of the public punishments was not that crimes against the sovereign diminished in number or severity, but rather that social control was achieved through the subjectivization of individuals.

## From the monarchy to the modern state

Since the 17$^{th}$ century there have been various attempts to replace the monarchy with a State based on disciplinary practices that combine the functions of surveillance, normalization, and control. Later discursive practices included punishment, correction and education. The result is the development of the modern state, with power resulting from these disciplinary practices, not merely from the object described by them. Hence, Foucault's focus on practices.

One example of such a change, from an absolute monarchy to a constitutional form, occurred during the French Revolution (1789–1815). This was at a time when Enlightenment writers were contributing to the development, exposure and documentation of new or renaissance philosophies. The power of the King was undermined when traditional explanations supporting his rule became redundant through the application of scientific rationality. Since the 16$^{th}$ century, scientific explanations about physical phenomena had begun to challenge the more traditional religious mythology which buttressed sovereignty. For the first time the rationality of the divine right of Kings and all its supporting structures became questionable. All of this suggests a point of crisis which forebodes a rupture in rationality.

A belief that science explains change in physical phenomena has been central to the Enlightenment. One alternative explanation is that change is discursive—it moves in all directions at once. In purporting to explain the world and the actions of individuals according to a *scientific* model, the writers of Enlightenment science changed the focus, location and application of power by providing a new rationality for power, but neither an analysis of its nature or explanation for its existence. The scientific explanation was also employed in the political arena when the methods and alleged value neutrality of science was adopted by the human sciences.

The argument here concerns only a limited notion of the Enlightenment, one strand of which led to scientism. Overall, the period was characterized by the emergence of liberal ideas (e.g., Rousseau, Voltaire) that even today we regard as progressive and necessary—liberty, justice and freedom. In this strand, Foucault's target was not science per se, but the kind of scientism that eventually underpinned the knowledges of the human sciences and which gave them, through their analogous reference to scientific method, their status as knowledge about humans.

In the modern regime of power, the popular but now anachronistic cry, give me liberty or give me death! might be usefully altered to read, give me liberty or give me life in a disciplinary block! But liberty is also a *disciplined* concept. An individual kept alive in a prison was able to be the object of power whereas in the previous power regime, death was the limit of power. In relation to the change in the focus from death to life as the object of power, Foucault (1978) gives a detailed account of the change from what he calls the *symbolics of blood* to the *analytics of sexuality*.

## From public spectacle to confinement

The focus of punishment later shifted from the body to the *soul* of the offender. The French Revolution altered the relationship between the King and subjects, the rationality of the King's divine right to rule collapsed, and with this change came new applications of power. Humanist reformers (e.g., Jeremy Bentham and his Panopticon) designed more humane forms of control, such as the prison. The soul was to be reformed through control of the everyday actions of the body in the disciplinary blocks (e.g., the prisons). Modern methods of punishment, supervision and constraint occurred in the disciplinary blocks, although carceral organizations were rare in medieval times.

Prior to the 17th century, gaols and dungeons existed, but they were few and far between, and not places in which convicted criminals served fixed sentences[1]. Prisoners were kept in them either as a means of stifling political opposition, to be tortured in order to extract information, or to await trial. The mentally ill either lived within the community, or were forced to roam the countryside. There were no asylums or mental hospitals. With the development of the constitutional monarchy, overt displays of power no longer had any rationality. The explanation of subjectivization in a liberal age lies in the power/knowledge regimes built around the practices that evolved from the humanitarian reforms of the 19th century. Public commissions and initiatives were set up throughout Europe to investigate such issues as the slave trade, prisons, asylums and conditions of work in mines and factories.

Under the rule of the King, the body of the subject (the offender) had been the object of punishment. Under the modern state, however, the reformers sought to make prisons into penitentiaries for the correction of the citizen offenders. With the Reformation in Europe came the growth of a variety of Protestant religions, which focused not on punishment for sins as in past practice, but on the prevention and reformation of bad habits. The focus was on saving the soul by the application of power to the body in a humanitarian manner. Through observation, power was exercised in order to change the behavior of the sinner. Behavior as presenting phenomena was presumably an indicator of the existence of a soul. The language for describing criminals also changed. Offenders were to be known as *delinquents* and this had some very real effects. The delinquent was not only the author of his acts (i.e., responsible in terms of certain free, conscious will), but became linked to his offence in terms of instincts, drives, tendencies and character. "An attempt was also being made to constitute a new objectivity in which the criminal belongs to a typology that is both natural and deviant" (Foucault, 1979: 252).

Where a biographical cause could be determined through psychiatric investigation, individual responsibility for the offence was reduced and there was thought to be an even greater need for strict supervision. The body was regarded merely as the instrument that allowed access to the soul which was to be corrected. Methods of discipline were to be instituted and new architecture was to be designed. It was thought that individuals who were continuously under observation would be on their best behavior, and constant good behavior was thought to inculcate good habits which would, in turn, indicate a retrained soul. Continuous observation also allowed for the development of knowledge about the behavior of those being observed. The knowledge could then be recorded, calculated and published in the form of statistical norms. The knowledge was produced by virtue of the power to incarcerate and observe. Such knowledge has been termed *classificatory*, as it is used to classify degrees of normality, and therefore, delinquency.

The ideal space for the exercise of power relations, in the form of a space for surveillance, was Bentham's panopticon, "the perfect disciplinary apparatus (which) would make it possible for a single gaze to see everything constantly" (Foucault, 1979: 173). First, the purpose of the prison cell was to prevent imprecise and dangerous distributions of people, uncontrolled disappearances, and diffuse and dangerous circulations. Second, the organization of the timetable allowed for precision and rhythms to certain controlled timings. Third, activities were broken down into stages so that particular skills, abilities or capacities could be developed in a given time through constant exercise. The final means of control was developed through signals such as whistles and bells that signaled the time for changes. The panopticon enabled larger groupings and more remote control. Through these four means of power relations, confrontation was minimized, but not at the expense of power.

> In short, to substitute for a power that is manifested through the brilliance of those who exercise it, a power that insidiously objectifies those on whom it is applied: to form a body of knowledge about those individuals, rather than to deploy the ostentatious signs of sovereignty. In a word, the disciplines are the ensemble of minute technical inventions that made it possible to increase the useful size of multiplicities by decreasing the inconveniences of the power which, in order to make them useful, must control them (Foucault, 1979: 220).

Crime was no longer to be punished. Instead, the criminal was to be redefined, analyzed and corrected according to the degree of variance from what had been classified as normal. Criminals were now seen to be delinquent, thus inventing work for psychiatrists. Psychiatrists were the new secular priests who, along with the other human scientists in the disciplinary blocks, filled the vacuum left when clerical privileges were outlawed by the French during their Revolution. Psychiatrists were now asked to classify prisoners according to the knowledge gained through observation in the disciplinary blocks and through subsequent calculations and normalization. In emphasizing the character of the criminal rather than the crime, "the 'juridico-moral' concept of the dangerous individual threatens us because it gives society the right to censure based on what the individual is" (Foucault, 1978: 125).

What may have started out as a humane intention of prison reform directed at the soul of the offender, became a powerful mechanism of social control—in a new form but with no lessening of power over citizens as subjects. The soul was to be reformed through the application of power to the body as it internalizes these disciplinary techniques. Other examples of disciplinary blocks are the military, schools, hospitals and asylums.

**Normalization and disciplinary knowledge**

The disciplinary effects of prisons, hospitals, asylums and educational institutions can be seen in their architecture. The walls of the military academies in France, for example, allowed no space for unobserved behavior; all recruits were observed at all times. Educational institutions today are similarly concerned with control over time, space, the development of capacities, and classifications according to statistical norms. 19$^{th}$ century statistics, calculation, population samples and normal curves of distribution all contributed to the development of disciplinary knowledge (Hacking, 1991).

The process of normalization structures the self to the extent that, through the technologies of self, individuals come to accept the normalized constructs as their own. Normalization, as a form of historically constructed rationality, gives to the notion of autonomy based on such rationality, a form of political domination. Allegedly using the methodology borrowed from empirical science and a performative use of language, the human sciences constructed a view of normality. The international DSM-IV psychiatry manual which classifies mental disorders is one modern legacy of the normalization process. What is not admitted in the human sciences is that normality is a statistical categorical construction brought about through performative use of language combined with the employment of empirical data gathered under certain social conditions.

We see here the beginnings of the professions within the developing human sciences which adopted the techniques of the physical sciences in an attempt to legitimate themselves. Within the human sciences, 'professionals' quantified observed behavior and calculated statistical measures of central tendency and dispersion, on the basis of their observations. These measures are converted into verbal descriptors of behavior, through which the features of normalized behavior become documented.

One source of difficulty arises when the normalizing effects become the standardized performative language for the 'correct' construction of the self. The problem is well laid out by Hacking as he argues that statistics "may think of itself as providing only information, but it is itself part of the technology of power in a modern state" (1991: 181). The norm for the behavior of each group is that which is described by the statistical measure of central tendency or dispersion. This translates into a descriptor in language that signals 'normal' behavior. Statistics thereby define the descriptive and performative use of language.

Individuals in these pre-defined categories take on the 'normal' performance through learning the language that describes and prescribes their selves—they come to think of themselves in certain predictable ways. This is based on the statistical concept of standard deviation in the social sciences, in which normality depends on the degree of deviation (although it is debatable whether deviation should be standardized). The language of normality and deviation becomes part of the prison or mental institution and fills textbooks in criminology and psychiatry for universities and the professions. The boundaries of professional interest become the boundaries of knowledge. Codes of ethics are set up to maintain practices derived from the language. These ethics are a politically dominant morality rather than a set of ethics acquired through personal action and experience. Sanctions are set in place to ensure adherence to the codes, so that the introduction of new practices through personal professional experimentation becomes risky. Generations of students of social phenomena are taught the distilled knowledge second hand, and schooled in what to look for. Their perceptions of *normal* are constructed through the given language.

From among the infinite classifications of possible practices in the world, some are deemed more worthy of analysis than others. In a particular context (e.g., prison), certain practices are more prevalent than others, depending on surrounding discourses and types of architecture which position each subject. The fact that the behavior occurs in any particular context is more of a commentary on the discourses in that context than it is on the actual existential condition of the individual. The inmates are acting out a political agenda that confirms the power that incarcerated them in the first place; they learn from the discourse what has been normalized. They probably seek comfort in acting as normally as possible as some parts of the 'normal' behavior earn merit points towards accumulated evidence of good behavior—their soul is deemed to be on the road to reformation. The accumulated merit points allow for early release or, as in education, certification.

The rationale for reform was that the body was merely the vehicle of the soul, the latter being the object of reform. In recent years, through the combined 'benefits' of behavioral technology and humanitarianism, the practices of parole and privilege have been introduced to reinforce the 'rationality' of the advantages of behaving in certain selected ways. Here, behaviorism has joined hands with morality, since the wrongdoer cannot be trusted to decide his or her own moral correctitude.

For Foucault, modern institutions subject people to constant surveillance. The disciplines are geared towards 'normalcy' as they redefine human beings as bio-power for the modern technological economy. In the modern era, important changes in the character of power take place. The examination is an example of modern disciplinary power that contrasts strongly with sovereign power. Sovereign power is made visible and "those on whom it was exercised could remain in the shade" (Foucault, 1979: 187). Disciplinary power on the other hand, reverses these relations. It is exercised through its invisibility and the objects of power—those on whom it operates—are made the most visible. "It is the fact of being constantly seen, of being able always to be seen, that maintains the disciplined individual in his subjection" (Foucault, 1979: 187). In fact, surveillance is the key to disciplinary technology.

The human sciences, including sociology and psychology, are enlisted in the effort to disclose everything possible about the so-called *normal* men or women, so that they can be properly adjusted to the imperatives of the technological system. The system, itself, lies hidden in the apparently beneficial institutions carrying out the disciplinary training needed to keep the system going. The human sciences even suggest what it means to be a man or a woman—the very insistence on a "true sex" (Foucault, 1980b: vii). Any admission of androgyny is an admission of a weakness in a binary sexual classification system. Foucault argued that power relations at work in the institutions of modernity are "unintentional and non-subjective. (And although) ... will and calculation were involved, the overall effect, however, escaped the actors' intentions, as well as those of anybody else" (Dreyfus and Rabinow, 1982: 187) [Author's enclosure]. But how can we speak of intentionality without a notion of a subject? Somehow, the disciplinary practices themselves embody the power that was the object of Foucault's investigations.

> Disciplinary normalizations come into ever greater conflict with the juridical systems of sovereignty: their incompatibility with each other is ever more acutely felt and apparent; some kind of arbitrating discourse is made ever more necessary, a type of power and of knowledge that the sanctity of science would render neutral (Foucault, 1977a: 107).

Disciplinary knowledge was developed in disciplinary blocks. Subsequent applications of knowledge saw individuals pathologised, incarcerated, categorized, and later *certificated*. The performative use of language by experts was one instance of such an application. Specialists in the disciplinary blocks used professional knowledge and control techniques to 'cure' inferred pathologies. The pathologies were seen to stem from such things as: abnormal behaviors, lack of 'proper' learning about the self, sexual preferences, and so on. The focus of the reformers was on correction and reform, a disciplinary (productive) use of power in the reforming of the self. But the application of such power is also a producer of discourse and practice which function as forms of social control. The self is thus defined by the knowledge of the human sciences.

Although it is not the main thrust of the argument of this chapter, it is interesting to note that the prevalence of recidivism in the justice systems in any Western society suggests that efforts to correct the soul through the punishment of the body have not been successful. For Foucault's argument about the strategic reversibility of power relations to hold, he needs to develop a theory of governance that requires and gains the co-operation of the subject. He does that through an account of technologies of self, and their intersection with technologies of domination, through the notion of governmentality.

*Notes*

[1] In some sense this is true today. The 'parole' idea is based on the admission of wrong doing and the promise from the delinquent to mend his or her ways. 'Parole' is from the French 'word'; words are in sentences and sentences are served by those who do not get 'parole'.

## Chapter Six: Technologies of Self

Foucault opens his discussion on technologies of the self with a critique of the so-called sciences through which we learn to understand ourselves.

> My objective for more than twenty-five years has been to sketch out a history of the different ways in our culture that humans develop knowledge about themselves: economics, biology, psychiatry, medicine, and penology. The point is not to accept this knowledge at face value but to analyze these so-called sciences as very specific 'truth games' related to specific techniques that human beings use to understand themselves (Foucault, 1988b: 18).

He believes that nowadays the self is constructed through dynamic interaction with the many discourses. For, he contends, it is in discourse that power and knowledge are joined together.

> Discourses are not once and for all subservient to power or raised up against it, any more than silences are. We must make allowance for the complex and unstable process whereby discourse can be both an instrument and an effect of power, but also a hindrance, a stumbling block, a point of resistance and a starting point for an opposing strategy. Discourse transmits and produces power; it reinforces it, but also undermines and exposes it, renders it fragile and makes it possible to thwart it (Foucault, 1978: 100–101).

In his later life, he queried whether he might not have insisted too much on the technology of domination and power, as he became increasingly interested in how an individual acts upon himself—in the technologies of self:

> ... not simply with the acts that were permitted and forbidden but with the feelings represented, the thoughts, the desires one might experience, the drives to seek within the self any hidden feeling, and movement of the soul, and desire disguised under illusory forms (Foucault, 1988b: 16).

According to Dreyfus and Rabinow (1982), his third set of studies is about the way in which human beings turn themselves into subjects. These studies include *The History of Sexuality, Vol 1* (1978), *Technologies of Self* (1988a) and *Governmentality* (1991b). In the later works, Foucault moves away from the construction of the self solely through applications of power on the body in the disciplinary blocks (which moved through the body, to the soul). As he writes, "I have chosen the domains of sexuality—how men have learned to recognize themselves as subjects of 'sexuality'" (Dreyfus and Rabinow, 1982: 208). Here, the self is seen and understood as constituted through interactive effects of technologies of domination and technologies of self, i.e., the individual is defined with a sense of agency and adopts particular practices. Since domination is inextricably intertwined with power, this subjugation is concerned with the integration within the self, by the self, of technologies of domination and the technologies of self.

Through technologies of self, individuals act upon themselves. Two important technologies of self are the examination and the confession. Foucault (1979) gives a detailed account of the disciplinary functions of the examination, a process that results in the self being constructed subject to the dominant political rationality—a means of correct training.

> The examination combines the techniques of an observing hierarchy and those of a normalizing judgment. It is a normalizing gaze, a surveillance that makes it possible to quantify, to classify and to punish. It establishes over individuals a visibility through which one differentiates them and judges them (Foucault, 1979: 184).

Because of the superimposition of power relations and knowledge relations within the disciplinary block, that notion of examination can be regarded as a technology of domination. The notion of examination in *The Technologies of Self* (Foucault, 1988b), however, is internalized within the self—the examination of conscience. This technology of self is a necessary precondition to modern confessional technologies.

## Knowing vs. caring for oneself

Examination of the self implies some sense of self-knowledge. According to Foucault (1988b: 22), "in the modern world knowledge of oneself constitutes the fundamental principle about the self". He presents several reasons why *know yourself* has obscured *take care of yourself* as the rationality of self. First, the Western tradition is essentially a Christian discourse with a Platonic notion of rationality based on a transcendent set of laws. The pleasures of the body are to be governed by the rational mind which purports to know what is best for the soul. Consequently, the notion of caring for oneself has come to be seen as a form of immorality, a means of escape from rules and respect for law. Second, we inherit a secular tradition which respects external law as the basis of morality. Caring for oneself may, from time to time, require a self to break with laws and rules. Third, in theoretical philosophy since Descartes, knowledge of the self (the thinking subject) takes on an ever-increasing importance as the first step in the theory of knowledge. The historical phenomenon in Western education of educating the mind separate from, even in spite of, the body is an obvious example of an epistemology that placed the ancient maxim *know thyself* at the center of the Cartesian universe. That center is the self. The maxim could not have been interpreted in terms of the human sciences as there was no *disciplinary* knowledge.

Foucault (1988b) found four techniques of the self in Stoic texts: (1) disclosure of self; (2) the examination of self and conscience, including a review of what was done, of what should have been done, and a comparison of the two; (3) *askesis* which is a technique, a remembering—rather than a disclosure—of the secret self; and (4) the interpretation of dreams. These Stoic techniques are applied not for deciphering the self or for self renunciation as for example in the Christian tradition, but rather, to activate the memory of what has been done. For the Christians, disclosure of self meant something very different. It meant you must decipher whether or not the root of your thoughts have evil origins which are perhaps hidden.

Foucault examines Plato's *Alcibiades* from which he isolates three major themes. The first is the relation between care for oneself and care for the political life. The second is the relation between taking care for the self and the problem of a defective education. The third is the relation between taking care of oneself and knowing oneself. In *Alcibiades* there is a close relation between taking care of oneself and knowing oneself. Foucault (1988b: 30) alludes to the idea that in the later texts of the Hellenistic and Roman period, *taking care of oneself* eventually became absorbed in *knowing oneself*. "In *Alcidiabes 1*, the soul had a mirror relation to itself, which relates to the concept of memory and justifies dialogue as method of discovering truth in the soul" (Foucault, 1988b: 31). The mirror relation between the soul and its examination can be thought of as a dialogue.

Later, different conceptions of truth and memory gave rise to another method of examining the self. Dialogue began to disappear and there was increasing importance placed on a new pedagogical relationship—a "new pedagogical game where the master/teacher speaks and doesn't ask questions and the disciple doesn't answer but must keep silent" (Foucault, 1988b: 31). The culture of silence is now the positive condition for acquiring truth. Listening is not that the learner is under the control of the teacher, but rather that the learner may listen and reflect on the logic of the rhetoric after the lecture. "This is the art of listening to the voice of the master and the voice of reason in yourself" (Foucault, 1988b: 32).

Listening to the truth from within oneself is the examination of conscience which has to do with purification and is concerned with memory and administrative stock taking. In this process, "faults are simply good intentions left undone. The rule is a means of doing something correctly, not judging what has happened in the past" (Foucault, 1988b: 33). In the Stoic view, we become permanent administrators of ourselves. Errors are errors of strategy not of moral character. Faults are a problem not so much for the faults themselves, but rather that the self had a lack of success in the day's activities. Retreats into oneself in the Stoic techniques of self, are not to discover faults and deep feelings, but to remember rules of action, the main laws of behavior. "It is mnemotechnical formula" (Foucault, 1988b: 34).

*Askesis* is a Stoic technique of self and unlike Christian techniques, means not a renunciation of self but the progressive consideration of self, or mastery over oneself. "It is a set of practices by which one can acquire, assimilate and transform truth into a permanent principle of action. It is a process of becoming more subjective" (Foucault, 1988b: 35). The principle features of *askesis* include exercises in which the subject puts himself (sic) in a situation in which he can verify whether he can confront events and use the discourses with which he is armed. It is a matter of arranging things so that one can test oneself with what one knows. There are two poles of the exercises of *askesis*. The one pole is *melete* and the other is *gymnasia*. *Melete* involved meditation which is the work one undertook in order to prepare a discourse or an improvisation by thinking over useful terms and arguments. At the opposite pole is *gymnasia* ("to train oneself"). While *meditatio* is an imaginary experience focuses on the training of thought, *gymnasia* deals with training in the real situation, grounded in a long tradition of "sexual abstinence, physical privation, and other rituals of purification" (Foucault, 1988b: 38).

Between these two poles of *melete* and *gymnasia* there are other possibilities. "Epictetus provides the best example of the middle ground between these poles. He wants to watch perpetually over representations, a technique which culminates in Freud" (Foucault, 1988b: 38). The control of representations means not deciphering, but recalling principles for acting and thus seeing, through self-examination, if they govern your life. Foucault (1988b: 38) calls this routine a "pre-Freudian machine of censorship"—you have to be your own censor. The meditation on death is the culmination of all these exercises.

Foucault (1978: 59) argues that the modern society is a confessional one. It is a commonplace belief that it is possible to tell the truth about one's self and, that with the help of professionals, truth about oneself can be discovered through self examination of consciousness and the confession of one's feelings, attitudes, desires, thoughts and acts. The truths are embedded in what Foucault calls sexuality and hence he investigates a genealogy of the history of sexuality.

> Since the Middle Ages at least, Western societies have established the confession as one of the main rituals we rely on for the production of the truth ... (it has) a central

> role in the order of civil and religious powers. ... The truthful confession was inscribed at the heart of the procedures of individualization by power (Foucault, 1978: 58–59).

Since the 18th century, these techniques of verbalization have become part of the human sciences and function to constitute a new self. To use these techniques without renouncing oneself constitutes, for Foucault, a decisive break. This long tradition of control through the confessional depends on inculcating in us the understanding that we have depths to ourselves to be revealed, which we imperfectly understand and need help to decipher and do justice to. In the late 20th century we came to know who we are partly by the way we construct ourselves through language. When we meet other people for example, we tell them who we are—we confess, and tell them the truth about ourselves (or what we select as truth). This construction of *self as truth* is an entrepreneurial confessional mode which is the antithesis of the notion of self held by the Stoics of uncovering through their various practices of self. Since the modern era is one of rapid change of materials, forms, signs and images, the modern self is constantly reconstructed and reconstructing itself for the changing circumstances within which it finds itself.

Foucault (1977a: 90) asserts that "power is war, a war continued by other means". Those other means are the practices that arise from the intersection of the technologies of domination and technologies of self. We need to continually deconstruct these technologies in everyday life because the politics and technology of each era interact with and change the presenting phenomena. Confession as a modern process is both therapeutic and controlling, involving the production of a self within the performative usage of language, and as Marshall (1995a) argues, when pronounced by an authority, the performative aspect of declaring something makes it so.

## The rational autonomous self

Foucault (1988a: 153) asks: "What kind of political techniques, which technology of Government, has been put to work and used and developed in the general framework of the reason of state in order to make the individual a significant element for the state?" He sees both technologies of domination and technologies of self as being the techniques of a new technology of power that was originally given the name *policing*, which historically in France was a far wider concept than we currently hold. Historically, *police* encompassed overall civil respect and public morality through the establishment of four boards of police to keep law and order (i.e., government). The individual became the object of the police in the application of power to make the individual a significant element for the State (i.e., a subject).

In his development of the concept of *governmentality* (a neologism for government rationality), Foucault investigates an historical shift from feudal power to a new police state, in which "the government begins to deal with individuals, not only according to their juridical status but as men, working, trading, living beings" (Foucault, 1988a: 156).

Foucault argues that there is no such thing as the humanist conception of the self (subject).

> The self is not an objective reality to be described by our theories but a subjective notion that is actually constituted by them. The self is an abstract construction, one continually being redesigned in an ongoing discourse generated by the imperatives of the policing process (Hutton, 1988: 135).

Given Foucault's notion of the self as a recognizable, socially constructed being, it would appear that the discourse, which is politically dominated by the imperatives of the policing process, in turn constructs the self. The self in this sense is politically dominated.

> I don't think there is actually a sovereign, founding subject, a universal form of subject that one could find everywhere. I am very skeptical and very hostile toward this conception of the subject. I think on the contrary that the subject is constituted through practices of subjection, or, in a more anonymous way, through practices of liberation, of freedom, as in Antiquity, starting, of course, from a certain number of rules, styles and conventions that are found in the culture (Foucault, 1989: 313).

According to Foucault, the idea that there is an essential human nature is false, and the rationally autonomous person of the humanist construction is "in himself the effect of a subjection much more profound than himself" (Foucault, 1979: 30). Foucault's genealogical research suggests that the autonomous rational self, free from historical and social contamination, is a fiction.

Foucault is not optimistic about the liberating potential of rationality because he sees rationality as socially and historically bounded—what is deemed rational in one era is not considered to be so in another. Post-enlightenment, the subject has been thought of as essentially subject to law, resulting in various forms of political domination. The notion of the rationally autonomous self grew out of the Enlightenment, which was "distinctive not for its faith in intellectual liberation but rather for its commitment to the disciplining of human behavior" (Hutton, 1988: 125). Consequently, integration of individuals into the modern state is not obtained by the form of the ethical community which was characteristic of the Greek city. It is obtained in the new political rationality by certain specific techniques called then, and at this moment, the police (Foucault, 1988a: 153).

The notion of the *free state* is appropriated to the individual who is not free, despite his/her belief to the contrary. The discourse of autonomy supports such a belief, masking the way that the individual is subject to political governance and effectively de-politicized. Foucault (1988a: 146) calls this process, whereby we recognize ourselves as part of the modern state, the "political technology of individuals" where political rationality is constructed within the reason of state. Foucault borrowed historical definitions of the 'reason of state' from Italian and German authors. The reason of state refers to the rationality specific to the art of governing states. He concludes (1988a: 148) that "the art of governing people is rational on the condition that it observes the nature of what is governed, that is, the state itself".

The knowledge produced by the human sciences which represent or carry the political rationality of governmentality gives us the discourse within which it is possible to think and act, and bears down on us as the only apparent form of power/knowledge available within which to construct ourselves. The rationality available for the construction of the self provides for autonomy insofar as the self is regulated within the law, but not for a self free of political rationality. Hence the conception of the rational autonomous self as a thinker or reasoner at a human level outside of the political rationality is false. The problem for individuals arising from this scenario is that the subsequent practices of governmentality, carried out in the name of morality, dominate their lives. Foucault acknowledged that he knew of other forms of power in modern society, but asserted that he was more interested in the "strategic reversibility of power relations" (Dreyfus, and Rabinow, 1982: 221).

Foucault asserts that in relation to an ethics of life, what we need today is a political philosophy not grounded in the problem of sovereignty. What we need to do, he says, is to "cut off the king's head" (1977b: 121). He is not, however, opposed to rational, intellectual authority and traditional forms of knowledge; his concern is about the regimes that legitimate truths. Knowing oneself and caring for oneself are two historical examples of regimes that legitimate truth notions of the self. The idea of knowing oneself has its origins in the epistemological notion of self. Self-knowledge is arrived at through self-examination—the internalization of the mode of examination which is "at the heart of the procedures of discipline, (and which) manifests the subjection of those who are perceived as objects and the objectification of those who are subjected" (Foucault, 1979: 184). In self examination, the self becomes the object of the examination. If, as Foucault suggests, the modern self is constructed subject to the law, this self-examination will reveal a version of self that mirrors the society it inhabits.

Patterned on Foucault's (1978) anatomo-politics and bio-politics, Ian Hacking (1995) has coined the phrase *memoro-politics* to refer to the human soul rather than the self or subject. In the face of criticisms that the soul is a particularly Eurocentric idea, he argues that "(o)ther peoples don't have anything like the historically situated notion of the soul that I have inherited from my culture. Good for them. Other peoples don't have memoro-politics or multiple personality disorder either" (Hacking, 1995: 215). Hacking advances four theses relating to the idea of depth and surface knowledge which illustrate how the *sciences of memory* have constructed the modern self since the late 19th century.

1. The sciences of memory were new in the latter part of the nineteenth century, and with them came new kinds of truths-or-falsehoods, new kinds of facts, new kinds of knowledge.
2. Memory, already regarded as a criterion of personal identity, became a scientific key to the soul, so that by investigation into memory (to find out its facts) one would conquer the spiritual domain of the soul and replace it by a surrogate, knowledge about memory.
3. The facts that are discovered in this or that science of memory are a surface knowledge; beneath them is depth knowledge, that there are facts about memory to find out.
4. Subsequently, what would previously have been debates on the moral and spiritual plane took place at the level of factual knowledge. These political debates all presuppose and are made possible by this depth (Hacking, 1995: 198).

It is the 'normalized' language and practices of the social sciences that provide the basis for judging social practices. For a self subjugated within society, the process of self-examination and the ways that one might 'know' oneself are, then, likely to be circular and self-reinforcing, with feelings of comfort arising from confirmation of what is already 'known'. *Knowing oneself* is, then, a technology of self with naive assumptions of: an essential self to be discovered; a rationality unfettered by historical and social constraints; universal notions of good and bad; objective examination on objective criteria that exist outside of the self; a dualism between oneself and the world; and a hope of progress towards enlightenment as salvation. By contrast, caring for the self in the Stoic sense is a technology of self with a different range of assumptions: no essential self and therefore no a priori moral truths, an ethics to be constructed through an aesthetics of experience, and a self with an accounting mentality that is making progress towards personal goals that will enable the self to be cared for.

A prevailing idea in society is that to know oneself, one must speak the truth. Truth-speaking situations are intentionally set up when participants in therapy groups relate their experiences through interviews or 'confessions'. Such therapy groups are set up to examine the truth of particular situations in the lives of those participants. The very idea of therapy comes from the *will to truth* which is presented by human sciences as liberating one's self from the repression through acts of speaking and reconstructing the self. Since we live in a confessional society, there is a continuous incitement to 'confess', in order to be understood, forgiven by oneself or others, and thereby be relieved of the symptoms. These truth-tellings are unpacked (deconstructed) and unloaded (catharsis) and many participants report a liberating effect. Their reported experiences are essentially reconstructions of the past generated in the present. Their reconstructions are examined, classified and objectified by the participant and others, in terms of the current discourses; their very experiences altered by the examination, and their selves reconstructed with what they believe is an autonomously, self-regulated process with a liberatory intent.

But Foucault believes that this modern self is not rationally autonomous insofar as it is the outcome of the human sciences. The language used by the participant to describe the liberation experience reflexively confirms the existence of the reported pathology. If a pathology is uncovered in the therapy of the essential 'conflicted' self, this process and conception of self may, in itself, be useful. Leaving aside Freud's theory of personality, there is no proof that an essential, conflicted self exists—only narratives of personal mal-adaptation in the face of the hostile power/knowledge regimes of the discourse within which one can *know oneself*. In the sense of *caring for oneself*, such mal-adaptation is presumably healthy—there is a refusal of domination.

Discourses other than the human sciences are therefore needed for liberation. In the study of the technologies of the self, it is not the self alone that is of interest, but the discourse that is made up of the governmental effect of technologies of self and technologies of domination. Foucault's key point is that it is political control and not freedom that has been the aim of the political technology in the construction of the self.

## Foucault's way out.

> Classical antiquity never problematised the constitution of the self as subject; inversely, beginning with Christianity, there is an appropriation of morality through the theory of the subject. Yet a moral experience centered essentially on the subject no longer seems to me satisfactory today (Foucault, 1989: 330).

If there is no rationally autonomous self, there will be no a priori moral truths upon which the self is to be constructed and there is no one true set of morals to discover in any examination. Foucault (1989) argues for an aesthetic view of the person as moral agent in which care of one's self was seen as the way out of such a difficulty in the construction of the subject. He sees the subject as politically dominated and the need to construct an ethics of self through inner dialogue.

If morality is the deliberate practice of liberty, the key idea is the slippage in modern usage of the notion of *care for thyself* into *know thyself*. This leads us to the human sciences, where political control and not freedom is the aim. In speaking the truth, in knowing one's true self, one constructs the experience, and one reconstructs one's self by adopting new descriptions and new practices. In order to behave properly, to practice freedom properly, it is necessary to care for the self—not merely to know one's self, but to improve, to surpass and to master one's self. This is achieved through a technology of self—the inner dialogue.

> The inner dialogue—what I say to myself and the self discipline—what I do to myself are the heartland of subjectivity. It is seldom force that keeps us on the straight and narrow; it is conscience. It is less knowledge produced in the human sciences that we use as our guide in life than self knowledge (Hacking, 1986: 236).

The inner dialogue indicates there is something 'in' there beneath the normalized or even the aesthetic self. We might ask, as in the case of Descartes' cogito, what is this entity that carries out the inner dialogue? Since logically there cannot be nothing, there must be something. How then is it to be characterized logically? Existentially, there actually is something, but there is not one truth about self.

According to Hacking (1986), the ethics of self consists of four elements: (1) ethical substance, the stuff that moral agents worry about, (2) the mode of subjection, whatever it is that is used to internalize these concerns and what is taken as the relevant truth about them, (3) how are we to get it to work? and (4) a teleology, the kind of being to which we aspire when we behave in a moral way. These elements can be analyzed for both their positive and negative aspects.

Foucault claims that we live in a confessional society, but that it is possible to retain the ability to control the construction of self through technologies of self which do not bind us into the technologies of domination. An example is the difference between the Christian juridical notion of confession based on the morality assumed to be inherent in the self, and the Senecan notion of confession as an administrative act. The administrative model of confession does not construct a dominated notion of self but allows for assessment of *self as a memory*.

One source of difficulty is that the construction of self through inner dialogue is bounded by language, which is ascribed meaning in the social discourse from the theories of the human sciences. The human sciences, in turn, create the power to legitimate the truth. Christian thought established sex as the truth about oneself and, as Poster (1986: 218) observes, "instituted an elaborate code, universally applicable, to regulate sexual conduct and thoughts". The idea of *sex as identity* is also a social construction—a *retail truth*:

> To care for oneself in the twentieth century has come to be to fit oneself out, retail, with a set of 'truths' which, by being learned, memorized, and progressively put into practice, construct a subject with a certain mode of being and a certain visible manner of acting (Marshall, 1996: 101).

Through technologies of self, the norms and principles of the retail truths then become the ethics of self. Therefore, extreme versions of autonomy in the volitional or motivational field may be construed as not caring for the self, if we accept that the rational autonomous self is politically dominated. A *normal* person (i.e., someone who is normalized) is the one who aspires to the statistical central tendencies of the group discourse. From this perspective, self evaluation (inner dialogue) is socially dependent, and politically controlled because it is grounded in a given set of norms and common principles.

An alternative conception or *way out* for the normalized self is a notion of social construction of the self, that acknowledges the self as a work of art forever in process. This fits neatly with Hacking's suggestion that we separate our ethical lives from what we know as science. Rhetoric about the good life usually references some claim to know the truth, but in Foucauldian terms, "there are no such truths to know" (Hacking, 1986: 239).

Foucault argues for an aesthetic view of the person as moral agent in which care of one's self is seen as the way out of accepting the notion of the politically dominated, rationally autonomous self. In a later interview, Foucault talks of a new ethics of sexuality with the need to replace socially constructed drives and satisfactions by bodies and pleasures:

> What we must work on, it seems to me, is not so much to liberate our desires but to make ourselves infinitely more susceptible to pleasure. We must escape and help others to escape the two ready-made formulas of the pure sexual encounter and the lover's fusion of identities' (Foucault, 1989: 206).

If Foucault is correct and we readily limit ourselves to two ready-made formulas, to that extent we are trapped in a polarity. And since the liberatory potential of fulfilling our desires with sexual encounters is necessarily limited (whether through lack of opportunity, imagination or energy), then in the interests of continued exploration of self, we are limited to only the other pole—a ready-made formula for a fusion of identities. This idea of fusion, though, contradicts the very meaning of identity, if identity signifies the essence of oneself. A loss of identity for an Enlightenment self may even be a recipe for madness, as identity is essential to its self-definition. Loss of identity would also mean loss of sexuality since identity and sex are so conflated in discourse. Under these conditions, the self is ordinarily likely to opt for *sexuality as truth*, leading, as it so often does, to a search for the essential, hidden self (with the help of professionals). It is not clear how one might explore possibilities outside known discourses, since one may not even recognize what they were. Foucault's (1988b) investigations into the technologies of self are certainly an attempt to construct something different.

How do we approach the study of the self and its practices in a manner that is not totally dominated by the discourse? With a notion of self in which sex is truth/identity, we could first make a distinction between the urge for sexual relief and the socially constructed objects of our sexual desire which we have internalized. If, as Foucault suggests, the self is socially constructed, the particular satisfactions we seek for the sexual drives are at least partially derived from our constructions. We project our socially constructed desires as if they are uniquely ours. And of course they are—we have constructed; and besides, the accompanying feelings do not belong to anyone else.

In order to unravel issues such as these, Foucault traced the technologies of the examination of conscience and confession back beyond the literature of the Stoics and early Christian times. Such technologies of the self permit individuals "to effect certain operations on their own bodies, souls, thoughts conduct and way of being" (Foucault, 1982: 18). They reconstruct and transform their selves to attain certain states of wisdom, perfection, purity and even happiness. But, as Hacking (1986: 236) points out, "to say this is not to return to subjectivity. There is nothing private about this use of acquired words and practical techniques. The cunning of conscience and self knowledge is to make them feel private".

Charles Taylor points out the difficulty inherent in disengaging from first-person experience. There is no way, he says, that my toothache can be experienced as a mere idea of the mind. In attempting to transpose first-person experience into an objectified, impersonal mode, we engage in what he calls a *radical reflexivity*, in that we have to focus on the first-person experience in order to transpose it. "Instead of being swept along to error by the ordinary bent of our experience, we stand back from it, withdraw from it, reconstrue it objectively, and then learn to draw defensible conclusions from it" (Taylor, 1989: 163).

> Disengagement and what we might call engaged exploration are two quite different things. They carry us in contrary directions and are extremely difficult to combine. The point of this contrast is to see that the option for an epistemology which privileges disengagement and control isn't self-evidently right. It requires certain assumptions (Taylor, 1989: 164).

These assumptions of course, parallel those of the Enlightenment. This raises interesting thoughts about what it means to be normal when there is an attribution under the law of individual responsibility for so-called sexual deviations and perversions. If biological sexual urges know no 'correct' object (i.e., whatever turns one on) and the sexuality of the individual is positioned by the discourse, it follows that logically there is no incorrect object of biological sexual desires—only degrees of agreement and consequences such as sexual satisfaction or lack thereof, imprisonment, castration, death penalty, or, what the individual will limit through their internalized acceptance of what is normal.

Failure of an individual to get sexual satisfaction from a socially approved object of satisfaction can also be construed as a failure of the discourse to correctly position the individual. The constructions of sexuality mediated by the discourse that are evaluated as abnormal, however, are usually seen as a deficit which puts socially constructed sexuality on the same level as biological urges.

It is possible, then, to distinguish between biological sexual urges in the first person stance on the one hand, and the disengaged notion of sexuality constructed through the discourse on the other. If we frame sexuality as a socially productive mechanism distinct from the biological urge, it may be difficult to know whether any personal satisfaction resulting from sexual activity will be as a result of a pre-determined biological urge, or merely an illusion of a creative aesthetic production of expression of sexuality. Expressions of sexuality (i.e., sexual acts carried out in the name of sexuality) can be viewed as discourse-bound and not necessarily a need for biological relief. However, first person experiences of biological sexual urges and a Stoic construction of a personal sexual ethics based on creative production are not normalized within the discourses of the human sciences. This creates a problem.

The danger, according to Foucault, lies in a conception of self in which pleasure alone was maximized at the expense of the aesthetic emphasis of caring for oneself. Foucault sees that the positive exercise of power in constructing an ethics outside the human sciences carries with it the danger of attending to one positive aspect of production of self at the expense of other aspects. "To this absence of a morality, one responds, or must respond, with a research which is that of an aesthetics of existence" (Foucault, 1989: 311). This position seems to underpin a way of constructing a personal ethics in the Western neoliberal societies.

There are limitations in real life to any rejection of the notion of the rationally autonomous self and its replacement with an aesthetics of existence. For Foucault, an aesthetics of existence implies the development of a personal style in the care of self. But because the capacity for care of self (i.e., through the language used for inner dialogue) is mediated within the available discourses, an individual can only take their stylistic and idiosyncratic care of self so far until the cultural norms within the discourse are being breached. Many such individuals have been observed, examined, labeled, classified, and moved to the margins as a result of a personal style that confronts the norms of societal practice especially when that practice is enshrined in law. Other 'abnormals' are marginalized and disenfranchised in terms of their culture through being unable to access the power of modern societies.

**An ethic of self**

Foucault understood that the origins of governance lay in the human science discourse, an understanding that avoids the elision between caring for oneself and knowing oneself. In terms of the current political rationality, caring for oneself in a Stoic sense has been appropriated by knowing oneself in the Christian sense. It is this latter sense that informs the technologies of domination that characterize the human sciences. Stoic techniques of self, with their ability to take the self outside the subjectivity implied in human sciences, offer a strong possibility in terms of how to proceed.

Foucault's critique of the Enlightenment self through a consideration of Stoic techniques suggests that the construction of the self is to varying degrees under the control of the individual. To the extent that individuals exercise technologies of self in the sense of the Stoic notion of caring for oneself, it is a message of hope. In Foucault's view, subjects continuously reconstruct their selves by the forms of self care they create. In this creative process, power is exercised as ethics are constructed. In an ethical sense, the value of an individual's life depends upon the way that power is deployed: it can, and usually is, appropriated for the purposes of governance by a conflation of caring for oneself and knowing oneself.

> In constituting the subject in these ways, in constructing the very identity of individuals, modern power produces governable individuals through technologies of individualization and normalization. According to Foucault the personal search for autonomy and identity, when mired in humanistic notions of the subject and liberal talk of rationality and emancipation, will only aid and abet such processes (Marshall, 1995a: 32).

The education system is now presented with managerialism as its disciplinary technology: theories of systems, organizational development models, behavioral technology, human resource conceptions of good employees and managers, and public service bureaucracy rationalism. Knowledge about teacher education programs based on social science is presented in a manner similar to the knowledge constructed about prisoners as investigated in *Discipline and Punish*. Enlightenment stories about students as rational autonomous beings are presented to student teachers through educational theories (e.g., theories of human development and child learning theories) which give a psychologized picture of students based on a priori constructions of self.

Foucault might accept novels as methods of investigation into the self but not psychology texts. Novels provoke feelings, are idiosyncratic, and are outside the social science disciplines. Psychology on the other hand, insofar as it presents its texts as rational accounts of human nature, is a form of disciplinary knowledge originating from the human sciences. But development of self knowledge arising from the Delphic dictum *know thyself* is a problem.

There are dangers with caring for oneself as a response. Although Foucault never made the law a principle focus of study, the theme of law as governance is of direct relevance to law and other societal regulation. Self-management, or caring for oneself, through processes that go back to antiquity, might engage people in ethical techniques of self that imply—or even more dangerously, demonstrate—that there is no unity of morality in political life. Caring for oneself in an ethical sense may, at times, be outside the law or the disposition of the modern, regulatory society. Modern societal arrangements of law and managed regulations are influenced by a human science conception of knowing oneself and how this self ought to be if it is to appear normal. But a shift of focus towards the governance of self through ethics does not announce a retreat to the private realm or a shift from the social to psychological inquiries. In an important sense, it is a return to what has been the core social question of the link between government and freedom. This apparent dichotomy between government and freedom does not imply opposition. Government is not necessarily opposed to freedom, just as freedom has never been the mere absence of government. Rather, the dilemma is that government and freedom each presuppose the other, while at the same time, threaten and challenge each other.

Foucault's genealogy of the constructivist view of the self is a critique of Enlightenment notions of the a priori, rational, autonomous self upon which the foundational principles of managerialism are based. There is no Enlightenment future for mankind, according to Foucault, because reason is embedded in socio-historical conditions and there is no rational unfolding of history in any development or improving sense. A real difficulty is that the assumptions underpinning disciplinary knowledge are occluded. Shades of sovereign power still support the ordinary discourse of managerial notions of authority and responsibility. And to change the discourse, an individual must become an element in the formation of a political will which, in turn, might reconstruct the discourse and its discursive practices. A private study of discursive practices does not necessarily yield discourse truth although it can reinforce or undermine for the individual the assumptions prevailing about the practices. Publicly displaying an 'abnormal' (i.e., aesthetic, or even an unfashionably contra) personal style under conditions of normalized disciplinary knowledge, however, is risky. In fact, risk management has become the new managerial technology for neoliberal government spaces.

In his later life Foucault advocated an ethics of self, although such advice has inherent difficulties. Implicit in such advice is the assumption of an unrestrained freedom, and the problem of detaching a notion of the aesthetic from the other strands in modern thought that he still wanted to attack.

Discussions about normality and the mediation of self through management of the various discourses apply, of course, to education. Foucault's critique has not produced any direct answers to the problems of education. It can, however, be regarded as pointing us towards inquiry, and even shaping the direction of that inquiry. The future of education is a problem very much in need of theorizing—based as it is, in Foucauldian terms, on carceral structures, a confessional ethos, normative constructions of the self and key elements of the Enlightenment notion of self.

## Chapter Seven: Governmentality

Foucault's account of governmentality provides a critique of the practices by which the management of self is sustained. The chapter locates Foucault's genealogy of the arts of government as a rupture with sovereign power. Foucault's approach to theories of state are discussed because he rejected these as attending too much to institutions and too little to practices. Theories of state also attempt to deduce the modern activities of government from essential properties of the State. Since for Foucault, the governmentalization of the State has permitted its historical definition and redefinition, it can be understood in its survival and its limits as the basis of the general tactics of governmental rationality. Foucault's attitude to liberalism is also examined—he thought that liberalism viewed as an ideology was preceded by disciplinary power and that it was not merely another grand narrative. A genealogy of neoliberalism is provided to critique the theoretical underpinnings of the recent reforms to New Zealand's economy and society. Foucault's notion of governmentality as a domain of research about government is discussed. The chapter then discusses Foucault's critique of the liberal individual, and then concludes with some implications of governmentality for self-management to illustrate the conditions of possibility available to the self under the busno-power regime in New Zealand.

### The arts of government

In his lecture entitled *Governmentality*, Foucault (1991b) undertakes a genealogical analysis of the emergence of the theme of the art of government in the mid 16$^{th}$ century where it was a dominant concern of numerous political treatises. Foucault utilizes the concept of government in two senses. The first concerns a dimension of experience, *the will to govern*. What makes forms of action and reflection *governmental* rather than theoretical or philosophical, is "their wish to make themselves practical" (Rose, 1993: 287). Actual practices in daily life become governmental. Reflection for example, becomes governmental to the extent that it seeks to render itself technical and realize itself as a practice. It is implicated in the construction of subjects who are not oppressed, but are capable of exercising a regulated freedom as well as caring for themselves as free subjects.

The second sense of government is an analysis of the problematic of rule. This refers to the ways in which rulers have posed for themselves the questions of the reasons, justifications, means and ends of rule, and the problems, goals or ambitions that should enliven it. This second sense of government addresses itself to the political which is a certain mentality of rule. In order to address this mentality, Rose (1993: 288) offers a set of focusing questions: What is the condition of the people? the economy? the family? What accounts for the problems and what would lead to their improvement? What effect have our strategies produced in the past? What can be done and should be done, and by whom in order to make things better?

Such questions seek to describe the ways in which mentalities of rule have intended, deployed, sought to utilize, or become dependent upon, various technologies which promise to connect up authorities with those over whom their authority is to be exercised. Such rule must be exercised in the light of the knowledge of that which is ruled. In the case of New Zealand, that knowledge is formed under the limitations of busno-power. Answers to the questions offered by Rose invoke desirable objectives within the limits of autonomy—interpreted as the liberal notion of freedom. Within education, (and still) under busno-power, therapeutic self-examination of the centered subject is the origin of self knowledge. This self and its knowledge is often erroneously represented as free from outside interference. In contradiction to this, Foucault's critique of the liberal individual shows that individuality as well as knowledge about how to be an individual, arise from the political rationality operating in any epoch.

The idea of the arts of government is formulated in opposition to a monarchical notion of power. The first key difference is that, whereas the prince is in a position of singularity and transcendence in relation to his principality, practices of government are many and immanent in the State and society. The notion of government derived from *The Prince* (Bull, 1961) is one of an essentially transcendent relationship between the prince and the principality that he rules. According to Foucault, the juridical theory of sovereignty and the doctrine of *The Prince* were obviously important and never ceased to function as the object of explicit or implicit opposition and rejection. Foucault argues that the issue re-emerged at the beginning of the 19$^{th}$ century in the context of many questions about the art of government. He says that all authors distanced themselves from the conceptions that took the sole interest of the sovereign as its object and principle of rationality. Regardless of the means through which the prince acquires his principality, the link remains a purely synthetic one, as "there is no fundamental, essential, natural and juridical connection between the prince and his principality" (Foucault, 1991b: 96).

The prince, then, stands in a relation of singularity and externality to his principality. A corollary of the external nature of the link between the prince and his principality is that the link is also fragile and under continual threat. The prince's main objective in the exercise of power must to be to strengthen and reinforce the principality, understood not as "the objective ensemble of its subjects and the territory, but rather the prince's relation with what he owns, with the territory he has inherited or acquired and with his subjects" (Foucault, 1991b: 90). The Prince is external and transcendent to his territory—the link is synthetic, external, fragile and continually under threat from within and without. Imperative to the exercise of power is the strength of the Prince's relation with the territory. "This fragile link is what the art of governing or of being a Prince as espoused by Machiavelli's text has as its object" (ibid.).

Therefore the mode of analysis is to identify dangers, and then to develop the art of manipulation of relations of force. But, "(h)aving the ability to retain one's principality is not at all the same thing as possessing the art of government" (Foucault, 1991b: 90). The art of government consists in identifying dangers and manipulating the relations of force that allow the prince to ensure the protection of his principality. In other words, under a notion of sovereign power the prince must maintain a certain level of force if he wishes to keep his principality. The force would be against any real or perceived competition. In the event he is successful, the ensuing stability of rule would therefore be relative to the force being opposed. As a mode of government then, this position of sovereign power is inherently unstable.

A second difference is that, in the juridical theory of sovereignty, a radical discontinuity is established and constantly redefined between the different forms of power that compose the arts of government. "The art of government consists of a plurality of forms of government and their immanence to the State" (Foucault, 1991b: 90). It is the multiplicity and immanence of these activities within the plurality of forms that distinguishes them radically from the transcendent singularity of the Prince. The plurality consists of (1) the art of self government which concerns issues of morality, (2) the art of properly governing a family which belongs to the economy, and (3) the science of ruling the State, which concerns politics. Each of the three fundamental types of Government relate to a particular science or discipline. The art of government is to establish a continuity in both upward and downward directions, i.e., among self, family and State. The prince is in a pedagogical relation (master or teacher) to the individuals, families and State, (in ascending order). The prince's pedagogical formation ensures the upwards continuity of forms of government. The model of the family is also used when the running of the State is transmitted as a model for the head of the family to look after the family and this in turn showed individuals how they should behave.

This descending line of continuity of governance was beginning to be known as police. The reason of state is government in accordance with the State's strength. Foucault suggests that the style of political thinking which enabled European reason of state to outgrow its Machiavellian limitations was contained under the rubric of the science of police. Police in this sense is equivalent to policy (policy as derived from police) in all areas of life. The police State is also termed the State of prosperity but Foucault (quoted in Gordon, 1991: 10) emphasises "that the real basis of the State's wealth and power lies in its population, in the strength and productivity of each". In contradistinction to the focus on death within what Foucault (1978) calls the symbolics of blood, life became the object of the police State which worked by the means of specific, detailed regulation and decree. "Foucault notes as a defining characteristic of the police State the marginalization of the distinction between government by law and government by decrees" (in Gordon, 1991: 11).

From the 16$^{th}$ century, the theory of the art of government was linked to the development of the administrative apparatus of the territorial monarchies and the emergence of governmental apparatuses. It was through notions of governmentality that the great forms and economies of power in the West were reconstructed. The juridical State was born in the feudal type of territorial regime, corresponding to a society of laws, reciprocal play of obligation and litigation. The administrative State was born in the territoriality of the national boundaries of the 15$^{th}$ and 16$^{th}$ centuries corresponding to a society of regulation and discipline.

The governmentalized State is defined in terms of population with territory as only one component, corresponding to a society controlled by apparatuses of security. At this point, the governmental State is no longer defined by its territory but in terms of its mass of population with its volume and density and with territory as one component. It was also connected to a set of analysis and forms of knowledge through the 16$^{th}$ and 17$^{th}$ centuries to do with knowledge of the State, in all its different elements, dimensions and factors of power, in other words, questions of statistics—the science of the State.

As the feudal order was replaced by the State and as capitalism began to expand, there was demographic expansion throughout the 18$^{th}$ century. The family as a model of government was unsatisfactory. From this time onwards, the arts of government were re-centered from the theme of the family to that of population. The theory of government moved from the privileged model of the father and the family to the problem of population, a view of the family as an instrument and a re-centering of the notion of the economy. The development of statistics enabled control through measurement and prediction. This enabled the art of government not as an end in itself but because it existed for the welfare of its people.

> Whereas statistics had previously worked within the administrative frame and thus in terms of the functioning of the sovereignty, it now gradually reveals that population has its own regularities, its own rate of deaths and diseases, its cycles of scarcity ... (Foucault, 1978: 101).

The population of the governed is likened to a herd as well as to a flock. Under this pastoral care, welfare is conjoined to exploitation, as the police thinkers are capable of understanding.

The assurance of order in the police State is an assurance of an order which the State itself has created. In this reason of state, the economy must be operated, but it also has to be continuously made by the government. The State referred to here is identical with the economy. Police government in this sense is a form of pastoral power, a government which defines itself as being *of all and of each*. Such a government is also an economy, through its way of equating the happiness of its individual subjects with the State's strength.

The police then, are a kind of economic, secular and pastoral priesthood. The individual here is very important as it becomes the object of the police. Policing was interpreted as fostering overall civil respect and public morality through the establishment of four boards of police to keep law and order. Foucault (1988a: 156) sees an historical shift:

> Feudal power consisted in relations between juridical subjects insofar as they were engaged in juridical relations by birth, status, of personal engagement, but with this new police State the government begins to deal with individuals, not only according to their juridical status but as men, working, trading, living beings.

A third difference between sovereignty and governmentality is that the central problem for theorists of the art of government revolved around the question of how to introduce economy. There was "an historical interconnection of the science of government, the recurring theme of economy on a different plane from the family, and the notion of population" (Foucault, 1991b: 99). The central term of this continuity is the government of the family, known as economy. To govern a State therefore means to set up an economy at the level of the entire State, which means exercising towards its inhabitants, and the wealth and behavior of each and all, a form of surveillance and control as attentive as that of the head of a family over his household and his goods. Economy became re-centered as an area of reality apart from the family through the development of the science of government.

Science allowed us to develop the notion of population and the problem of government came to be thought, reflected and calculated out of the juridical framework of sovereignty. Statistics now became a major technical factor of this new technology of the science of government. In this new scientific State (or more aptly, the state of science) the notion of economy is re-centered outside the model of the family through administrative science. Statistics which previously worked inside sovereign interests, reveals that population has its own regularities that are not reducible to those of the family. Knowledge became power, as sovereignty no longer had exclusive control of the information. Those who had the knowledge could rationally defend their position if not retain their heads in the face of sovereign power. That knowledge in part was created through the development of statistics.

The use of statistics, which created the concept of population, showed that population was not reducible to the family, but ironically it was statistical data extracted from the family that provided the means for knowing population. The family was no longer the model for government but rather the instrument. The individual was the unit of statistical analysis, but it was the family that tied the individual to others—structurally, emotionally and sexually. The family also had a religious tradition and was a stable unit to be employed as an instrument of government. The idea that the family had any intrinsic worth had now died; hence, concern for the family from about the middle of the 18$^{th}$ century as a means of social control (Foucault 1989: 17). The population now appears more as the aim of government than the power of the ruler; the population is the *subject* in terms of needs and aspirations, but it is also the *object* in the hands of the government, aware of what it wants but ignorant of what is being done to it. Government through population, however, does not eliminate the problem of sovereignty.

There was a transition in the 18th century from the art of government to political science, and from structures of sovereignty to techniques of government. The transition turns on the theme of population and the birth of political economy resulting in government through knowledge and information. Population was now the object of government. In contrast to sovereignty, government aimed at the welfare of population. The means used by government to attain welfare ends are immanent in the needs of the population. Whether it knows it or not, the population (and thereby the individual) is the object of government. Without its awareness for the most part, the population is analyzed and operated on by government, through calculated public relations, marketing campaigns, awareness raising, advertizing, budgeting, and more overtly, inoculation. This kind of government operation is now regarded as an integral part of the research, design and implementation of government policy.

In order to govern in a conscious and rational manner, "the constitution of a savoir (knowledge) of government is absolutely inseparable from that of a knowledge of all the processes related to population in its larger sense, that is to say, what we now call the economy" (Foucault, 1991b: 100). The new science of political economy now emerges out of the existence and intersection of several factors. There was a perception of new networks of continuous and multiple relations between population, territory and wealth. This was accompanied by the formation of a type of intervention characteristic of government in the field of economy and population.

With the displacement of the model of the family by that of the population, new forms of study arose which led to the analysis of the population in terms of its own regularities. There were a series of crises in the 17$^{th}$ century: Thirty Years' War, peasant revolts, urban rebellions and financial crises. The art of government needed support and expansion because of military conflicts and political and economic tensions. Mercantilism developed as a response to these crises, both itself and its art of government derived from a renewed version of the theory of sovereignty. Yet, the framework of sovereignty was too large, abstract and rigid, and new knowledge emerging from statistics undermined the theory of mercantilism as a theory of governance. In response, jurists began formalizing the theory of contract, enabling the "mutual pledge of ruler and subjects, to function as a sort of theoretical matrix for deriving the general principles of an art of government" (Foucault, 1991b: 98). Contract theory remained at the stage of general principles of public law.

A fourth difference between the Machiavellian notion of juridical sovereignty and the arts of government emerges in connection with the nature of the object over which power is exercised. "Government is the right disposition of things, arranged so as to lead to a convenient end" (Foucault, 1991b: 93). Unlike sovereignty, government is not about promoting the common good, but of disposing of things, using laws as tactics, for the ends of each thing to be achieved. The finality of government resides in the things it manages and in the pursuit of the perfection and intensification of the processes it directs, including the management of property and territory. The instruments of government, instead of being laws, now come to be a range of multi-form tactics. In governing, wisdom is a combination of diligence and service to those who are governed. In some sense, the governor has the freedom merely to rule within the constraints that are inherent in the thing being governed. If this is accepted, we might say that we are caught with the way things are. But the discussion of marketing provided later in this book indicates that governance is a little more complex than that.

**Theories of State**

For Foucault, theories of State could not explain the practices of government. Theories of State attend too much to institutions and too little to practices, and rely on the State having some essential properties. Foucault holds that the State has no inherent propensities or essence and is, itself, a function of changes in practices of government. Although noting a propensity for the State to colonize all outside itself, Foucault argues that the State cannot be relied upon as a means of describing the ways in which power is actually exercised, because the State is, itself, the *object* of power. The idea of State intervention, then, is problematic, in that it implies intervention *by* the State which is, itself, an entity that exists on the basis of intervention. The State might usefully be considered as a set of practices comprised of a certain power/knowledge discourse of how things are at any one time.

The central concern of political philosophy is to investigate the legitimate foundations of political sovereignty and political obedience. It is about the best government. Political sovereignty cannot be relied upon as a means of describing the ways in which power is actually exercised under such a sovereignty. Foucault, in contrast, asks *how* questions to find the immanent conditions and constraints of practices. An examination of practices allows for thinking differently about government. They give us the actual happenings without limiting us to a pre-conceived theory. Since practices are infinitely variable, they change with such things as technological developments, political desires, wars and ideas. There is always scope for further investigation as new forms evolve. In our time, (re)form is the rationale and practice of government and therefore, the need for research is greatly intensified.

Governmentality is not limited to traditional political philosophical methodology and dialectical assumptions about the 'naturalness' of duties and rights, and repression of rights. *How* questions do not create immediate polemical implications between 'how' and political philosophy. *How* is not a concern with the purely expedient or factual. Governmentality, rather, is about critique, problematisation, invention, imagination and changing the shape of the thinkable. The perceived internal constraints are just as capable of carrying normative meaning and content as principles of legitimation. The content and object of governing as bio-politics is itself already ethical. Governmentality is not epistemological as it does not address pre-conceived theories of knowledge about the State. *Government as knowledge'* carries a concern with truth which exceeds the merely utilitarian in power/knowledge. Foucault advances an interdependence between government and truth. Government has a need for knowledge as truth.

Today the State still exercises power and commands attention. But an excessive valorization of the State raises two problems. The first is an image of a cold cynical monster confronting us both effectively and tragically. The second is a paradoxical move at the same time towards a minimalist State. This reductionist vision of the relative importance of the State's role invariably renders it absolutely essential as the target needing to be attacked and a privileged position needing to be occupied.

But "the State today, no more than at any time in its history, does not have this unity, this individuality, this rigorous functionality, and importance" (Foucault, 1991b: 103). The State today is a composite reality and a mythicized abstraction and of limited importance. What is important is the governmentalization of the State, i.e., what has permitted the historical definition and redefinition of the State. Thus, the State can be understood in its survival and its limits only in terms of the general tactics of governmental rationality.

## Liberalism and neoliberalism

Foucault adopts a distinctive approach towards the analysis of liberalism. "Liberalism can be analyzed from the point of view of governmental reason, i.e., from the point of view of the rationality of political government as an activity rather than as an institution" (Burchell, 1993: 269). Liberalism for Foucault is a rationally reflected way of doing things which functions as the principle and method for the rationalization of Governmental practices. Rose (1993: 283) argues that "liberalism is not to be considered as a political philosophy nor a type of society but as a formula of rule".

Rose advances three schematic propositions about liberalism. The first is that $19^{th}$ century liberalism (from 1780–1850) as a rationality of rule, produced a new modality of authority and a new authority for authority. It produced a series of problems about the governability of individuals, families, markets and populations. Expertise arose to provide solutions to these types of problems. The second proposition is that $19^{th}$ and early $20^{th}$ century (1850–1930), liberal formula of government was perceived from a variety of perspectives to be failing to produce the necessary economic, social and moral consequences. Governance could be provided at a distance through the knowledge and evaluations of 'experts' who set the social norms. During this time there was a rise of the welfare State under professionals within society. The third proposition is that advanced liberal rule (1930–1989) depends upon expertise and articulates experts into apparatus of rule through the regulated choices of individual citizens. "It detaches the substantive authority of expertise from the apparatuses of political rule, relocating experts within a market governed by the rationalities of competition, accountability and consumer demand" (Rose, 1993: 285).

Rose further argues that these propositions are not to be regarded as periodization. They are rather a schematic way of identifying a number of distinct problematisation of rule: ways of asking what should be ruled, by whom, and through what procedures; what is intelligible and possible; what can be counted as problems, failures and solutions. What we inhabit as the present is a virtual space composed of residues of past rationalities. Examples of these are structural oppositions such as: Marxism versus powerlessness; public versus private; compulsory versus voluntary; State versus market; and domination versus freedom. Such foundational, rhetorical elements, however, have difficulty in analyzing their own conditions of possibility.

Liberalism, according to Rose, has four key features. Firstly, liberalism inaugurates a new relation between government and knowledge. It ties government to positive knowledge of human conduct developed within the social and human sciences. Government is now connected to theories, diagrams, techniques, experts, i.e., government through knowledge. Knowledge is the apparatus for the production, circulation, accumulation, authorization and realization of truth. Truth is the technical know-how which promises to make government possible.

Secondly, liberalism depends upon a novel specification of the subjects of rule as active in their own government. In this view, free subjects are invested with great hope. Free subjects in a liberal space are shaped and regulated through norms, capacities, devices in disciplinary blocks and will regulate and shape themselves in terms of knowledge gleaned from human sciences. Under liberalism, the national objective of the good citizen is fused with the subject's personal objective for the good life.

Thirdly, government is inherently bound to the authority of expertise. Foucault argues that there is no single logic for the rise of the expert. Frictions and disturbances were recorded as social problems through the proselytizing effects of independent reformers. These events had consequences for national well-being and thus called for authoritative intervention and attention by experts. Relations between legal, economic, financial, and other spheres of society were brought into being and produced regulations, legislation, funding and organizational capacity. The authority of experts became hegemonic through bureaucratization and professionalization.

The fourth feature of liberalism is that it inaugurates a continual questioning of the activity of rule itself, e.g., it confronts the question, why rule? There is a constant scrutiny over rulers' activities with questions about who can rule. Questions of legitimacy must be answered practically. There is a constant suspicion of rule. There is a fear of not governing enough versus the fear of going too far. There is a perpetual dissatisfaction and questioning of the desired results. The imperative is not necessarily more government but better government. This continual questioning is exemplified in Foucault's advice that we are in need of the Enlightenment attitude of permanent critique.

The experience of liberalism has been fundamental in the shaping the government rationalities of the West. For Foucault, liberalism is specified in opposition to a notion of police. As a mentality of rule, liberalism

> abandons the desire and possibility for a totally administered society which, in this view, is theoretically impossible. It is a rationality of rule which sought to limit the scope of political authority and to exercise vigilance over its exercise (Rose, 1993: 289).

Under the rationality of liberalism, government also acquired the obligation to foster the self-organizing capacities of markets, citizens and civil society now seen as natural spheres. This can be contrasted with the artificial and arbitrary constructions of the markets and civil society set up within the current neoliberal rationality.

Liberalism repudiates reason of state as a rationality of rule as well as abandoning the rationality of sovereign power. Within liberalism, subjects have inalienable rights and sovereigns face the reality that they do not have the requisite knowledge and capacities. Within the notion of bio-power, the disciplines of the body and the bio-politics of population intersect and interact to produce the significant condition, forms of self mastery, self reflection and self control, necessary to govern a nation now made up of 'free' citizens. Politically and socially, citizens have a form that is normalized and to which they subject themselves. Bio-political strategies are invented such as statistical enquiries, programs for the enhancement or curtailment of rates of reproduction, or the reduction of illness and the promotion of health. Bio-politics seeks to render intelligible the domains whose laws liberal government must know and respect. Arbitrary sovereign power is out maneuvered by intelligent use of knowledge.

Foucault sees in the early modern State, the conjunction of the reason of state and science of police as important, both epistemologically and ethically. That conjunction constitutes the activity of government as an art with its own distinctive and irreducible form of rationality. It also gives to the exercise of sovereignty the practical form of a pastorate, a government of all and each for the purposes of secular security and prosperity.

Some of the attributes of the welfare State can be seen to originate from the police State, but more is needed to fully explain the rationality of the development of the modern welfare State. Foucault's (1978; 1991b) lectures on modern governmental rationality pay as much attention to a further intervention, that of liberalism. What is distinctive about Foucault's approach is his concern to understand liberalism as a style of thinking concerned with the art of government. Liberalism can be characterized in Kantian terms as a critique of State reason, a doctrine of limitation and wise restraint, designed to mature and educate State reason by displaying to it the intrinsic bounds of its power to know. Foucault sees the problem of liberalism as how a necessary market freedom can be reconciled with unlimited exercise of political sovereignty (Burchell, 1993: 269).

This problem is already a criticism of the police State under earlier reason of state. It is impossible for the State to be totally known, therefore police reason of state has a suspect rationality. In the police State, tables of data were drawn up to allow for a complete account of all the economic processes within the State. This can be regarded as a notion of economic sovereignty. Once again we are faced with the problems of sovereignty discussed earlier in the chapter. Under economic sovereignty it was thought that the ruler was in a position to permit economic subjects freedom of action because, through the data table, the ruler still knew what was happening. But Adam Smith's *invisible hand* is a critique of the notion of the table because it admits to there being more to the economy than can be counted and measured. The idea of the 'invisible hand' suggests there is something outside of control, and therefore the theory of the police State does not fully account for what is happening. To the extent that absolute control is thwarted, so is sovereignty. The invisible control is not known about and consequently is not available for the exercise of sovereign power.

Early Anglo-Scottish liberalism, as espoused by Adam Smith, sets limits to the State's capacity to know and act by situating it in relation to the reality of the market (or more pointedly, commercial exchanges of civil society), as a set of quasi-natural dynamics, with its own intrinsic forms of self regulation. Laissez-faire is, in this sense, both a limitation of the exercise of political sovereignty through the government of commercial exchanges and a positive justification of market freedom. Paradoxically, freedom is guaranteed by governing less. "This notion of liberalism regards the market as an already existing quasi-natural reality situated in a kind of economic reserve in a space marked off, secured and supervised by the State" (Burchell, 1993: 270). Liberalism undertakes to determine how government is possible, what it can do, and what ambitions it must renounce to be able to accomplish what lies within its powers.

Neoliberalism can be seen as a Western phenomenon. Also known as economic liberalism or economic rationalism, it provides reason to limit government in relation to the market. Starting out from the neo-classical formula that economics is about the allocation of scarce resources to alternative ends, economics becomes an approach "capable of explaining all human behavior" (Gordon, 1991: 43). And yet, the role of government remains important.

> Neoliberalism defines a general problematic of governmental invention and experiment. It becomes a question of constructing the legal, institutional and cultural conditions which will enable the artificial competitive game of entrepreneurial conduct to be played to best effect. In this view, society is the product of government's intervention (Burchell, 1993: 174).

Neoliberalism seeks its own ways to integrate self conduct of the governed into the practices of their government and through the promotion of correspondingly appropriate techniques of self. It constructs ways in which individuals are required to assume the status of being the subjects of their own lives—entrepreneurial selves in an enterprise culture. Government impinges upon individuals in their individuality, in their practical relationships to themselves in the conduct of their lives and at their very hearts, by making its rationality the condition of active freedom. It opens up a new, uncertain, often critical and unstable domain of relationships between politics and ethics, between government of others and practice of self.

Gordon (1991) explains the origins of three strands of neoliberalism: German, American and French. The German strand is concerned with how to create a State on the basis of an economic freedom which will secure the State's legitimacy and self limitation. The neoliberal argument is that the Nazi development was an example of the exorbitant growth of the State through anti-liberal policies. In this instance, the growth of the State has been attributed to several factors: national protectionism, welfare policies of the Bismarckian State, Keynesian interventionism and wartime economic planning and management. Since the 1960s in Germany, jurists and economists attribute governmental meaning to the idea of market. Unlike the theory of the unseen hand in liberalism, the market is not spontaneous and natural. The government sets up conditions for the existence and functioning of the market. The conception of the open space of the market and its competitive freedom functions as the principle of a possible new political legitimacy. From a neoliberal perspective, the major problem with a notion of society is its anti-competitive effects.

> In order to survive, capitalism must embrace competition as a system within a framework of positive institutional and juridical forms. Not only is the juridical domain not to be regarded as a mere superstructure of the economic, but an economic government conducted in the name of the market must accord a central role to a new kind of legal activism a conscious notion of economic right (Gordon, 1991: 42).

Extensive juridical interventionism is required to further the game of enterprise as a pervasive style of conduct, diffusing the enterprise form throughout the social fabric as its generalized principle of functioning. Under neoliberalism, the whole ensemble of individual life is to be structured as a pursuit of a range of different enterprises: a person's relation to his or her self, his or her professional activity, family, personal property and environment are all to be given the ethos and structure of the enterprise form, impacting significantly on ethical and cultural values within society. Foucault points out that the principle of enterprise carries its own contradiction since the idea of enterprise "seems in large part designed to palliate the desegregating effects of market competition on the social body" (Gordon, 1991: 42).

The American origin of neoliberalism involves a global redescription of the social as a form of the economic. It uses the neo-classical formula that economics concerns the study of all rational conduct. It envisages, therefore, the purely economic method of programming the totality of governmental action. It is both a reactivation and radical inversion of the economic agent as conceived by the liberalism of Smith and Hume. Reactivation consists in positing a fundamental human faculty of choice, while radical inversion involves re-interpreting the idea of order as meaning a commodified supply of law abiding behavior. The common problem is the question concerning the extent to which competitive, optimizing market relations and behavior can serve a principle for not only limiting governmental intervention but also for rationalizing government itself. The market only exists under certain political, legal and institutional conditions that must be actively constructed by government.

This version of neoliberalism claims to enrich economic understanding of human work. Economic activity is seen as a discriminating use of available resources. For neoliberals, work for the worker is not the Marxist theory of abstract labor value. It is, rather, the use of resources of skill, aptitude and competence which comprise the worker's human capital to obtain earnings which constitute the revenue on that capital. Human capital accumulated as a result of investment in the self extends the work on the self to more than an enterprise. It makes the individual an entrepreneur of himself or herself, i.e., a mode of continuous self motivation to accumulate abilities. The features of bio-power explain the re-emergence of Human Capital Theory within all three versions of neoliberal theory.

The French origins of neoliberalism involved an acceptance of mass unemployment as politically acceptable, because the individual is continuously employed in the enterprise of improvement of self. The preservation, reproduction and reconstruction of one's own human capital can be seen as *care of self* which governments commend as the corrective to collective greed. Gordon (1991) observes that where the right to permanent retraining became an institutional reality (as in the tentatively neoliberal France of the 1970s), its technical content has relied heavily on the contributions of culture of psychology and its techniques of the self (self-awareness, self-realization, self-presentation, etc.).

Common to all three neoliberal explanations is but one available subject position—the limited notion of the rational, self-interested, utility maximizing individual, *homo economicus*. Individualism is a methodological doctrine about how social events and situations are to be explained, with all explanations reducible to the individual as the unit of analysis. Being rational means that the explanation forms a logically valid argument such that if the premises of the argument are all true then the conclusions logically derived will also be true. Such logic is considered universal. In higher education, the individual would, through the faculty of rationality, maximize the utility to be had from education. In neo-classical economics, the individual's aims are identified with the individual's faculty of utility. The rationality that assures universality and uniqueness of choice is therefore, fundamental to neo-classical economic theory.

*Neoliberalism in New Zealand*
Economic rationalism has not always been regarded as capable of explaining all human behavior. In fact, as Sen (1987) has argued, economics was

derived originally from ethics about how we shall live. In other words, the ethics of ordinary life shaped the economy. New Zealand has had a tradition of organic solidarity which found expression in the welfare State. Now though, under New Right policies of deregulation and privatization, New Zealand has experienced a growing internationalizing of its economy and significant participation by multinationals as key players. New Right explanations focused on a challenge to such things as the documented inequities evident in, and admitted to by, the welfare State. New Zealand Treasury documents (1984; 1987; 1990; 1993), are an articulation of such neoliberal challenges.

Neoliberalism is a radical challenge to the philosophy underpinning the welfare State. Neoliberal philosophy has been used in New Zealand as a critique of State reason in an attempt to legitimate the minimization of the State in terms of its restructuring through corporatization and privatization (Peters et al., 1993). Through the application of neoliberal theories, government was to be made strong by limiting its powers and responsibilities. A number of indicators are used to measure the level of government intervention: government spending and taxation expressed as a proportion of gross domestic product (GDP); the size of the publicly owned sector of the economy; public employees as a percentage of all employees; and estimates of the range of government responsibilities and powers. And yet, despite the professed minimization of the State, "all these indicators show a substantial enlargement of the role of government in the twentieth century" (Gamble, 1988: 347).

The neoliberal challenge was introduced by the New Right with extensive academic theorizing about the apparent failures of the public services. Their main theoretical sources were monetarism, Austrian school economics, public choice theory and libertarian theory. Pollitt (1990: 43) argues that, "in the hands of its interpreters this body of knowledge and polemic was changed into an apparently simple but radical program for addressing the major perceived contemporary problems".

The prescriptive dimension of this program for public sectors is based on a diagnosis of the governance of Western liberal democracies which focused on at least seven key issues. The first point was an identification of pluralism and corporatism which leads to public sector interest groups obtaining a level of resources that, it was thought, would involve more public spending than the median voter would have supported.

The second issue was the presentation by the New Right of an extremely unfavorable account of the normal role of public bureaucracies (Niskanen, cited in Aucoin, 1990). Public officials were seen as being principally concerned with maximizing their own budgets and status. Typically, they were seen as being in league with special interest groups who were pressing for public subsidies. Politicians in turn were seen as anxious to satisfy these vocal groups. Because of lack of competition it was also suggested that many public bureaucracies were extremely inefficient and wasteful.

The third and fourth point is that the professions came in for special criticism for their alleged monopolization of the provision of particular services. From the standpoint of liberal economics this restriction on trade was bound to produce an undersupply of services which would be unnecessarily expensive. There was a double problem perceived here: the professionals who had captured the provision of services were likely to be both unnecessarily costly and deeply inadequate. The rising costs could be ascertained from an empirical evaluation of government expenditure.

The fifth problem was a result of too much reliance on the State. There was here a threat to the freedom of the individual and a subtle undermining of enterprise and self reliance as more and more citizens were tempted to take the easy way out and become salaried public servants themselves or to accept the generous public handouts (perhaps in the way of contracts) which those bureaucrats provided.

The sixth issue concerned the level of government responsibility for a minimum standard of welfare. The New Right did not see it as a legitimate function of government to seek some egalitarian concept of social justice. This would undermine freedom and result in open ended government expenditure.

Finally, the overall growth in the public sector, especially government borrowing to finance its own programs, was held to stunt private sector growth. Pollitt (1990: 44) reports that "such an unrelenting critical analysis could only lead its believers towards policies for cutting the size of the public sector and increasing the efficiency of what was left".

## Governmentality

From his work on the theme of 16$^{th}$ century government, Foucault developed a new paradigm for understanding power in modern society. In this new paradigm, power is seen to operate as a triangular complex, involving sovereignty, discipline and government—what Foucault called *governmentality*. The notion of governmentality is counter-posed to Statist conceptions of power, which in Foucault's view erroneously dominate modern understandings of social relations. The theory of power surrounding the modern State is a problem. Foucault argues that the State and sovereignty both rely on juridical conceptions of power as a negative or repressive force.

The limited conception of power as an institutional and prohibitory phenomenon cannot adequately explain the range of power relations that permeate the body, sexuality, the family, kinship and discourse. The notion of governmentality extends this critique of the State.

By governmentality Foucault means governmental rationality. The term refers to a domain of research about the rationality of government, about the nature or practice of government. In Foucault's terms, governmentality meant both governance of self and others. Its domain would include the self as the politically constituted subject of busno-power. Foucault says that governmentality means three things:

> The ensemble formed by the institutions, procedures, analyses and reflections, the calculations and tactics that allow the exercise of this very specific albeit complex form of power, which has as its target population, as its principal form of knowledge political economy, and as its essential technical means apparatuses of security.
>
> The tendency which, over a long period and throughout the West, has steadily led towards the pre-eminence over all other forms (sovereignty, discipline, etc) of this type of power which may be termed government, resulting, on the one hand, in the formation of a whole series of specific governmental apparatuses, and, on the other, in the development of a whole complex of *savoirs*.
>
> The process, or rather the result of the process, through which the State of justice of the Middle Ages, transformed in the administrative State during the fifteenth and sixteenth centuries, gradually becomes 'governmentalized' (Foucault, 1991b: 102).

For Foucault, the target of the analysis of governmentality is not institutions, theories or ideology, but *regimes of practices*; practices understood here as "places where what is said and what is done, rules imposed and reasons given, the planned and the taken for granted meet and interconnect" (Foucault, 1991b: 75).

## Governance and discipline

The technologies of self are those things that the individual does to implicate his or her self into accepting, or even promoting, the technologies of managerialism in such a way that managerialism becomes freely chosen (albeit in an illusion of choice) as a subsequent way of thinking and acting. Exposing the technologies of managerialism allows for the unraveling of the governmentalizing practices by which the self becomes implicated in its own management under a discourse of managerialism. In this sense, self-management is ordinarily promoted as an apparently self-evident, unproblematic and politically neutral mode of governance to be applied to educational institutions. This application is a practice that, depending on an individual's relative position in the managerial hierarchy, is to be enjoyed differentially.

On the accounts provided of standard managerial practices since 1870, managerialism can be regarded as a form of governmentality. As a mode of governance, managerialism has remained implicit, preferring instead to account for itself explicitly within explanations of accountability, efficiency, productivity and economic growth. But managerialism is fraught with notions of self discipline which present themselves as practical rather than as discursive and conceptual.

I want to develop the idea that managerialism is a regime of governmentalizing practices rather than a meta-narrative of administration that is often inadequately promoted as politically neutral for its explanatory value in rhetoric such as: *in the interests of the students, efficiency, upskilling* or even *education*.

Through the reforms to education, the introduction of managerialism is an attempt to legitimate a new type of governance that encourages educators to treat all tasks and processes as if they were production problems. The subsequent production problem, of constructing a managerial culture to support the development of a new self that manages various subject positions, demands that a range of institutions be overhauled. It demands that those institutions reconfigure themselves in ways conducive to self-management.

The meta-narrative of self-management, derived from managerialism, implies a subject to be managed. New legal, institutional, structural and cultural arrangements demand new modalities of existence and, as Huczynski (1993: 192) asserts, "managerial action cuts across many widely held liberal democratic values such as liberty, fraternity, freedom of choice and defense against exploitation". Arguably, then, a government intent on reforming attitudes, desires, values, expectations and goals must present a well articulated, internally coherent and psychologically plausible metaphor, to direct people to the desired end. New thoughts, desires, reasons, attitudes and behaviors, will be required to facilitate change. In the reformed structures, the acquisition and exercise of autonomous qualities in the individual will be encouraged.

The new discourse will require a de-legitimation of all the values that might inhibit the acquisition and promotion of autonomy. These inhibitory values are the values inherent in the notion of the dependent self which, like the previous so-called dependent welfare culture, are asserted by neoliberals to be no longer appropriate. Autonomy enhances productivity in the State sector where the discourse of self-management locates responsibility for productivity ultimately with the self-manager. What that productivity in the education discourses consists of is not clear in managerial discourse.

The phrase *self-management* in education has many possible meanings which relate to subjectivity, education, and management, in ways that ordinarily are not differentiated from each other. This non-differentiation conflates, or at least does not encourage, analysis at the level of practice. To the extent that the possibilities for self-management are not defined, neoliberalism has not constructed the space where the self can legitimately manage itself. Without an accepted boundary and sets of power anchored in public knowledge, it is not clear how the self is to act.

It is important therefore, in the absence of legal or regulatory guidelines, to examine what it is possible to say about self-management. There are many nuances that can be postulated using words *self*, *management* and *education*: (1) *self-management* in education; (2) self-management in education; (3) 'self-management' in education; (4) self-management in *education*; or, (5) self-management *in* education. When we use the phrase *self-management in education*, it is not immediately clear what we are talking about. We could be talking about, for example, the self, the management, the educational nature of the management or the self. We could perhaps focus on the non-Cartesian concept of 'inness' as Heidegger (1962) does in Being-in-the-World, and so on. This multiplicity of formulations of self-management, is indicative of the capacity of language as a practice. Semantics, metaphor and interpretation are all issues for the governance of/in education insofar as they are the site of the interaction of technologies of domination and technologies of self.

The apparent freedom alluded to through the language of self-management masks or distorts some underlying assumptions. For example, through the attribution of culturally value laden notions of freedom to the idea of self-governance through the practice of self-management, the subject comes to believe in autonomy of choice as a source of sovereign power. Within the notion of management then, a certain sense of origin or author(ity) that inheres within the individual, is implied. Corporate management theory is replete with references to the manager as all powerful. This is part of the attraction of management as a practice, especially to males who occupy the vast percentage of management positions. Mintzberg (1974) found that managers prefer action to reflection and behave accordingly. As managerial action can be interpreted as a behavioral manifestation of executive decision making. Self-management implies authority.

Managerialism, in this sense, is about the power that is implied through the autonomous decision-making competency of the manager. The notion of author embedded in the word *authority* implies that the manager is the autonomous and sole author(ity) of the decision. The notion of author is also employed here in the sense of an executive originator. Autonomy signifies the exercising of a human faculty of choice that itself is also assumed to be part of the constitution of the subject (Marshall, 1996). One widely-read management text, *The One Minute Manager* (Blanchard and Johnson, 1983), provides an example of the autonomous subject which portrays the manager as having a sense of sovereign control over the world merely on the basis of the decision to exercise that control. The very title of that text, in keeping with its contents, asserts that the manager is the authority, an assertion that all managerial evaluations depend on.

What is absent in these accounts of managerialism is any critique of the differences between managers and others (i.e., those who are not managers). This raises questions about why managerialist accounts of autonomy imply that non-managers have less powerful, and therefore less valuable, subjectivities. Otherwise, why would managers be privileged as they are with higher remuneration, better security of tenure, and more status? We might ask whether the difference might be explained by the genealogical accounts of managerialism that construct subjectivities, or whether those accounts themselves are but manifestations of presumed essential a priori phenomena that characterize business literature. The presumptions favor managers over workers. And yet, as Foucault has observed of managerialism, "this machine is one in which everyone is caught, those who exercise power as well as those who are subjected to it" (Foucault, 1977b: 156). Executive managerialist discourse then, reinforces its own privileged position as a form of sovereign power. Nevertheless, for the reasons discussed in this chapter, governmentality trumps managerialism as a way of explaining the world.

If we concede that a map *engenders* the territory as much as it *describes* the territory, then it is important to enquire of what the map consists. Otherwise, we may be accepting a poorly described territory as the basis for our reality. This has clearly been the case with the introduction of managerialism into education. Neoliberalism provides a limited account of society or of education, with its subject of economics (*homo economicus*), or what Sen (1987: 15ff) refers to as a "rational, self-interested, utility maximizer". By contrast, because it focuses on practices such as the infinite relations of power that are not subsumed to neo-classical economics, governmentality allows for the possibility of other-than-economic explanations of the self. In this respect, it provides a more satisfactory account than neoliberalism of the way in which subjectivities are developed.

Foucault's notion of governmentality provides a strong basis for critique of practices by which the neoliberal subject is constructed.

## Chapter Eight: A Genealogy of Managerialism

Chapter eight is a genealogy of the managerial discourse introduced into the reform of New Zealand tertiary education after the restructuring of the core State sector. Hood (1990) refers to this form of managerialism as the *New Public Management*. Two key texts in the reform process were the New Zealand Treasury publications *Economic Management* (1984), and *Government Management* (1987). There was no introductory public debate about the value of managerialism, its origins, its legitimating rhetoric or even its role in governance, apart from the standard account of *homo economicus*. Nevertheless managerialism as part of a more comprehensive package of new institutional economics was 'given' to us through legislation (Boston 1991). Very little management literature is concerned with the ways in which the discourse of managerialism appeals to common sense understandings about the world and hence, among other things, functions as a technology of self.

The chapter discusses the way in which managerialism is usually—and inadequately—explained as a meta-narrative in various attempts to legitimate the governance of individuals, societies, their organizations, and even the world. An alternative characterization of managerialism is as a form of governmentality which implicates the subject in its own governance. The idea of governmentality is that it can account for the way in which individuals construct themselves subject to the prevailing political rationality—in this case, neoliberalism. The language of management appears as common-sense, but on reflection, is both historically and materially located. A description of the historical surges in the rhetoric of managerialism therefore provides a basis for evaluating the assumptions within this form of domination. The discourse of managerialism is largely assumed to be describing self-evidently *good* things. As managerialism is employed in current education policy it needs to be examined for its intended and unintended effects and possibilities.

### The context of capitalism

Liberal or competitive capitalism is a notion of capital formation that Habermas (1988) argues takes place in a situation of unlimited competition. Liberal capitalism came into being as governments intervened in the market, granting incorporation to firms which led to the concentration of large amounts of capital as investors invested jointly. In this phase theorists had to come to terms with the process of industrialization and the concomitant creation of large workforces concentrated at particular sites of production. In the United States and in Europe in the 1870s and 1880s doctrines of Social Darwinism were widely expounded: ideas of competition and natural selection suggested that entrepreneurs and owners need have little regard for the welfare of their workers. Nature's laws would ensure the survival of the fittest, and the sensible employer should therefore manage with this *natural legislation* by retaining the healthiest, strongest workers and disregarding the rest (Perrow, 1979).

The next phase in the development of capitalism is sometimes referred to as state-regulated capitalism in that it admits to the need for state intervention. On the one hand, this phase involves the process of economic concentration—the rise of national and multinational corporations and the organization of markets for goods, capital and labor. On the other hand, we see the State intervening in the market as functional gaps develop.

> Capital formation takes place in a situation of unlimited competition. However, the supporting conditions of this competition—the social foundations of the production of surplus value—cannot themselves be reproduced by capitalist means. They require a state that confronts individual capitalists as a neo-capitalist order to carry through vicariously the 'collective capitalist will' absent in the competitive sphere (Habermas, 1988: 50).

The move in the discourse from other-management in a welfare model to self-management in an enterprise model indicates that welfare can be understood as an instrument of government. Some writers (e.g., Kelsey, 1995; Peters, 1995; Sharp, 1994; Rosenberg, 1993) argue that the welfare State was not the failure that many supporters of the introduction of managerialism in the State sector have claimed (e.g., Treasury, 1984, 1987; Deane, 1986; Pollitt, 1990; State Services Commission, 1991). What the supporters of reforms miss (in a genuine sense) is that the very success of the welfare state may have been its problem. Where liberal capitalism was seen to fail in terms of its unintended social problems, welfare capitalism emerged to restrain its worst effects and offer a collective security (Habermas, 1988). The welfare 'problem' and its subsequent conversion into a neoliberal *economic recovery* may have had more to do with the idea that "political rule was given the task of shaping and nurturing those domains that were to provide its counterweight and limit" (Rose, 1993: 290). Capitalism had therefore provided welfare to legitimate itself.

Welfare can be interpreted as a governmental device that covers up the way in which organized capitalism fails to provide security for the individuals. I suggest that the problem was not the failure of welfare by omission, but rather the success of its processes that required reform.

Increasingly welfare had a totalizing governmental effect in the form of a technology of domination with accumulation, statisticalization, and implementation of knowledge created from data.

Welfare in this sense is not a moral political stance but an adjunct to the economy. It offered collective security to the workers within organized capitalism at the same time as that security created a new space for the subject. The neoliberal criticism is that welfare capitalism takes away capital from investment in production and diverts it into welfare. Neoliberalism avoids paying welfare because it requires the subject as a condition of its very essence to produce its own welfare through enterprising thinking and activity within the current economic base.

Managerialism is the new face of capitalism. The self-managing subject which is the "counter weight and limit" (Rose, 1993: 290) allows for the reduction of the welfare State under neoliberal political rule. The so-called *dependent* subject of welfare is on this account a construction designed for a market space that has been constructed in order to facilitate production.

Managerialism is situated within an account of the development of organized capitalism. A combination of forces generated a need to separate the ownership of capitalist enterprise from its operational function which was the stimulus for the employment of a managerial hierarchy in the organization. The growth of the modern business enterprise can be located in this broad institutional context, and the bureaucratization of its surveillance capacities can be linked specifically with two phases in the development of the capitalist economic system. These are referred to as competitive and organized capitalism respectively (Habermas, 1988).

The practices of rule that liberalism specifies are concerned with knowledge of human activity. In his study of the 18$^{th}$ century French health system, Foucault (1976) illustrates how welfare organizations gather information for this purpose. In this sense the welfare mechanisms function like a panopticon (Foucault, 1979) as they govern on the strength of the practices of individuating and normalizing from the gathered data. Such a notion of power is *productive* rather than *repressive*.

The productive power of welfare, for example, developed a totalizing effect which did not allow for an account of technologies of self in the relations of power. Managerialism as governance, without a credible account of technologies of self, is unstable. Through its emphasis on neoliberal technologies of self-management and freedom (of choice), the State is purportedly restoring the proper space for the practice of individual responsibility and autonomy.

This role for the State, according to Hood (1991), is a return to history in that neoliberalism has many of the features of cameralism. Judging state control as improper in comparison with the proper domain of self-managing individuals, still involves the application of disciplinary power and is reliant upon an opposition between society and the State. Foucault transcended disciplinary power with his notion of governmentality which incorporates a notion of technology of self.

## The discourses

At the level of specific techniques and practices, the ideological components of managerialism are frequently difficult to discern. A particular performance indicator in education for example, such as staff to student ratios, appears on the surface, to be a relatively neutral and technical artifact. Yet, to appreciate its full significance, we need to take into account the techniques which accompany it, the model of management within which it is deployed and the broad assumptions about the role of management underlying it.

The essence of managerialism lies in the assumption that there is an activity entitled *management*—a generic, purely instrumental activity, embodying a set of principles that can be applied to public business, as well as in private business. At the level of meta-narrative, managerialism has been described as "an international ideology on which the economic, social, and political order of advanced industrialized societies is actually based" (Enteman, 1993).

There is much confusion and uncertainty as to the essential character and significance of management. It has for example, been characterised as a "set of beliefs and practices, at the core of which burns the seldom tested assumption that better management will prove an effective solvent for a wide range of economic and social ills" (Pollitt, 1990: 1). It may also introduce "an elite social grouping which acts as an economic resource and maintains the associated system of authority" (Child, 1969: 13).

In terms of the modern corporation, managerialism signifies the shift within the corporation from the owner to the professional manager as the key figure in the enterprise. Some large-scale economic enterprise and management techniques were well known, through the Catholic Church and the army, but managerialism in its modern form is a new phenomenon.

> There is a sense in which the genesis of management in the factory enterprises of modern industrial capitalism was a distinctly new development. This was because of a conjunction of social forces which hitherto had remained relatively separate: the concentration of ownership of the workplace, the means of work, source of

power and raw material in one and the same hand. This combination was only exceptionally met with before the eighteenth century (Dandeker, 1990: 161).

As capitalism became more organized, business enterprises were called upon to provide for mass markets rather than a narrow range of consumer wants. The discipline of formally-free labor was one of the central administrative problems of these organizations (Dandeker, 1990). To ensure production from large concentrations of workers and arbitrary work routines, a new disciplinary force was required: managerialism. According to Pollit (1990) managerial thought grew hastily in the final decades of the 19$^{th}$ century and has since moved into at least six broad phases.

Barley and Kunda (1992) challenge the prevalent notion that managerial discourse has moved progressively from coercive to rational and ultimately, to normative rhetorics of control. They argue that since the 1870s, managerial discourse has been elaborated in waves that have alternated between normative and rational rhetorics. They attribute changes in managerial discourse to fundamental antinomies in Western industrial societies: the opposition between mechanistic and organic solidarity and between communalism and individualism. This view supports Enteman's contention that managerialism can cope with communitarianism as well as individualism. Barley and Kunda argue further that the timing of each new wave is shown to parallel broad cycles of economic expansion and contraction, cycles in which the various rhetorics continue, despite being overtaken by new fads. The following rhetorics of managerial discourse are currently discerned in the modern economy, characterizing *management* as a subject within universities and other teaching institutions.

*Bureaucratic theory*
The era of state intervention was the beginning of bureaucratization of the capitalist business enterprise. Weber's theory of bureaucracy derived from his interest in the process of social change, and in particular, in the effect of rationality on religious thought and capitalism. By rationality he meant the kind of action or modes of organizing in which goals are clearly conceived and all conduct not designed to achieve the particular goal, eliminated (Pollitt, 1990).

From this historical perspective Weber designated different types of authority as charismatic, traditional and legal-rational. In the legal-rational form of authority, orders were obeyed because people believed that the person giving them was acting in accordance with legal rules and regulations. The organizational form built upon pure legal-rational authority was bureaucracy. Fully developed and in its most rational form, bureaucracy necessarily presupposes the concepts of legitimacy and authority. This notion of bureaucracy offers a stable and predictable world which provides the blueprint for rationally designed structures in which rational individuals carry out their prescribed roles and actions. In this type of structure the rationality of any action had to be judged against some objective standard and this formal rationality was reflected in the management thought and literature that succeeded it. The bureaucratic form of organization possesses the features of specialization, hierarchy, rules, impersonality, full-time officials, career focus and a split between public and private activity.

The principles of bureaucracy are evident: the notions of rules and regulations and the idea of categorizing employees. Tasks are divided in order to increase predictability of behavior, speed up skill development, and facilitate the surveillance and evaluation of staff. Managers appreciate that, in attempting to control outside influences, bureaucratic organizations seek to stabilize and routinize their own processes in the interests of internal efficiency. Bureaucratic practice treats the individual as a system given rather than as a variable. This key feature serves to differentiate bureaucracy from other management rhetorics. An essential characteristic of the ideal type of bureaucracy is a coherent, common set of goals which gives a clear direction and which formally translates into the various sub-tasks to be achieved.

Organized capitalism demanded more surveillance than liberal capitalism by definition. The growth of bureaucratic surveillance within the firm involved a shift from personal to bureaucratic control. The entrepreneurial ownership and direct control of small enterprises gave way to the impersonal control of large enterprises by a directorate employing a managerial hierarchy. According to Chandler (1977), with the growth of the firm, the invisible hand of the market became internalized to the organization as the visible hand of management. This process meant that the organizational boundaries of the firm, or the divisions between internal and external changed over time. The emergence of a managerial hierarchy involved an occupational differentiation of functions once performed by a single individual. This division of labor resulted in a separation of line management and staff management and the development of corporate planning of the firm's operations and strategy.

*Welfare capitalism*
With the move to organized capitalism, employers wanted to develop a workforce that was bound to the company so they developed an approach that contained elements of welfare capitalism. Prior to the American Civil

War in America and in the mills of England, little attention was paid to working conditions or employee welfare. Welfare capitalism linked religious visions of morality to a new stage of evolution premised on the principle of co-operation. Firms built libraries and recreational facilities. They offered classes, established social clubs and instituted profit sharing and benefit plans. They also improved sanitation and aesthetics of factories. In Barley and Kunda's (1992) account, the rhetoric of welfare surged from about 1870–1900, with some of its key advocates being substantial figures in the American establishment, and over a hundred major firms providing welfare facilities. Its espoused central values were organic solidarity and communalism. There was, however, no doubting the economic object of such welfare:

> Philanthropic businessmen established industrial welfare schemes in part in response to work-place conflict, to control local labor markets, maintain managerial prerogative and ameliorate work-place disaffection. As one of Melling's businessmen put it 'there is no need for us to appear as philanthropists first and businessmen afterwards—we benefit the workman incidentally but our motives are selfish to begin with' (Cantor, 1991: 226).

Organized capitalism was supported in the private sphere by the dominant Christian Protestant notion of duty towards those who had worked to make the profits. The rhetoric cultivated notions of the *working man* combined with religious and moral values, and unlike Marxist theory, did not challenge the prerogatives of the ownership of the means of production. In this view, lack of frugality, industriousness and temperateness of the *individual* lay at the root of industrial unrest. Systems based on co-operation were advanced as morally superior to those built on conflict. Through the rhetoric, workers' interests and values were brought into line with those of the owner, thus achieving moral authority, and procuring loyalty and commitment. Co-operation in this context meant between workers and the owners of capital rather than between worker and worker. These notions of the individual are not available in an ideal bureaucracy where individuals are merely system givens.

One would think that this rhetoric contained the idea that contented workers would remain loyal to the boss. It did, but it did not remain dominant for very long. The Pulman Palace Car Company's welfare efforts were insufficient to avert the strike of 1894. In the economic depression of 1896, reform-oriented firms were as vulnerable as any others. Attacks were made by journalists, and trade unions on the moral grounds of paternalism, feudalism and authoritarianism. Scientific management was seen as superior to the systematic "industrial betterment" approaches of the time (Huczynski, 1993: 120), because it addressed itself to the issue of the control of the work process. Attacks were also made by industrial and mechanical engineers which eventually gave rise to a more *systematic* or *scientific* management.

*Scientific management*
The next phase introduced the detailed, practical body of thought most commonly associated with the work of Frederick Winslow Taylor. Scientific management from 1900–1920 eclipsed welfare capitalism as the dominant rhetoric. The central value of scientific management is rationality. Engineers applied the principles of academic disciplines to the organization of production. The key advocates of scientific management are cited in Barley and Kunda (1992) as Frederick Taylor, the Harvard Business School, and the Carnegie Commission. Interest in scientific management was not confined to the so-called capitalist countries. Bell (1976) argues that Lenin was strongly attracted to the scientific management ideas of Taylor. Marxism, after all, claimed to be a scientific social mechanism. The Carnegie Commission in 1910, involved in reform of higher education, showed that scientific management had utility beyond the factory as a *progressive* political agenda.

The publication of Taylor's *The Principles of Scientific Management* (1911) presented schemes for improving management's coordination and control, cost accounting systems, production control systems, wage payments, and plans to enhance productivity by specifying cause and effect in the production process. By the 1920s unions embraced scientific management as a way of preventing despotism in the factory and of controlling the work of their own members through providing clear rule definitions, explicit job delineation, detailed rules governing wages and working conditions, and a grievance procedure based on division of labor (Huczynski, 1993).

Taylor is perhaps best known as a pioneer of time and motion techniques, in studies of the detailed movements of workers dealing with well defined tasks. Taylor wrote his work on the principles of scientific management to point out and promote efficiency through systematic management, rather than in searching for some unusual or extraordinary man. In particular, he was intent upon proving that science was the model for management.

> The best management is a true science, resting upon clearly defined laws, rules and principles, as a foundation. And further to show that the fundamental principles of scientific management are applicable to all kinds of human activities, from our

simplest individual acts to the work of our great corporations, which call for the most elaborate co-operation (Taylor, 1911: 5-7).

Two of Taylor's claims are of particular importance. First, there is the assertion that management can be a *true science* with all the connotations of discovering precise, impersonal laws. Second, a parallel claim is made for universality of application. All human activities are subject to the laws. This claim is extensive and has moral implications.

The rhetoric of scientific management involves several key features: a belief in the utility and morality of *scientific* reasoning, the axiom that people are primarily rational, and the supposition that all people view work as an *economic* endeavor. There is also a sense that these claims do not need to be justified and can, therefore be accepted as natural. Such 'natural' laws offered managers limited options, thereby suggesting to them that there were only a fixed number of possible actions. Organization of work in this schema is a rational technical problem informed by scientific approaches to efficiency. Since scientific thinking is seen as incontrovertible, effective management is reduced to the exercise of demonstrable expertise. Scientific management produces a need for a new way of thinking, not just a set of techniques. Managerial rhetorics of efficiency provided a political platform for a progressive notion of governance by educational elites, the superiority of scientific reasoning, and authority of expertise.

*Administrative theory*

From Taylorism flowed many attempts to identify and enumerate the correct principles for the design of organizations. This literature of the 1920s and 1930s, has become known as *classical management theory*. One very well known formulation which attempts to promote management as the science of administration is *POSDCORB* which is an acronym for planning, organizing, staffing, directing, coordinating, reporting and budgeting. From such lists of key tasks a manager might get some clues about how to function. Typical lists of activities for managers include

> the need to set clear objectives, communicate them throughout the organization, allocate resources to ensure their achievement, control costs, motivate staff, improve efficiency, and especially for senior managers, move strategically and proactively to shape external relationships with customers, suppliers, and other organizations (Pollit, 1990: 5).

The primary focus of this management idea was the determination of what types of specialization and hierarchy would optimize the efficiency of organizations. The application of these two concepts produced a very mechanistic form of organizational design which paid little attention to people except to see them as cogs in a wheel. Administrative management is built around four key principles. These are the division of labor, the scalar and functional processes, organizational structure and the span of control. Other important concepts include discipline, unity of command, unity of direction, remuneration, subordination of the individual interest to the general interest, centralization and a focus on the *esprit de corps*. It was believed that the techniques of successful management could be described and taught and that managerial organization was a valid area of study .

*Human relations theory*
Scientific management generated its own counter-ideology in the form of the rhetoric of human relations. By the 1920s several government studies cast doubt on Taylor's claims to substantially reduce waste or power costs. Labor had achieved collective bargaining and union participation in corporate governance. There was fear of unrest among workers based on the Bolshevik revolution in Russia—workers had to be made content. Welfare capitalism, which focused on the human aspects of production, was also still widespread in the 1920s.

The value position of human relations managerial rhetoric, dominant from 1925–1955, is normative, seeking to transform the firm itself and its management into a cohesive collective. Human relations basically held that the industrial society was a shaky fabric: scale, diversity and constant change frustrated basic human desire for intimacy, consistency and predictability in social living. People were to look to their jobs instead to manufacture the conditions to meet these needs. Workers were held to be more responsive to the social forces of their peer groups than to the controls and incentives of management. This perspective is of Freudian psychoanalytic origins evident in the work of two key advocates: the 1940s empirical research of Sheldon, Parker-Follett, and the multi-disciplinary approaches of Mayo and Lewin (Barley and Kunda, 1992).

Mayo's (2003) work, commonly known as the *Hawthorne Studies*, established the idea that informal relations within and without the organization are of considerable importance. Individuals are seldom motivated by rational argument alone. Some of the intellectual heritage of the human relations school extends to such notions as job enrichment, participative management styles and self actualization. Productivity, however, is still the name (and the reality) of the game.

In the 1950s the human relations rhetoric reached, and was promoted by, management consultants and business colleges. Human relations rhetoric supports an assortment of technologies; interest in work groups, theories of self actualization, promotion of similar conceptions of workers, managers and views of organizations as primarily social entities. Work groups are thought to have norms which are not necessarily consistent with managerial objectives. Therefore, in order to align workers' values with the structures of the organization, management is conceptualized as synonymous with leadership. The function of leadership is to unleash the power of the normative system to enhance the firm's integration. Effective management is equated with cohesive collectives.

One key difference between the human relations school and scientific management was the advancement of a considerably more sophisticated model of the individual worker. Whereas in early scientific management the worker was treated as an individual unit responding directly to simple incentives and punishments, the human relations school substituted a model of a rather complex being who responded to a much wider variety of environmental factors, including behavioral norms created and sustained by fellow workers. Human relations created the worker who wanted to feel good about work and fellow workers. Scientific management posed the solidarity of a group as an obstacle to be overcome rather than a phenomenon which could be understood and turned to management advantage. The human relations school made use of such political features as group solidarity. The key idea of the human relations school was the rational assessment of the whole person set in a context of the social relations of the workplace (Perrow, 1979: 49).

*Systems rationalism*
Challenges to the rhetoric of the human relations approach to management included criticisms of loss of individuality especially among white collared employees. The unintended consequences of cohesion and loyalty within human relations were thought to produce a notion of *group think* or *The Abilene Paradox* (Harvey, 1974). These shortcomings were thought to undermine the values of democratic society. Managerial theorists claimed that the human relations approach was cost inefficient and did not 'deliver'. The means—the process of being at work—became the ends. The development of computers also posed a challenge. Science and engineering became economically and culturally central in the Cold War. Managerial education emphasized statistics and quantitative methods. The human relations movement was also accused of the disintegration of families through techniques of psychoanalysis that were employed to improve relationships. If true, this would undermine another dominant rhetoric of

Western society—the family. Lindsey (1987) reports how psychoanalytically oriented management consultants changed the values of individuals in AT&T personal growth workshops. Some of the values constructed within the management groups were very effective and, the workers argued, contradicted those required for commitment to the family. Subsequently some of the workers sued the company on the basis of the American Constitution which guarantees respect for their values.

The humanizing tendencies of the human relations school had its limits. Although management has a definite interest in recognizing that production is a social enterprise, and that workers are not merely commodities but can also contribute with their thinking, they also have an interest in limiting the development of human potential which expressed oppositional cohesion and solidarity. It might suit workers to act as if socialism really operated inside work, but the manager must operate in a world in which market forces are material and govern what is possible in the development of a co-operative environment. Employment was no longer a social responsibility of the business.

The rhetoric of systems rationalism dominated from about 1955–1980. Its key value system is rational. Management was now conceived of as a science with its use of operations research, process theory and contingency theory as instances of a broader trend of systems rationalism. Its central tenet is *management by objectives* (Barley and Kunda, 1992). Management literature on systems rationalism in the Business Periodicals Index peaked in 1980.

The rise of the rhetoric of systems rationalism coincides with technological developments inevitably associated with modern warfare. During World War 2, the military employed mathematicians, physicists, statisticians to devise methods for solving logical problems. *Operations Research* teams were established in industry to solve managerial problems. In the mid 1960s, queuing theory, network analysis, simulation techniques and linear programming were introduced into corporations and universities. The core curriculum of elite business schools consisted of operations research, management science, finance, accounting and statistics. Process theories provided management with a definition of itself consistent with the tools of operations research and management science. Systems rationalism prescribes rational and calculative activities as antidotes for human relations excesses. It incorporates insights of the human relations school in a dynamic relationship with systems modeled on cognitive and decision making processes. Thus, instead of arriving at a set of administrative maxims, systems rationalism adopts an approach more related to the context. It presents principles to enable managers to plan, forecast and act more effectively. It drew moral if not technical inspiration from scientific management, with ideas like Critical Path Method and Program Evaluation Review Technique. In a manner similar to that of managers within the scientific management rhetoric, managers under systems rationalism must also be experts, but that expertise is generic, and abstract, not merely functional. Managerialism can therefore be applied generically to any place and time: hence the rise in explanations of professional management.

One well known approach that reflects this relativism is known as *contingency theory*, reflecting the idea that the optimal internal structure for an organization will be determined by the setting of "key environmental contingencies" (Pollitt, 1990: 19). Systems rationalism lacks an explicit model of the workforce; workers are seen as rational actors and their involvement in work as purely instrumental. Managerial analytic orientation could effectively manipulate structures and decision processes. The theory implies that employees are instrumentally motivated, and that efficiency is a matter of means/ends calculations or inducement/contribution ratios. Micro-organizational behavior was now interpreted as psychological theory.

*Culture management*
The dominant rhetoric since about 1980 is the normative theory of organizational culture (Barley and Kunda, 1992), with competition from Japan and West Germany in American industry, lower labor costs in South East Asia, and high inflation in the United States. There was a large increase in US service industries and professional workers (Bell, 1976) whose identities extended beyond the firm. These people were motivated differently through their possession of abstract generic skills and were less amenable to control or exercise of traditional authority. Culture management is a form of social action that espouses a voluntaristic epistemology, legitimating differing perceptions of organizational realities, and emphasizing individual ethical choice over institutional imperatives (Pollitt, 1990). The rationality for the change in rhetoric from systems rationalism to culture management is that systems rationalism neglected the importance of symbolism and ritual in organizational life. Handy (1976) argues that the idea of culture refers to sets of values, norms and beliefs: far from there being one best culture, cultures may legitimately vary both between and within organizations. In pursuit of *excellence*, Peters and Waterman (1982) are more prescriptive, claiming that the task of shaping the organizational culture is one for senior management.

Culture management can be regarded as an attack on systems rationalism which sacrificed moral authority, social integration, quality and flexibility.

Systems rationalism was also criticized for rewarding specialization, parochialism and calculative involvement at the expense of loyalty and commitment. Culture management promotes views of organizations as socially constructed systems influenced by anthropology and symbolic interactionism. It contains notions of symbolic leadership, concern for employee's values, and enhancing competitiveness, on the lines of the culture of the Japanese work-place. The British Periodicals Index shows that by the late 1980s, corporate culture was as common a discourse as systems rationalism. Reed (cited in Pollitt, 1990: 23) however, asserts that since the 1970s, the field of organizational studies became a "melee of competing theoretical perspective that jockeyed for intellectual 'poll position'".

The rationale of organizational culture is that economic performance in turbulent times requires the commitment of employees who make no distinction between their own welfare and the welfare of the firm. Unity and loyalty are thought to counteract the unintended consequences of rational design. Such commitment is said to enhance individualism and autonomy. Culture in organizations is a dominant notion of the fully fledged collective which can be designed and manipulated. Value systems can be formulated and inserted to the advantage of the firm, at the risk of promoting 'cults', 'clans', 'mythical heroes' and 'religious conversions'. Value conformity and emotional commitment support financial gain. Organizational effectiveness now becomes organizational transformation for the firm, where the emphasis is on "loving each other in a brotherly manner, incorporating spiritual values into work, and doing something physical together" (Huczynski, 1993: 170).

**Principles of managerialism**

According to Enteman (1993), managerialism is an international ideology on which the economic, social, and political order of advanced industrialized societies is actually based. It rests on the impoverished notion that societies are nothing more than the sum of the decisions and transactions which have been made by the managements of organizations. Managerialism is both a normalizing force and a form of disciplinary knowledge. As a consequence, social decisions in education are seen as the interactions of managers, not necessarily the will of the community, the students or the needs of its teachers. From this perspective, the nature of the institutions has become a function of changes in management practices over time.

A managerialist society is not one which responds to the needs, desires, and wishes of the majority of its citizens. In a managerialist society, influence is exercised through the managerialist structures of organizations. Society responds to whatever the managements of various organizations can gain in their transactions with one other. If people belong to an organization where managements effectively represent their interests, they are likely to respond appropriately.

Managerialism is both a process and a substantive ideology (Enteman, 1993). It renders the individual an empty abstraction and the organic existence of the State an abstraction without any correspondence to reality. Social decisions arise out of transactions in which managements of organizations are engaged. The movement from individual values to social choice is through organizations, arranged in the transactions of the managers of the organizations. Managerialism is not simply a technique or an attitudinal shift. Enteman considers that attitudinal shifts are not merely perturbations in an otherwise stable situation but are manifestations of a radically changed society.

Managerialism presents neither an atomistic nor an organic view of society. It shares elements of both, but moves beyond them. Previously it seemed that all ideologies relevant to industrialized societies should fall into one or other of those two categories. Managerialism falls into neither, but is not simply a compromise. It makes a break from the past but does not merely carry it forward into the present. Managerialism appropriates representative democracy for its own purposes. Managerialism is organic in that it recognizes that social organizations can take on organic characteristics which cause people in them to rise above their own individualism. Individual preferences are seen to be expressed through organizational units and larger social choices are made as those units interact with each other. In spite of this genuflection towards an organic view, managerialism accepts that there is only a *will of all* rather than the *General Will* in Rousseau's terms. The will of all is not grounded in the preferences of individuals. It is rather the result of interactions among the social subunits.

Capitalism was grounded in the assertion that economic activity results from the purchase and sale decisions of individual consumers. Managerialism does not recognize much effective power in individual decisions. It finds the social decisions including economic ones arise out of the transactions among units which encompass individuals. It is not the organizations, however, that interact to create a social decision—it is the managements of those organizations. In order to capture both the atomistic and organic perspective within an institution, Enteman (1993: 158) claims that managerialism is "polyorganic". It is important to note that the managerialist perspective does not reach the conclusion that all units develop an organic structure. Some of the units may be internally quite atomistic, with members refusing to subscribe to an overall view or position which does not suit their own personal interests.

While the metaphor of a management team is currently popular, not all managements operate as teams, and those who claim to operate as a team are not all successful. Management structures can develop where each of the participants acts only out of self-interest, with no concern for the overall direction of the organization. Managerialism is atomistic then, in that it declares that a society is nothing more than the summation of the decisions and transaction which have been made by the managements of the organizations. In this respect, social choice results from numerous transactions among managements.

Managerialism is not deterministic, however, as its efforts at control are not always predictable or successful. In democratic politics for example, managements of organizations lobby political candidates for their respective organizational interests. The political candidates, in turn, shape their responses to the electorate so that their message does not offend their critical constituencies, i.e., those organizations that want their views put forward and who in turn provide much of the funding for the political process. Political candidates become packaged by their own parties to cope with these demands and end up being undistinguishable from one other on most substantial issues since they are all in the grip of managerialism.

From this account of political lobbying, we may be tempted to suspect managers of engaging in a complex, hidden conspiracy that enables them to govern the country. This is not so. In the sense that managerialism is atomistic, it describes a situation in which the managements of organizations try to make the best possible arrangements for themselves first and for their organizations second. In making these arrangements, managements find it necessary to negotiate, bargain and transact with the managements of other organizations. Groups and individuals who are not represented at the bargaining are unlikely to have their interests represented. Interdepartmental power, as well as individual power, is at stake. Individual managers compete with one another inside the company. They seek to improve their unit's bargaining position within the organization.

Accounts of scarcities (within the rationale of economic theory) increase internal bargaining for resources which affect the daily quality of life, as well as the ability to produce accomplishments that might produce career advantage or simple productivity of the organization. Turbulent environments also keep shifting the focus of relevance of positions and make whole departments, even organizations, relatively essential or inessential, depending on their control over critical issues. Since the views of managements are developed in large part as a function of contest with many other individuals and managements (with varying degrees of success) this process is far from conspiratorial. Management cannot be understood as merely technical:

> In addition to its technical function, management is a system of authority through which policy is translated into the execution of tasks; and ... an elite social grouping which acts as an economic resource and maintains the associated system of authority (Child, 1969: 13).

Drucker (1994) extends this transcendent analysis when he asserts that the post-capitalist society will be divided by a new dichotomy between intellectuals and managers, the former concerned with words and ideas, the latter with people and work. Apart from its implication that managers are not intellectuals, this idea implies a meta-narrative. "Post-capitalist society requires a unifying force ... a common and shared commitment to values, onto a common concept of excellence ..." (Drucker, 1994: 193). Managerialism, on these accounts, has emerged as an ideology in the wake of the so-called breakdown. It has remained implicit as a mode of governance, however, preferring instead to account for itself explicitly as a mode of efficiency and productivity in the interests of economic growth. In an earlier work, Drucker (1974: 19) defined management as "an economic organ, indeed the specifically economic organ of an industrial society. Every act, every decision, every deliberation of management has as its first dimension an economic dimension". In terms of the modern corporation, managerialism signifies the shift within the corporation from the owner to the professional manager as the key figure in the enterprise. This is clearly a competitive view of the world where the fittest survive. Managerialism, it would seem, can be characterized as Darwinian, in its promotion of the notion of the survival of the most adaptive groups and managements within and between organizations and groups.

### Illusions of freedom

The attempts by management theorists to capture the high ground certainly indicate a sense of grand theory or what Lyotard (1984) terms a meta-narrative. Taken together, these characterizations envisage an important role for managerialism. On the one hand, neoliberal explanations for the insertion of managerialism into the public sector, attribute to the manager (the subject *homo economicus*), a faculty of choice which is assumed to be a inherent, or a birthright. This faculty is merely seeking a suitable territory within which to exercise itself. This explanation implies that neoliberal structures, including the constitution of the self, are rational and that the operator is merely an ideologically driven technician. If, on the other hand, accounts of managerialism are simply descriptions of an individual functioning within a territory appropriated by the power of certain groups, we have a different issue for the self. In this case, the self needs an ethic that implicates itself in its own governance.

If the accounts of managerialism are acknowledged as maps that engender the territory, within which managers can then manage, a different picture begins to emerge. That is an image of a semiotic cartographer designing the chart, creating the space in which attempts at autonomy are to be exercised. The discourse of managerialism which relies on the metaphor of autonomy is problematic indeed. Neoliberal self-management is State-induced, discourse-bound and subject to governmental discipline. Managerialism appeals to a new level of freedom for the individual, by providing more choices and opportunities within self-management as part of a reason of state, but such appeal is illusory. The actual specifications for the freedom of the individual provided through the reforms are nothing more than a moment in an individualizing and totalizing process.

In terms of education, although the New Zealand regulatory environment is designed to facilitate the development of a market, it has been established through State intervention. The national economic growth desired by government must be achieved, it seems, not by state funding support but through *neoliberal* State interventions. The marketisation of higher education in New Zealand then is a neoliberal experiment (Peters et al., 1993). If, as neoliberalism suggests, the individual must manage his or her self, the technology of managerialism is problematic.

## Chapter Nine: The Management of Human Capital

Chapter nine explores certain neoliberal aspects of governmentality legislated into the education discourse to control the bodies and minds of individuals. The chapter critiques Human Capital Theory and then outlines notions of bio-power, busno-power and busnocratic rationality to critique the rationality of government adoption of the notion of humans-as-capital.

What is needed in an information society is an account of power that explains how Human Capital Theory has captured the hearts and minds of individuals. Accordingly, the chapter draws on Marshall's (1995b) notions of busno-power and busnocratic rationality to address the inadequacy of bio-power as an explanation of human capital and its management in what Poster (1990) calls the mode of information.

Neoliberal rhetoric concerning the reduction in the size and scope of the State is discussed. Despite neoliberal claims to the contrary, the busno-power of Human Capital Theory functions paradoxically to increase the power and pervasiveness of the State. The so-called minimalist neoliberal State increases its power through management of the definition and regulation of its stock of human capital. Busno-power functions as a form of governance and provides a grid of intelligibility for the self under these conditions.

The chapter then discusses the ways in which Romer's Endogenous Growth theory (1990) is employed in an attempt to shift other understandings of the notion of human capital. The essential differences are the attempts to separate the individual from his or her own knowledge and the attempts to shift knowledge into a notion of information. This separation of the individual from knowledge re-conceptualizes both the individual and knowledge, and is a radical departure from other versions of Human Capital Theory. This development is not discussed in OECD reports on Human Capital Theory or elsewhere in the literature. There is also no acknowledgment by Romer, by the OECD, or by government, that under Endogenous Growth Theory, a shift from knowledge to information is required if the shift is to be successful.

The chapter problematises the governmental effects of Human Capital Theory, including that of the self. The explanation offered here is non-dialectical in that the self, under busno-power through busnocratic rationality, is also implicated in its own governance. Control over, and through education and training, lies with control over the curriculum and funding. Therefore, under busno-power, delivery of education and training is seen as a merely technical exercise and well within the capability of most interested people in the accredited managerial system. The busno-power regime retains the management of the education and training curriculum (including funding) at the center, and locates the responsibility for their delivery (and increasingly their governance) at the periphery. Since there is no internal space within which to critique its form and content (busnopower's positivistic philosophy removes this possibility), this technical form of management is problematised in the chapter as busnocratic.

## Human capital theory

Human Capital Theory has been critiqued by Marginson (1993) as the most influential economic theory of Western education, setting the framework of government policies since the early 1960s. Marginson identifies three phases in the application of Human Capital Theory to government education policy.

The first phase, in the 1960s, was one of public investment in human capital, dominated by claims about a link between education and economic growth. The second phase was a period of eclipse, in which the earlier policy assumptions were abandoned and the rates of return equations were confined to a modest place with the body of neo-classical theory. The third phase (not completed) saw renewed policy commitment to investment in human capital. But in the free market climate now prevailing, the emphasis is on private rather than public investment. In this latest phase, of which the policies pursued by the Government are a prime example, education in human capital terms is seen as a source of labor-market flexibility in relation to technological and social change.

In terms of structural reform, the OECD identifies the following four elements as the basis for the Government's structural policy framework:

1. Enhancing labor flexibility—through regulatory reform in the labor market, as well as raising skill levels by additional investment in education, training and employment schemes, and immigration focused on attracting high-quality human capital;
2. Promoting participation and self-reliance—through reforms to the welfare system;
3. Improving the overall competitiveness of the economy—through continued supply-side reforms including the legal framework, resource management, and tax policy;
4. Strengthening international linkages—by encouraging foreign investment and trade development

(OECD, 1993: 55)

The OECD identifies human capital development as a crucial issue. Workforce skills and management are seen as the "key determinant of economic performance" (OECD, 1993: 69), and human capital development as a "factor which enhances labor-market flexibility and facilitates structural adjustment" (OECD, 1993: 69). The OECD argues that while the educational system and formal qualifications represent significant factors in the fabric of human capital there are important elements outside these realms. Human capital is "the sum of the skills embodied in its people, with the value of that capital dependent on the opportunities people have to use those skills" (OECD, 1993: 69-70). Those opportunities are to be constructed in a neoliberal world through the market.

Clearly, such a definition includes skills acquired in the workplace as well as those acquired within the *second chance* system. On this basis, the OECD makes a case for the importance of skill development, particularly in nations with perceived low participation rates in education. In the 1990s the OECD expressed concern about the high proportion of people without formal qualifications, and relatively poor performance in terms of growth in total factory productivity (i.e., output growth unexplained by additional labor and capital inputs). One report states that

> in the past, benefit structures, a lack of vocational focus in the school curriculum, inadequate integration between different forms of post-compulsory education and training, labor-market regulations, and the highly protected economic environment all lead to poor skill development (OECD, 1993: 103).

The OECD (1993) identifies poor skill development, skill shortages and skill mismatches as primary constraints facing future economic performance. In keeping with the images of Deleuze (1990), we might say that skill mismatches are *perpetual shuffling* back and forth until a match is made. The same report identifies necessary reforms such as greater speed and *adaptability* over *detailed prescription*. It identifies scope for a coordinating role for government in the move to an industry-led training system. In the absence of significant private sector competition, the report also recommends lower per-student subsidies, a capital charge regime, and the elimination of any restraints on competitive practices, as policy means for encouraging the sector to respond to the training needs of industry. Subsequent OECD (1994; 2007) reports continued this theme of Human Capital Theory.

*The self as capital*
Traditional Marxist theory has a notion of the self as an abstract form of labor power. Human Capital Theory, however, has changed the self into a form of capital that can, like financial capital, be invested. According to Gary Becker, Nobel Prize winner for his work in Human Capital Theory, the

theory is a study of the general theory of investment in human capital with its ramifications for a variety of economic phenomena.

> Investment in human capital is concerned with activities that influence future monetary and psychic income by increasing the resources in people. Schooling, a computer training course, on-the-job training, migration, information about prices and incomes, expenditure on medical care, and lectures on the virtues of punctuality and honesty are capital in the sense that they improve health, or raise earnings. These forms of investment differ in their effects on earnings and consumption, in the amounts typically invested, in the size of returns, and in the extent to which the connection between investment and return is perceived ... all these investments improve skill, knowledge, or health, and thereby raise money or psychic incomes (Becker, 1994: 11).

In a pre-emptive strike against any accusation that Human Capital Theory is unadulterated utility, Becker argues that work and money are not all that concern Human Capital Theory. The theory also claims to consider culture as a matter for research. It considers that education can be subsumed as a cultural artifact within the economy. Studies funded for research within the human capital domain show that education "promotes health, reduces smoking, raises the propensity to vote, improves birth control knowledge, and stimulates the appreciation of classical music, literature, and even tennis" (Becker, 1994: 21).

Becker's explanation suggests that Human Capital Theory advocates a perspective on culture that equates with the picture of *the good life* promoted by its main beneficiaries, i.e., the financial capitalist investors who discern that there exists an all embracing purpose for human beings, especially those who would be educated. That purpose is to accumulate capital inscribed in their selves. Since, within neoliberal Human Capital Theories, all facets of life are subsumed under the economic investment in the self, by the self, is the essential purpose of life. This appears to be a self independent of political, economic or cultural circumstances.

In this individualized culture of accumulation, the self is dominated by a discourse that equates existence with improved productivity. And, since human beings are thought to be infinitely malleable, the process of improving productivity knows no bounds. This requirement for performance, Lyotard (1984) calls *performativity*. No longer is government funding to be provided merely for Being; continuous individual performance is required. Education and training are themselves constitutive of that performance, in that they are implicated in power relations that set up the conditions of possibility for the existence of that performance.

## Bio-power

Bio-power is a form of bi-polar technology that generates political counter-demands, providing for the possibility of a "strategic reversibility of power relations" (Foucault, 1982: 221). Bio-power is about power over life, in contrast to previous regimes of power over death. With this contrast, Foucault (1978) marks a shift in history from the *symbolics of blood* to the *analytics of sexuality*. Whereas the symbolics of blood focused on death as the ultimate power, the analytics of sexuality focuses on control over life as the ultimate source of power. According to Foucault (1978: 138), "one might say that the ancient right to take life or let live was replaced by a power to foster life or disallow it to the point of death".

Bio-power can be defined as the way in which current life practices function so as to bring about an order within which individuals will be healthy, secure and productive. Bio-power is not a notion of power as repression but rather designates forms of power exercised over persons specifically insofar as they are thought of as living beings. It is a politics concerned with subjects as members of a population, in which issues of individual sexual, and reproductive, conduct interconnect with issues of national policy and power.

Foucault proposes two poles of bio-power in the modern regime of power over life. He argues that these bi-polar technologies of life are not antithetical. There are two directions of bio-power development. In the first pole of bio-power, the focus is centered on discipline of the body, optimizing its capabilities, the extortion of its forces, the parallel increase in its usefulness and its docility, its integration into systems of efficient and economic controls. Foucault details the procedures of power that characterised the disciplines of the human body. Particular technologies include discipline through the army, apprenticeships, reflection on practice, practices of the care of self, education, disciplinary blocks and power/knowledge.

The second pole of bio-power is population control, made possible by the emergence of demography, statistics, evaluation of use of resources, tables of wealth, circulation, actuarial tables of longevity and risk. In the second pole the body is imbued with the mechanics of life and serves as the basis of the biological processes: propagation, births and mortality, the level of health, life expectancy and longevity, with all the conditions that cause it to vary. Supervision takes place through a series of interventions and regulatory controls—a bio-politics of the population. There are strong traces of Becker's Human Capital Theory in bio-power.

In relation to this second pole, Foucault sees the belief that it is possible to tell the truth about oneself. This belief is concerned with the possibility and not the empirical facts. Through the discursive practices associated with this belief, individuals become objects of knowledge both to themselves and also to others. Telling the truth (discursively, circumscribed and constructed) can be both therapeutic and controlling. Eventually, individuals learn through these practices to subjugate themselves into an object of these 'truth' constructions. Here, the subject and object become one and we can celebrate the death of the subject. This is the essence of the interactive effects of technologies of domination and technologies of self, which Foucault refers to as governmentality.

Human Capital Theory then, can be interpreted as a form of bio-power, with control of the body as its focus. Science and technology provide control over life and were instrumental historically in the creation of the possibility of thinking in this manner about humans as capital and through the possibility now of the value of life expectancy being able to be calculated. Life insurance is predicated on this idea. The development of electronic technologies has made it possible that virtually everything about life can be calculated, and therefore theoretically available for investment and integral to the economy. By contrast, a power focused on death would not be a good investment because of its unknown risk factor. It is on the basis of the worker's life then, rather than the Marxist notion of abstract labor power, that the recent versions of neoliberal Human Capital Theory have been built. This focus on the body of the worker has had a rationale in the past in terms of the mode of production:

> We pass now from the accumulation of capital to the other aspect of industrialism: 'the accumulation of men', as Foucault put it, so that the time of individuals is integrated into a production apparatus, turning them into labor power. Foucault suggested that the disciplinarianism of the work force may have been a precondition for industrialism rather than the other way around (Horne, 1986: 67).

Bio-power, with its focus on the body as an element of population, has been an indispensable element in the development of capitalism. It allowed the controlled insertion of bodies into the machinery of production. In the case of capitalism, bio-power dealt with living things through knowledge/power, control, and delivery, of the right number, and correctly disciplined supply, of working bodies. Here we have the beginnings of the notion of people as capital, as an investment category calculable through an analysis of capabilities, training, integration and control. The calculation and investment potential of human capital is infinitely enhanced by electronic technology.

## The management of busno-power

Developing and extending upon Weber's notion of technocratic rationality and Foucault's notion of bio-power, Marshall (1995b) provides an account of busno-power, imbued with a busnocratic rationality, that underlies neoliberal theories of human capital. Marshall's account refers particularly to radical economic liberalization in New Zealand since 1984. As has been argued elsewhere (see Fitzsimons and Peters, 1994), these changes have been explained as a result of introduction of institutional economic practices into public sector restructuring, and since 1987, into education. The reforms were underpinned by a particular mix of neoliberal theory, including Public Choice Theory, Human Capital Theory and the New Public Management. Busno-power focuses on the mind in the mode of information and accounts for the ways governmentality operates in a neoliberal regime in which the body is not available for control and where the self is electronically distanciated and instantiated.

We can see busnocratic rationality inherent in the government's industry training strategy; in the drive for mass participation in tertiary education; and in regulation of qualifications. These function as technologies of domination at one pole of Foucault's bio-power—the pole of population. Both poles (population and individual) are accommodated by busno-power. Some of the ways in which the technologies of self function as the other pole, to implicate students as consumers and choosers, will be detailed in the practices described and critiqued in the following chapters.

Busno-power produces and reproduces the very form of the self. Its control is exerted at both poles of the individual/population continuum. At the one pole, busno-power directs itself at the subjectivity of the person, not through the body, but through the mind, through the electronic forms of educational practice and pedagogy that shape the subjectivities of autonomous choosers in their educational choices. But against this, education in a marketised world is a captured choice. Education, embedded as it now is in the frameworks of busno-power and busnocratic rationality, is an important step in the individualizing and totalizing functions of busno-power.

At the other pole, busno-power addresses the demands of governmentality for the integration of the self into the forces of domination, where the individual is redefined, along with the culture within which the individual is situated. Busno-power is

> directed not only at individuals to turn them into autonomous choosers and consumers, but also at the population as a whole, by a total immersion in the

enterprise culture of the social, the economy and the new rationality of State. In the exercise of busno-power there can be seen then a merging of the economic, the social and the activity of government (Marshall, 1995b: 6-7).

The introduction of busnocratic rationality implies a culture change, integrating the concepts of enterprise culture into the very practices of the self. It involves a penetration into the very basis of human nature, reforming relations between individual and society. It also involves and promotes new forms of governmentality or rationality of State.

> Central to busnocratic rationality are these emphases: the concepts and stances taken in promoting skill, as opposed to knowledge; information and information retrieval, as opposed to knowledge and understanding; and the view that it is the consumers (especially industry), as opposed to the providers, that define and determine quality in education. It is the particular ways in which business values of skill, important 'knowledge', and quality, are intertwined into this form of rationality which distinguish it from technocratic rationality (Marshall, 1995b: 7).

In developing a notion of busno-power that implicates the mind rather than the body as a technology of self, Marshall has opened up a notion of power that explains the way in which the mode of information functions. Just as busno-power requires the mind on the one hand as a technology of self, it gives rise on the other hand to a technology of domination where the self is identified as an invisible individual element of the statistical population on any electronic network.

The OECD (1993) version of Human Capital Theory which underpins government policy is able to be explained through busno-power and busnocratic rationality. In the busnocratic rationality underpinning human capital policy, we can see a merging of the economic and the social through busno-power. Human Capital Theory is certainly underpinned by technocratic rationality in its attention to skills, outputs, standards and frameworks of knowledge. In the technocratic rationality, delivery is separated from the conception of the curriculum, instrumental outcomes and behavioral discourse. Weber's iron cage of bureaucracy comes to mind in attempts to standardize knowledge as a commodity in the interests of efficiency. Traditional liberal versions of education policy were also imbued with technocratic rationality—there is no internal space for critique. In the previous liberal education regime, however, the technocratic rationality usually allowed the ends to be separated from the means, and, even though it was not always successful, there is at least an external space within which to contest its values (Marshall, 1995b).

What distinguishes the OECD account of Human Capital Theory from traditional liberal accounts of education, is that it is heavily permeated with the values of busnocratic rationality "at a microscopic level" (Marshall, 1995b: 9-10), making debate and contest difficult. By its very nature, busnocratic rationality acts through its capacity to appeal superficially to agreed ends (such as those of efficiency and quality), but at the same time conflating its means with its ends. So, to define a system as a *quality* one (as in a quality assurance system, the mere existence of which is said to ensure what counts as quality) is to valorize the notion of quality in such a way that it is unable to be critiqued from within that system. This capture of the discourse, however, has not stopped others from critiquing what counts as *quality* (see Marshall, 1993).

Distinction between policy regimes is more than a mere exercise in semantics. In the rhetoric of the OECD, the purpose of this change is to enable individuals (with certain predictable higher socio-economic status) and the nation to take advantage of the modern technological economy within competitive international markets. In this sense, the neoliberal policy context is argued as a busno-power policy regime that promotes Human Capital Theory as a form of governmentality. Just as the previous liberal education in the name of Enlightenment did not provide the notion of personal autonomy with freedom, neither (despite its rhetoric) does the new busno-power regime with its underlying busnocratic rationality. Rather, it shapes individuals as particular kinds of subjects so that they will choose in certain general ways.

The neoliberal theories of human capital inherent in the restructuring of education require the construction of a new, or at least a severely reconstructed, culture. And a new culture requires the acquisition of new subjectivities. Insofar as the subject is actively engaged in its own governance, explanations for the constitution of the self are contestable. Because it is limited to the subject position of *homo economicus*, neoliberalism cannot be said to have captured the hearts and minds of individuals. What is still needed is an explanation of the practices through which the subjects of busno-power are implicated in the mode of information.

Through neoliberalism, busno-power has installed a free market economic agenda at the heart of education policy. This has had profound consequences for both the academic and the democratic project (Marginson, 1993). Through the application of Human Capital Theory in particular, education policy is now interpreted as economics. And, under this new busno-power policy regime, the notion of student has been transformed into an autonomous, rational, self-interested, utility-maximizing, verbal juggling, revenue-generating unit[1]. This transformation in the notion of the student indicates the power of neoliberal philosophy to name, and therefore govern, education. Deleuze's (1990) notes the self-perpetuating nature of the regime in his reference to *perpetual training*.

But for busno-power to function as governmentality, the liberal rationality of the self and its culture, or at least its account of culture, needs reforming. To this end, new language and practices imbued with busnocratic rationality have been inserted into life in the form of a new policy regime. In an effort to change the culture (and the self), since 1984 in New Zealand, existing arrangements have been unsettled. The remainder of this chapter critiques a sample of practices that have been employed: (1) to rationalize the unsettling of the existing policy regime; and, (2) to rationalize the introduction of new technologies of domination and technologies of self.

The technologies of domination are the discourses of the key change agents. The technologies of self are the language and practices that individuals employ as a result of changes and through which the self becomes implicated in reform. Since technologies of domination and technologies of self are involved in this production of governmentality, there is no dichotomy in practice between domination and self. By definition, if culture is reformed so are its constituent selves, and vice versa. Busno-power produces, and is produced, through the practices of domination and the practices of self.

## The management of education

### The management of perpetual training

Insofar as a neoliberal regime is implemented, busno-power requires an enterprise attitude centered on the discipline of the mind, optimizing its capabilities, the extortion of its forces, a parallel increase in its usefulness and its docility, and its flexible and enterprising integration into systems of efficient and economic controls. Busnocratic rationality is inherent in enterprise culture because an enterprise culture demands enterprising behavior; in turn requiring perpetual training in the face of continual restructuring, new electronic technologies, and changes in the discourse.

The methodology itself for change is clearly articulated. Enterprising behavior can be encouraged through such managerial notions as performance pay, perpetual training, and continuous control.

> The modulating principle of 'salary according to merit' has not failed to tempt national education itself. Indeed, just as the corporation replaces the factory,

perpetual training tends to replace the school, and continuous control to replace the examination. Which is the surest way of delivering the school over to the corporation (Deleuze, 1990: 4-7).

Busnocratic rationality can be seen in the corporate regime of practices such as the claim to measurability of unit standards, the perpetual training and upgrading of skills, continuous and centralized control through such things as accreditation systems, and the continual assessment of skills. Perpetual training is thus part of the new corporate rationale for education and training systems in advanced countries. It provides the link between education (in the broadest sense), and the economic system. It motivates both policy and practice. In terms of the prevailing Human Capital Theory, perpetual training is the basis for a vocational reorientation of the education system to meet the needs of the new economy.

Under government management skills are to be standardized. Here we have the appearance of a notion of skill that has been emptied of its contents. Skill in this sense has no knowledge and appears as low level behavior. How, one might ask, can a skill be improved in this sense other than through mindless imitation? But without a theory for interpretation, how would the individual understand what counts as success? If skill acquisition came about simply through trial and error, we are left without a theory for interpretation. All we are left with are explanations about the activation of some primordial brain stem that reacts in a survival mode on the basis of its genetic structure and is thus impervious to training efforts. This conjures up an image of learning as instinctive drift. How then, would transfer or generalization occur? Are we to say that it is through proper breeding? The problem with that explanation is that it leads to eugenics.

A totalizing focus on education and training, i.e., the policy regime within which the human capital is managed, fails to recognize the cultural nature of the outcomes. Instead of addressing the social, cultural and political issues inherent in the employment and social world, government policy concentrates on the skill levels of the individual within an education and training discourse, a focus that precludes addressing structural issues.

A key policy question that is often addressed is whether or not State intervention in training helps disadvantaged individuals into employment. In a labor market that is expanding, the answer will probably be yes. In a labor market that is shrinking, the answer may be no. After surveying the results of various broadly based training programs for unemployed adults in New Zealand, the training-friendly OECD was forced to conclude in 1994 that "there was markedly meager support for the hypothesis that such programs are effective" (Economist, 1996: 19).

The same results are true for studies in America. There, in a study of the largest job training program, it was found that "for those aged under 21, training had no effect at all, and may have caused young men to lose earnings" (Economist, 1996: 19). Britain's experience is similar. Youth Training, Britain's flagship program for 17-18 year olds, enrolls about 200,000 youngsters a year. A government evaluation in 1994 found that "almost half of those who joined dropped out before the schemes had ended. Unemployment rates of those who did finish, at 27%, were higher than for the age group as a whole" (Economist, 1996: 19).

Summing up the British experience in a paper for the London-based Employment Policy Institute, Peter Robinson of the London School of Economics argues that after accounting for deadweight (programs helping those who would have found jobs anyway) and substitution (finding work at other people's expense), "hardly any benefit remains from Britain's training schemes" (Economist, 1996: 20). And part of what does remain seems to come from a small but telling detail: a few hints about deportment and interview skills.

Of five Australian training programs studied during 1989-1992, only one could report that at least half of its participants were either working or studying three months after completion (Economist, 1996: 20). In Australia, there were complaints from the unemployed that they are being recycled from training schemes to short term subsidized jobs and back again. Converting long-term unemployed into short term unemployed serves a political purpose—to be seen to be doing something for the long-term jobless. And "by maintaining some contact between the unemployed and the world of work, it serves an economic purpose too, but a disappointingly limited one" (Economist, 1996: 20).

In 1995, a Swedish study, commissioned to evaluate the country's long admired active labor market programs—including job-search assistance, training and relief work, concluded that "while retraining might raise, slightly, the chances of employment, it does so at higher cost, and to less effect, than simple job-search" (Economist, 1996: 20). The OECD reported research that evaluated four German programs, two offering further training and two retraining for the unemployed. The result: No type of training was found to have any significant impact on the flows out of either short or long term unemployment, nor on the flows into unemployment. Arguably, the closer training is to general education (as in Germany), the more likely it is to succeed. But even if education and training are working as they should expect, there will be no miraculous falls in unemployment until the costs of labor to employers, and the benefits of the labor to workers, have been shifted to levels the market can bear. It is possible then, that a focus on government policy about training and on individual skill levels is merely a distraction from the real problems of unemployment and the lack of a broad general education. The type of analysis quoted from the Economist (1996) refers to training programs which might be seen cynically as a process of *warehousing*. Programs are seen as effective at the margins but might otherwise be regarded as 'parking lots'. It is seen as a policy regime under which individuals are 'parked' in active labor market training programs in a cost efficient manner until a job is created by an upturn in the economy. Consequently, the course *outcome* of employment may bear no relationship at all to the training program undergone by the trainee. Any evaluation that touts a successful outcome from national training schemes and does not distinguish between these structural unemployment and skills training issues will be more illusory than real. Politically, the problem will *appear* to have diminished, but beneath the appearances, structural problems will still be hidden behind the rhetoric of training.

*The management of participation*
In order to achieve the Ministry of Education (1993) vision of increasing the value of the human capital, participation in tertiary education was increased. Participation was expected to supply, control, deliver and monitor the variable requirements of the correctly disciplined minds for national economic productivity.

Mass tertiary education was reported as a means of upskilling populations to take advantage of the development of modern, complex, technological economies (OECD, 1993). To OECD commentators (e.g., Smith, 1993, Shapiro, 1993), mass participation in education represents a move away from the previous elitism of universities. The movement towards mass tertiary education is represented by the OECD as a third wave within the history of modern Western education. The two previous waves were the development of mass secondary education in the mid $20^{th}$ century, and the move towards mass primary education towards the end of the $19^{th}$ century. Since the early 1950s and in line with increased participation in primary and secondary education, the level of public funding of education in most industrialized countries has risen markedly.

Participation in tertiary education has also risen in almost all Western industrialized countries. In contrast to the historical and corresponding increases in funding for the increased participation in primary and secondary education, however, the level of public funding per student is to be reduced. The funding regime in tertiary education is not commensurate with the expansionary rhetoric of the OECD. The idea that each individual will maximize his or her utility in the face of reduced funding per student is fundamental to the Human Capital approach to education.

To facilitate this increase in participation, a few possible provision arrangements are outlined below. The first, and least likely, mechanism is to increase public expenditure on education. This was the preferred option under the Keynesian model of the Welfare State. A second mechanism is that the student contribution could be increased, although participation levels are likely to be inversely proportional to fee increases. A third approach is to increase system efficiency through the use of performance indicators. However, as Peters (1990) observes, such indicators are mostly of a quantitative nature and do not measure the actual essence of the educational process. Another strategy is to reduce the cost of provision through competitive tendering, a marketised option in which curriculum design may be decoupled from delivery. The use of information technology and computers in education makes this option a possibility. Alternative private provision of delivery could be promoted, with the expansion of approved accreditation system to harness the willingness of the private sector to compete in the delivery of training and qualifications. More fundamental still, there could be a radical review of undergraduate curricula and a closer alignment with the OECD emphasis on the needs of the economy for human capital. Auctioning courses to the lowest bidder among the institutions is also a possibility.

A drive for mass tertiary education, rationalized upon a need to compete in world markets, indicates busnocratic rationality. In order to compete, nations must increase human capital. There is an apparent contradiction, however, between the State adopting neoliberal policies which argue for the construction of a minimalist State, while at the same time arguing for increases in State power through taking responsibility for increases in tertiary education on the other. Human Capital Theory assumes that education is a private good that will be accessed evenly and rationally in the light of the evidence presented by its exponents (e.g., Becker, 1994). What this approach ignores, though, is that behind every economic theory or schema is a society.

Busnocratic rationality increases busno-power through strategic planning in commodity production. In the case of education, one set of commodities are the students, referred to during the 1990s education reforms as *revenue generating units*. The message is clear: as a matter of policy, participation in tertiary education is to increase and is an investment; formal education is an arm of economic policy and a part of the social process of commodity production.

The OECD (Marginson, 1993: 20), has argued that the development of contemporary economies depends crucially on the knowledge, skills and attitudes of their workforces—in short, on human capital. It is of further interest to note that rates of *participation* are now being regarded as indicators of *quality*—the section in the report on rates of participation is entitled "education standards by international comparison" (OECD, 1993: 85). This suggests that the OECD (1993) equates participation with quality.

It is in *disciplinary blocks* (Foucault, 1979) that human capital is currently circulated, reformed, certificated and finally screened to develop its maximum investment potential. The point nowadays is that busno-power and modern information technology no longer require the carceral function for the body of these disciplinary blocks.

Through busno-power, certain forms of language are indicative of the busnocratic rationality of human capital policies such as those involved in the promotion of increased participation in tertiary education: subsidies, student loans, full fee paying students, tuition fees, income contingent loans, equivalent fulltime student, targeting, income threshold, abatement, consumer price index, real value, supply and provision, performance indicators, auctioning, competency, efficiency, vouchers and choices. Prior to 1984 this language was not prominent in the educational discourse.

**The management of growth**

Technological change, research, innovation, productivity, education and competitiveness are all central concepts in the economic rhetoric of Romer's (1990) Endogenous Growth Theory. The theory creates demands for a new subject position, the subject of economics, a commodity to be circulated in the market as human capital independent of its own knowledge, i.e., it is commodified. The individual is separated from his or her own knowledge, constituting a radical departure from other versions of Human Capital Theory. This development is not discussed in promotional literature; neither is the underlying shift from knowledge to information on which the new subjectivity depends.

The OECD asserts that Romer's Endogenous Growth Theory is a means of improving national economic performance through human capital development, as a "key input to the research sector underlying productivity-enhancing technological process" (OECD, 1993: 69). In alignment with the OECD, nations harness tertiary education systems as economic devices in the interests of national economic growth. The subject of human capital is a key determinant of economic performance, so the demand for a new subject position is a seen as a moment of governmentality.

*Economic terminology*
Economists attribute two fundamental characteristics to any economic good. (1) The degree to which it is rivalrous and (2) the degree to which it is excludable (Romer, 1990: S73). Rivalry is a purely technological attribute. A purely rival good has the property that its use by one firm or person precludes its use by another. A purely non-rival good has the property that its use by one firm or person in no way limits its use by another. Excludability is a function of both technology and the legal system. A good is excludable if the owner can prevent others from using it. Conventional economic goods are both excludable and rivalrous. Public goods are both non-excludable and non-rivalrous.

*Romer's Endogenous Growth Theory*
The notion of endogenous indicates that economic growth affects, and is affected by, other variables within the system rather than being dependent on a variable outside the model. Four basic inputs in the model of endogenous technological growth are: capital, labor, human capital and an index of the level of technology. Capital is measured in units of consumption goods. Labor services are skills of the healthy body, and are measured by counts of people. Human capital is a distinct measure of the cumulative effect of activities such as formal qualifications and on-the-job training and is distinct from labor services. Labor, for example, is more or less productive (all other things being equal) depending on the variable of the human capital. It is interesting to note that, in Romer's (1990) theory, labor is separated from human capital. By contrast, it was one of the innovative formulations of Human Capital Theory to integrate labor through redefining it as a notion of capital. Under Human Capital Theory, an index of the level of technology could be, for example, the count of the number of new designs in an economy in any given period.

Growth in this model is technologically determined, in that it is limited by technological change arising from intentional investment decisions made by profit-maximizing agents. The distinguishing feature of *technology as input* is that it is neither a conventional good nor a public good: it is rather, a non-rival, partially excludable good. Romer's main conclusions are that: the stock of human capital determines the rate of growth; that too little human capital is devoted to research in equilibrium; that integration into world markets will increase growth rates; and, that having a large population is not sufficient to generate growth (Romer, 1990: S71).

Romer outlines the historical development of three types of human capital. The first two types of human capital implicitly combine a notion of knowledge that can outlive any individual, with a labor market notion of human capital that cannot do this. Romer seems to imply that these two types of human capital contain inherent contradictions. Human capital models, such as those presented by Becker (1994), treat all forms of intangible knowledge as being analogous to human capital skills that are rivalrous and excludable. Romer's model emphasizes the importance of human capital in the research process. Earlier models showed that scale is an important determinant of the rate of growth, and now we see the correct measure of scale not as population but as human capital.

Non-rival goods can be accumulated without limit on a per capita basis. Since human capital is finite to the individual, it is a rival good. Treating knowledge as a non-rival good allows us to conceptualize that there is an imperative that knowledge will expand because of the magic that non-rivalry imposes on the profit-maximizing agent. The profit-maximizing agent will multiply the knowledge (design), providing conditions for unlimited growth when that knowledge is combined with human capital in the research of production process. Treating knowledge as a non-rival good also makes it possible to talk sensibly about knowledge spillovers, i.e., incomplete excludability—appropriatability (Romer, 1990: S75). These two features—unlimited growth and incomplete excludability—are generally recognized as being relevant for the theory of growth. Knowledge, then, is a non-rival good that is able to be combined by preference to produce growth. In the case of Romer's (1990) model, knowledge is combined with a notion of human capital that has been redefined and enhanced in the production process itself.

*The separation of knowledge (design) from human capital*
The model of endogenous growth defines knowledge as equivalent to design and separates the rival component of knowledge, from the nonrival, technological component. Because it has an existence that is separate from that of any individual, the technological component (i.e., knowledge) can grow without limit. Each new unit of knowledge corresponds to a design for a new good. The measure of the technological component is the count of the number of designs in an economy. Once a firm has produced a design for a durable good, it can obtain an infinitely lived patent on that design. Romer argues that an educated person working today and one working 100 years ago have the same human capital, measured in terms of foregone participation in the labor market. The educated worker today, however, is perceived as more productive on the basis that he or she can take advantage of all the additional knowledge accumulated as design problems were solved

during the last 100 years. This reasoning suggests that knowledge is separate from the knower.

The design of a new good is non-rival. The vast majority of designs result from the research and development activities of private profit-maximizing firms. A design is non-rival because once it is created; it can be used as often as desired, and in as many productive activities as desired. A design in this sense differs in a crucial way from a piece of human capital such as the ability to add—the design is non-rival whereas the ability to add is rivalrous. The differences as laid out by Romer (1990) are set out immediately below.

| **Design (Knowledge)** | **Human Capital** |
| --- | --- |
| non-rival | rivalrous |
| disembodied | embodied |
| used in many locations | one location at a time |
| non-excludable | partially excludable |
| able to be copied | privately provided |
| used in many activities | traded in competitive markets |
| cheap to replicate | costly to replicate |
| accumulated without bound | finite to each person |

A crucial feature of the specification employed by Romer (1990), is that knowledge enters into production in two distinct ways. Firstly, a new design enables the production of a new good that can be used to produce output. Secondly, a new design increases the total stock of knowledge and thereby increases the productivity of human capital in the research sector. The owner of the new design incurs the development costs, which means that the benefits from the first productive role of that new design are completely excludable. There is a secondary role for the design because, in practice, it is not possible to stop the spread of knowledge. As knowledge spreads and other types of designs are invented or production benefits are gained, the benefits from the second role are completely non-excludable. This means that the non-rival design inputs are partially excludable. The new knowledge is a nonrival good that is partially excludable and privately provided (Romer, 1990: S85).

*Economic growth through technology*
The relationship between investment in knowledge (design) and the resulting productivity is clearly represented in the tables on the following page.

In Case A, the research investment in terms of hours produces a design for a 20 megabyte hard drive for a computer. Along with the other inputs (D), (F) and (W), the production in one year equals 2 trillion megabytes. If the inputs (F), and (W), were doubled the second year, the production would be 4 trillion megabytes—twice as much. In Case B, however, the investment in research is 20,000 hours and, as a result, a better research design is produced. The production in the first year is 3 trillion megabytes. But if the inputs of (F) and (W) were to be doubled as in Case A in the second year, the production would be 6 trillion megabytes—three times the original output of Case A in year one. These tables show that (1) technological change drives growth (which is the first premise of Romer's (1990) argument) and (2) that the technology is a non-rival good but is inconsistent with the second premise of Romer's (1990) argument. Both premises, however, deny the role that private maximizing behavior (i.e., agency) plays in generating technological change.

| Case A | Inputs | | | | Outputs |
|---|---|---|---|---|---|
| | (R) Research hours | (D) Design product | (F) Factory investment | (W) Number of workers | Production |
| Year 1 | 10,000 | 20 megabyte | $10M | 100 | 2 trillion megabytes |
| Year 2 | 10,000 | 20 megabyte | $20M | 200 | 4 trillion megabytes |

| Case B | Inputs | | | | Outputs |
|---|---|---|---|---|---|
| | (R) Research hours | (D) Design product | (F) Factory investment | (W) Number of workers | Production |
| Year 1 | 20,000 | 30 megabytes | $10M | 100 | 3 trillion megabytes |
| Year 2 | 20,000 | 30 megabytes | $20M | 200 | 6 trillion megabytes |

*The subject of economics*
Neoclassical economists often work with abstract models or so-called perfect economies that obey strict mathematical laws. When these abstractions neglect reality, the theories can have negative effects at worst; at best, they can be discarded as irrelevant. Since Romer's (1990) Theory of Endogenous Growth is important to OECD policy advice it needs to be examined for its effects.

Romer's Endogenous Growth Theory can be seen as a example of the type of practices which Foucault (1991a: 75) argues "possess up to a point their own specific regularities, logic, strategy, self-evidence and 'reason'". Romer's theory has been articulated within a neoliberal account of reform that explains its totalizing effect through the authority ordinarily attributed to government reports. Through the government's acceptance of the OECD report and the government's many references to the technological growth rhetoric in many of its communications, Romer's theory can be viewed as governmentality that has a *totalizing* effect. There is a question, however, about the way in which Romer's theory of endogenous technological change accounts for the transformation of the subject if that subject position is only explained from a perspective of domination. Such an emphasis on domination would unrealistically serve to deny agency.

What we need is an account of the way in which the self is involved in its own governance that is not technologically determined. What is needed is an account of the conditions that initiate, promote, enhance and allow such practices as imposed theories to be seen as *natural* and *real*. Foucault's notion of governmentality is such an approach.

*The subject of human capital*
Romer's Endogenous Growth Theory is the subject of an impoverished notion of human capital. The notion of the human capital subject that is minus the ownership of its own knowledge is metaphorical. Donzelot (1991) describes the ideology behind the techniques that are used in modern management development programs. The aim of these programs is to modify the relation of individuals to their work—to breakdown the statutory perception the worker has with the psychological ties he or she establishes with their work. Workers are helped to reconceptualize the idea that work defines individuals and stamps their place on them like a destiny, robbing them of their identity if they lose their jobs, and making a change in the place or content of work potentially threatening. The new approach involves putting the accent instead on individual autonomy and the capacity to adapt. The individual is invited to become an agent of change in a world of change. Instead of defining individuals by the work they are assigned to, the new approach regards productive activity as the site of deployment of personal skills. Whereas individual freedom previously meant the possibility of either accepting or refusing an assigned status, it now signifies the flexibility to permanently redeploy one's capacities according to the satisfaction one obtains in one's work, one's greater or lesser involvement in it, and its capacity to thoroughly fulfill one's potentialities. Thus we have continued retraining within a whole new psychological culture. This approach assumes a change in the status of work and the management subject. It is, in fact, a culture change.

Substituting the term *information* for *knowledge* in Donzelot's (1991) account, we can see that Romer's theory contains similar assumptions about the nature of the subject. In Romer's case, it is adaptability rather than knowledge that is to count as a career, with deployment of skills emptied of their knowledge content.

The idea of productivity can be seen as metaphorical. Under Romer's theory, all human capital is now able to be either involved in research about technology, or in the use of technology, to facilitate productivity. Productivity ultimately comes from within the model and is not stimulated from variables—that is the meaning of endogenous. It represents an exemplar of productivity fully under the control of human agency, where private, profit-maximizing agents make investments in the creation of new knowledge and earn a return on these investments by charging a price for the resulting goods greater than the marginal cost of producing the goods. The endogenous nature of the model suggest ideological comfort in what Lyotard (1984) critiques as outmoded meta-narratives of human agency, in this case, the profit-maximizing agent.

The notion of human capital employed in Endogenous Growth Theory suggests a new position for the subject. Romer provides us with a conceptualization of human capital that allows for the separation of the knowledge—a non-rival and non excludable good—from the 'knower', thereby making 'knowledge' available to all ready and upskilled human capital. In Romer's (1990) view, nations will gain most from investing in research from where new knowledge is developed. The speed of design and accessibility of research knowledge is what creates economic growth. On this account, the human capital subject is redefined as an input, in possession of a set of non-cognitive skills—labor redefined as an adaptive information handler. The human capital subject is now required to adapt entrepreneurially to all new and continually developing external information through the continual enterprise of themselves (Gordon, 1991). Under Romer's theory, the individual is continuously vulnerable to the technologies of domination.

**The management of the State**

In this chapter, Foucault's notion of governmentality has been interpreted as operating through busno-power, i.e., the State run by an economy largely controlled by business interests. The governmental reform practices in relation to perpetual training are not primarily about enhancing individual learning, transforming educational institutions, increasing national wealth or even dealing with international competition—those ideas have been discounted as rhetorical by influential commentators. They are, rather, about busno-power. Marshall's notion of productive busno-power, through the theme of governmentality, takes agency as central (because technologies of self are integral to it), and allows the critical reactions of well informed commentators to be seen as an indication that busno-power is a more complete explanation.

The notion of a relationship between national economic growth and education is a major platform in the government's busno-power policy regime. On this basis, public policy designed to stimulate economic growth includes measures to develop human capital. The government's position is that human capital must increase in the interests of national economic productivity. For government to argue that education is solely about productivity or national economic growth is to resort to busnocratic reasoning. In the absence of empirical evidence of the positive relationship between education and economic growth, busnocratic rationality based on Human Capital Theory is, at best, questionable. In fact, one reconstructed Human Capital theorist even argues against this idea (Blaug, 1987).

Although it is often argued that the neoliberal State has been minimized, there has not been a naive return to the Classical State of history. The modern State and its policies are constituted by experts, discourses and technologies, themselves subject to busno-power, and integral to governmental practices. The State remains the effective broker in the contest between private and public goods in the economy. Any reform of policy is integral to what Miller and Rose (1993) call the *programmatic* character of governmentality: programmatic in the sense that reforms tend to be linked to explicit programs, and also in the sense that a better reality is programmable. When policies or reforms fail, what the State does, of course, is to develop more reforms.

> When transformation actually happens it will not be because a plan of reform has found its way into the heads of the reformers. It will be when all those who have to do with the reality of (in this instance, education), have come into collision with each other and with themselves, run into dead ends, problems and impossibilities, been through conflicts and confrontation; when critique has been played out in the real, not when reformers have realized their ideas (Foucault, 1991a: 84).

Foucault's analysis of reform suggests that words and programs of reform won't change much. Rhetoric simply will not do. The practices must change and something must cause them to change, but Foucault has his doubts about reform. Although neoliberalism provides a rationale for the introduction of technologies of domination such as the legislated decrease in the size of the State, the increase in busno-power afforded by the human capital policies of the government suggest that neoliberalism is an insufficient account of reason of state. This chapter concludes therefore, that Marshall's formulation of busno-power and busnocratic rationality (as extensions of Foucault's notion of governmentality) are more than adequate explanations for the State and its promotion of Human Capital Theory, especially in dealing with the conflation of education, skills and training. What busno-power and busnocratic rationality provide is an account of the actual practices that are worked out by those who are subject to them.

*Note*

[1] Revenue Generating Unit (RGU) was, for a time, the New Zealand Ministry of Education designation for a student within the education funding regime.

# Chapter Ten: A Poststructuralist Critique of Managerialism

## The rational subject of managerialism

The term *subject* refers to something quite different from the more familiar term *individual*. In Latin, subject means thrown under and refers to the practice where Romans forced defeated armies to pass under a yoke of spears as a symbol of defeat. The term *individual*, however, dates from the Renaissance and presupposes a free agent with thinking processes not coerced by historical or cultural circumstances.

This view of reason is articulated by Descartes who assumes that the *I* that does the thinking—'the thinking thing'—assumes itself to be fully conscious and hence self knowable. It is also coherent. Descartes' subject is a narrator who imagines that he or she speaks without simultaneously being spoken. In this view of the universe, we speak ourselves into existence. This creates the illusion that, a priori, individuals are fully responsible for all their thoughts and actions.

There are inherent problems in this subject position. The often contradictory positions evident in life may militate against the Cartesian notion of rationality. The choices that an individual makes may be based on rational analysis, but that rationality may be subverted by desire. And reason, itself, is not without its problems. As Taylor (1991: 28) argues, "self-determining freedom has been an idea of immense power in our political life. ... (and) ... has been one of the intellectual sources of modern totalitarianism ..." A critique of the neoliberal subject is therefore required, if we are to unravel the defining power of managerial approaches to education.

Within a neoliberal environment, self-management presents itself as rational. The phenomenon of the neoliberal subject of managerialism as a rational, self-interested, utility maximizer can be differentiated into several strands. Peters (1993) identifies four: (1) The strand which can be traced to Hobbes and his view of human nature in a form of pre-social life where human beings were seen as essentially egoistic, concerned only with their self preservation; (2) The form of individualism identified by Hayek, which descends from Locke, Hume, Smith and Burke, and highly influential in some New Right accounts ...as explaining the spontaneous order of market exchange; (3) The strand of individualism descended from Rousseau and Marx, in which societal order is designed by human reason; and (4) the strand, again descended from Locke, seen in the work of Nozick, where individualism is defined in terms of property rights. In neoliberal thought,

Peters argues, the individual is considered free inasmuch as he is proprietor of his person and capacities.

Three key concepts within these strands of individualism are rationality, individualism and maximization. These concepts can be regarded as technologies of self and can be deconstructed to examine their basis and connections with each other and the way in which they function in the management of the self in the image of the neoliberal economy. Rationality and individuality imply autonomy. But an unproblematic belief in personal autonomy masks the fact that the very idea of choice is integral to neoliberal rationality philosophy.

Sen (1987) points out two predominant views of rational behavior in mainline economic theory. One sees rationality as internal consistency of choice, and the other identifies rationality with a maximization of self-interest. He argues that internal consistency, no matter how defined, could itself be sufficient for guaranteeing a person's rationality. Similarly, Sen questions the demand for external correspondence between the choices that a person makes and the self-interest of the person, particularly the idea that one should pursue one's own self-interest to the exclusion of everything else. With regard to rationality, "the real issue is whether there is a plurality of motivations, or whether self-interest alone drives human beings" (Sen, 1987: 19).

Two types of choice can be discerned from Sen's argument about rationality. The first is the idea that rationality of choice is a function of its internal consistency. The second is that rational choice occurs when a subject makes a choice between two options. In practice, there may be only one option available, or alternatively, there may be several which require a ranking of preferences rather than an absolute choice. Further, the preferences of others may need to be taken into account as part of ethical community relationships. Ethical relationships challenge the predominance of rationality in both in the sense of absolute consistency, and in the maximization of self-interest. This ethical focus is missing from a neoliberal economic picture, which posits individuals in a 'natural' state of perpetual maximization of self-interest, with an essential element of consistency in order to achieve that end. A notion of community under neoliberal regimes is merely a collection of separate entities contracting with each other, an arrangement in which value is calculated in terms of rationality.

There are pitfalls in attempting to achieve economic efficiencies through the application of rationalism. Through the domination of systems rationalism, community-based work organizations devoted to rationalist values can eventually end up corrupting the very values they aspire to.

Kieser (1987) describes an entertaining example from the Christian Church where the development of asceticism was a reaction to the material world of the Romans. During the Roman Empire and beyond, religious ascetics or hermits provided examples of impoverished life styles. Maintaining that life style, however, was difficult. Even hermits had to work for food and that work diminished the time available for prayer. Time spent on work corrupted prayer, so a solution was required if the religious account of poverty was to remain intact. The hermits also found that regular exposure to daily life caused a diminution in the hermit's time for contemplation.

Benedictine monasteries were subsequently developed to support a contemplative lifestyle with rules for a work organization that could provide sustenance as well as space and support for asceticism. Monasteries, as work organizations, developed job rotation and multi-skilling, their success predicated on self-management. But a concentration on manual labor undermined prayer and contemplation. In order to ensure the observance of the correct values, external rules were imposed, hierarchies, and controls were installed to replace the previous self discipline. The external rules specified behavioral performances, installed hierarchies of punishments for non-compliance, and most importantly, promised an imaginary reward of life after death for voluntary compliance. With disciplined work and low levels of material consumption, the monastery 'business' flourished. They began to generate enormous wealth. One monastery would develop another as its numbers and wealth grew. The parent monastery loaned money and the new monastery repaid it. Economic rationalism was alive and well. The behaviorism of the Benedictine Rule was now connected to the community (monastery) economic enterprise.

Benedictine monasteries were a feature on the European landscape for 1200 years. These monasteries were very successful and spread over Europe under the power of Charlemagne who built his empire on the strength of them. Serfs were engaged to do the manual work. The monks then had more contemplative time. This should have released the monks to concentrate on a religious lifestyle. The wealth should have minimized working time and maximized prayer time, because the monks' basic needs were met. There was no rationale within the vows of poverty for consumption or for private ownership, but community ownership of wealth was regarded as a corruption of the values of poverty—the wealth was contrary to their raison d'être. The wealth could not be given away, as that would have corrupted others' values of poverty. Even those who had not vowed poverty were seen as in need of conversion to the virtues of poverty and so there was no point in giving the wealth to them either. In these ways, the monastery rationality had reached an impasse through its own success. Benedictine Rule, as the ethos was known, still operates today and provides a useful comparison with today's managerialist technologies of control through performance indicators and performance standards.

## An analytics of preference

I will now examine the idea of preference as a necessary condition of rationality in a neoliberal configuration. Choice, for *homo economicus*, is dependent on a system of rationality without a theory of preference. Preferences are not necessarily rational, and an individual may prefer not to maximize his/her self-interest, although it could be argued circuitously that following such a preference *is* a form of self-maximizing. It would then be difficult to distinguish between preferences and self-interest in any serious way. In this sense, *homo economicus* loses its force as the limit explanation for the self. To this extent, neoliberalism is weakened.

In economic theory, it is argued that consistency of choice is a condition of rationality. Often, consistency seems to imply a notion of an organic unity within the subject: there is said to be some connection between events in time or elements in a series. Organic unity may imply rationality in that the same object of preference is chosen on the basis of internal consistency, although there is some argument about what is meant by consistency.

> The very idea of purely internal consistency is not cogent, since what we regard as consistent in a set of observed choices must depend on the interpretation of those choices and on some features external to choice as such (e.g., the nature of our preferences, aims, values, and motivations) (Sen, 1987: 14).

It might also be argued that in order to qualify as a condition of rationality, consistency is required between the actual elements within a series, regardless of time or social considerations. And further, it might be argued that rationality, in this sense, is concerned with the variation in these elements, and their consistency (or lack thereof), in terms of some overarching principle or underlying essence. What this move ignores are Lyotard's (1984) arguments that meta-narratives are discredited. And, since there is no overarching principle or underlying essence of rationality to appeal to (except what might be argued for within any particular series of elements), rationality in this sense is constructed, localized, not universal, and restricted to what might be said about any particular set of elements in the series under consideration.

If rationality were to depend on internal consistency of choice, the implication is that one choice event is able to be evaluated against another. A particular choice may even have an impact on the next choice merely because of agency (i.e., I chose). This situation is not independent of time or culture. A choice made at a particular point in time (T1, say), may be regarded as a rational choice at that time. In order for consistency to be a condition of rationality, all subsequent choices would need to be in a consistent relationship with the original at T1. Here, rationality is dependent on the degree of consistency between the first and second choices, regardless of conditions prevailing at the time each choice was made.

However, a choice made at T1 may not appear rational at a later time (T2), when different circumstances apply. A subject may make a different choice at T2, inconsistent with the choice made at T1. If one accepts consistency as a condition of rationality, the subject at T2 does not now appear to be rational, although he or she may be merely expressing a different preference at the later time. Consistency, as a condition for rationality, is in conflict with maximization of self-interest. Self-interest may demand a change of preference not consistent with an original choice.

It is, however, commonplace for individuals, out of habit, to not change their preferences. Individuals may not even recognize their own preferences, i.e., they don't know what they want. A habit is initially a set of choices for handling recurring practical problems and situations. Over time, the reasons for the choices are forgotten and in place of choice the routine takes on a life of its own, precluding thoughtful options and providing a set of secondary justifications for the existence of habits. Other habits at the personal, institutional or societal level develop on top of the original choice. Similarly, social practices often depend on habit, starting out as an exercising of preference, and later developing as ritual or religion. So, an action is not necessarily the result of a free or non-subjugated choice in the present. Habits, in many instances, help reduce complexity and overload in the interests of self-management.

Advertising may reduce my agency in terms of thinking rationally and maximizing self-interest, and I may find an irrational habit better than thinking through all the options. In addition, given the technical capacity of marketing to construct certain effects, I may not have enough of the right information to inform my choices. I may also have set up a network of friends (perhaps people of similar persuasion) to advise me on what choices to make. My friends' choices, although not necessarily rational, may express similar preferences, thereby confirming our friendship. This is a common social interactive process and is well documented in psychology. If consistency is a condition for rationality, my friends' choices are not rational, but it still may be what they do. Such are the governmental effects of marketing.

Paradoxically, neoliberal self-interest changes the meaning of friendship, a social relationship previously based on altruism. But, if friendship is redefined in terms of self-interest alone, then friendship becomes purely contractual rather than altruistic. Neoliberalism then, alters culture here at the intimate dyadic level. This signals a problem with the way busno-power policy regimes utilize the family as a social unit upon which to build public policy.

A consideration of marketing as a feature of modern life directs the discussion about rationality away from the context of the individual towards the context of culture. Choices made by an individual are very often influenced, even constructed, by marketing, not necessarily in a rational manner. Although the choices may be absolutely consistent, they may or may not maximize self-interest. The consistency of the choice may largely depend on evaluation of external evidence of choices that conform to the *marketised* culture. The very object of marketing is to shape preferences over time and, as a result, even what we are able to perceive in our world has been shaped in certain ways.

If, for instance, we look at the 'world' of Coca Cola we see that their advertizing tactics insert the product into the culture. Coca Cola assumes a familiarity like air and wallpaper; it is always with us. When we choose Coca Cola, this is not necessarily a rational choice made from a position of maximization of self-interest. There is no choice point here, only habit that is based on an illusion of choice, an illusion reified by Coca Cola advertisements which sing, 'It's the real thing'. The very mention of Coca Cola here suggests that marketing is an influence on choice. I expect the reader to be familiar with the product and its marketing regime. Coca Cola has become an example of what might be termed the collective unconscious—the moral wallpaper of life, although individuals who choose Coca Cola are not necessarily irrational.

The value of consistency as a condition of rationality can be evaluated further by examining means/ends rationality—adaptation of means to ends. Ends, at least in this relationship, justify the means. Cynically, we might say that this type of rationality can only be opposed by those who think it a self-evidently good thing that individuals should choose means which do not realize their professed ends. It is difficult to argue logically against this type of reasoning. The rationality of making choices consists in having foreseeable results based on those choices at the very least appear desirable from the standpoint of self-maximization. Reason here is presented as a slave of passion in the sense that its function is to make sure that a person's desires are satisfied (the maximization of self-interest). But how can choices be regarded as rational when controlled by the passions? These are, by definition, not rational.

Self-management then, can be said to be generated from both cognition and the passions, neither of which offers a guarantee of rational options. Because of the possibility of a conflation between ideals and norms, it is difficult to know in what way individuals (on an individual level) might choose means that will satisfy their ends. One function of means/ends arguments is to inform us that to act rationally is to act so as to achieve our ends, and, it follows logically, that if we want to achieve our aims, we will thereby want to be rational. Of course, empirical evidence or ethical argument may lead us to choose different ends, but what needs to be questioned is the necessity for giving pre-eminence to cognitive activities and standards, of which consistency and self-interest maximization are but two. Consistency and maximization of self-interest are part of a wider picture of life of which *homo economicus* is but a part. If an individual operates on the assumption that ignorance is bliss, it may be considered irrational for that individual to seek *the* truth, because that may put an end to the blissful state.

There are further distinctions to make. When I am faced with a choice between two similar things, reason neither forbids nor requires that I actually *make* a choice. The choices are merely *allowed* by reason. Choosing not to maximize self-interest is not therefore, necessarily irrational. It would depend on the reasons advanced for the choice and what was meant by self-interest. Here we are into criteria well beyond *homo economicus*. Reason signifies the choices of the right means to an end in the sense of an outcome. It has nothing whatever to do with the choice of those ends.

Which brings us on to the idea of the role of intentions and emotions. In view of the ends the individual happens to find appealing, certain actions may appear rational, but the ends themselves are neither rational nor irrational. Means/ends rationality is attractive because it allows individuals to make judgments about rationality without committing themselves to value judgments that are controversial or not susceptible to empirical verification. On this view, to know which action is rational does not require that one judge whether the individual's aims themselves are valuable. Often, what determines the choice of ends are the emotions, the particular desires or aversions the individual may have. Rationality in this sense, has something to do with making choices regarding our means of satisfying those desires, aversions and so on. Ends, by definition, exist outside the individual, independent of their choices.

## Rationality, choice and autonomy

A second sense of rationality (self-interest maximization), can be explained by evaluating the choice made between two options at one moment in time, in terms of how well self-interest is maximized. Self-interest may be disguised as altruism where an individual chooses what looks like an ethical option. What may, in fact, be happening is that the individual chooses the option that looks ethical, purely to maximize self-interest: appearing ethical may be an attractive quality. This is an element—some would say the driving force—of politics.

There will be cases where self-interest is maximized and the choice is entirely rational when viewed from the point of view of the individual. But when that same choice is evaluated against a criterion of its cumulative effects on others, it may be characterized as irrational. If, for example, we examine the maximization of self-interest that occurs when an individual driver takes his or her automobile to work, even in a congested transport system, the choice is perfectly rational. There are many comforts and efficiencies for the individual in having an automobile, especially in a society that functions as a collection of neoliberal atoms, where there may be no, or very little social or collective means of available transport. In this instance, it may be rational to drive to work.

However, when this same choice is critiqued ecologically (e.g., considering its effects on motorway congestion or pollution), the choice is collectively irrational and many of the individuals involved know this. The choice that is in the self-interest of the individual on the one hand, is also not in the interest of the individual on the other. In this account, the same choice is at one and the same time both rational and irrational. This paradox challenges the idea of unity of the subject—something cannot at the same time be both rational and irrational. What might change the degree of rationality would be something like central planning that would make it more or less rational to take individual transport, a community in which individual and social goals are aligned. But neoliberalism does not admit to such notions of community; individuals are entirely responsible for their own rationality. Rational choices at the individual level may be consistent and may actually maximize self-interest, but as in the transport example above, such choices may be irrational in a collective sense and a recipe for societal and ecological disaster.

Viewed in this way, rationality is more a function of discourse than of any psychological or pathological state of the individual. Rationality does not arise from the internal organic unity of the individual. It arises, rather, from the context within which the individual finds him/herself. It seems, then, that the maximization of self-interest a particularly useful criterion for evaluating rationality.

Individual notions of choice imply a sense of autonomy. The notion of the *autonomous consumer* has been appropriated by Marshall (1995b), who coined the phrase *autonomous chooser*, to illustrate the requirement to exercise the faculty of choice in order for the neoliberal subject to be fully human. If partial choice were to be exercised, it might also be asked if this implies partial humanness. In education, the rhetoric of managerialism relates to a situation in which managers are said to be *managing*, ostensibly to provide a commodity for the autonomous consumer. The autonomous consumer is said to *know*, through its a priori faculty of self-interest, what it wants, independent of education. If this is so, we might say that marketing has replaced education.

Marshall's shift in nomenclature from the autonomous consumer to the autonomous chooser is more than mere semantics. *Consumer* implies the absorbing or consuming of something from the exterior. *Chooser* signifies an interior process: a chooser is said to exercise an internal part of the self. Being a chooser suggests the exercise by the subject of a faculty of choice. Whether such a faculty exists a priori within the subject is not the question. What is at issue here is the argument that underpins the subject which is said to *have* a faculty of choice.

Scarcity of resources is a key theory in neoliberal economics; choices are made among various scarce resources. Such choices are pertinent to the notion of productivity under neoliberalism where individual behavior is the basis of economic activity. Because resources are scarce, the most maximizing individuals would become more fully human as they choose more effectively and thereby ensure more efficient use of resources. The implication is that they might not be fully human prior to the choosing, in need of caring or therapy to improve their choice making capacity.

A variety of initiatives in the recent education reforms in New Zealand are designed to enhance the productivity of the subject through the way in which the subject functions to choose autonomously. The initiatives include the following: contestable funding, the establishment of private training establishments that operate with government funds, the standardization of qualifications and notions of consumer choice through NZQA, and the restructuring of councils of tertiary educational institutions to represent business interests. All these initiatives suggest the development of an enterprise culture in which the consumer is sovereign.

Skepticism may be expressed, however, towards the idea that consumers possess any significant form of autonomy in contemporary capitalist economies. For autonomy to be significant, consumer preferences in education would at the very least have to be generated independently of the plans and activities of the producers (i.e., managers, or professionals). They would also need some say over the choice regimes. Yet, the reverse is increasingly the case. There are comparatively massive resources available to the government in its attempts to shape and control the so-called choices of consumers, including such things as the control and provision of funding, the promulgation of regulations and legislation, and the sophistication and effectiveness of marketing campaigns. Through legislation, regulation, and acquiescence to the desires of powerful vested interests within the political economy, government controls the production and marketing of education as a commodity, and is, therefore, by definition, the most significant producer. The insertion of notions of consumer sovereignty into education is problematic in that it defines consumers in modern capitalist society as actors who can exercise autonomy in a meaningful way. Clearly in the face of government power, that is not possible.

Advanced capitalism requires a state that, "confronts individual capitalists as a neo-capitalist order to carry through vicariously the 'collective capitalist will' which is absent in the competitive sphere" (Habermas, 1988: 50). In a modern capitalist economy then, it is the mode of production that determines the consumption, and not vice versa: the autonomous consumer is a fictitious being. In addition, public choice theory predicts that there will be a constant tendency for governments to expand (Gamble, 1988: 349). Despite the current attempt by neoliberals at an explanation of a reduction of the State, the State in New Zealand is still the monopoly supplier of the funding for tertiary education in both the public and so-called *private* realms. Following the enactment of the *Education Amendment Act 1989* there are now several hundred accredited private training establishments who obtain most of their funds from government, raising questions about the distinction between notions of public and private.

The State is the monopoly supplier of education. All providers operate under the same regulations, legislation and standardized curriculum delivery systems of accreditation. This monopoly severely limits the capacity for autonomy or self-management, among education providers and 'consumers' alike. Education as a consumable represents the imposition of an individualizing and totalizing, economic, instrumental meta-narrative of education, inimical to meaningful notions of autonomy and free choice.

An explanation is needed to account for the willing cooperation of the subject to continue to believe in autonomy under contrary and antagonistic conditions. In Foucault's (1991b) terms, the existence of a subject implies that power is required to construct or exercise a technology of self. New Right accounts of consumer sovereignty in the governance of education do not appear to allow for the exercise of power through the implication of the subject except under the condition of *homo economicus*. The consumer merely consumes within a given range of options without being aware of the very limits that are constituted by those options.

Foucault's contention is that freedom is a pre-condition for power.

> A power relationship can only be articulated on the basis of two elements, ... that the 'other' (the one over whom power is exercised) be thoroughly recognized and maintained to the very end as a person who acts; and that, faced with a relationship of power, a whole field of responses, reactions, results, and possible inventions opens up (Foucault, 1982: 220).

In Foucauldian terms, the consumerist interpretation of education might even be said to not allow for a conceptualization of power at all. It suggests rather an idea of oppression or domination.

## The subject of consumption

The neoliberal subject, which must continuously produce and reproduce itself, can be said to consist (among other things) of an intersection of the faculties of rationality and choice. This formulation of choice and rationality can be said to maximize the subject's self-interest. The neoliberal subject has an additional requirement of productivity. The output that results from combining the notions of *homo economicus* and productivity might then be characterized as *homo productus*—one who produces goods or services for exchange. In fact, the making of a choice itself may be construed as a moment of production. The production of choice is a moment in Foucault's governmentality.

Neoliberalism is said to be the "generalization of an enterprise form to all forms of conduct and the promotion of enterprise culture through invented forms" (Burchell, 1993: 276), but there is no legislated demand for the subject to produce. Despite the absence of such legislation, the subject is nevertheless not free, insofar as it is still required to respond on the basis of its very reason for existence. In other words, there is a requirement for the subject to produce behavior appropriate to the requirements of the Classical State—for external security and for arbitrating between citizens where there are disputes they cannot settle for themselves. It may be claimed that at a minimal practical level, the subject must choose in order to live. But to live or demand how another ought to live, is of no necessary concern to neoliberalism. For governance, however, the subject must be enticed to choose through its own efforts. In this way, technologies of domination are integrated with technologies of self and produce governance.

The illusion is that, under neoliberal government by the market, the State has limited functions, outside of which the free market is the primary mechanism of exchange. By its very nature the market is defined as *free*; so is the subject that chooses to produce or not, as it sees fit. Paradoxically, the subject of neoliberal reform is also involved in a continual re-production of self within an enterprise culture set up under Government intervention. However, the re-production of *self* requires both consumption and reconstruction of the existing self.

In this sense the neoliberal subject is continuously employed in the enterprise of consuming its own production by using its reconstructed self as both a production and a moment of consumption. *Homo productus* might also be characterized as *homo consumptus*. The next construction might now be *homo cyclicus,* a creature that goes around in circles. In this last circular version of the individual, in a quality system, the consumer would at least know who to complain to. The neoliberal aphorism might now be expressed as: a subject must learn to change (it)self continuously in a continuous world of change.

Another way to think of the slide of *homo economicus* into *homo consumptus* is to recall Plato's simile of the cave found in *The Republic*. In a cavern deep beneath the surface of the earth sat prisoners, fixed by chains, who saw reflected on the cave walls shadows of wooden figures which in total represented a reality which existed outside the cave, and which was only knowable by those lucky enough to escape the cave, and who upon reaching daylight could see the True, the Good, and the Beautiful, and thereby became enlightened. The subject of managerialism suggests a slightly different version of the cave. Now there is no outside. The subject wanders within, choosing appropriately and often, still taking the shadows of its own imitations as constituting history, meaning, and even itself. It gazes at the shadows and affirms its freedom and individuality by perpetually consuming and producing itself in ever newer forms.

Through a requirement for perpetual responsiveness, then, the self has become its own illusory enterprise. In business idiom that self might be represented as *Self Inc*. In terms of the degree of self-absorption, this type of self-management might also be a recipe for self-isolation. And, since, in an ideal neoliberal world the notion of society is de-emphasized, this result seems entirely rational.

Since autonomy is accepted as a priori, the idea that the so-called neoliberal free market (constructed though Government intervention) is an illusion escapes the notice of this subject of 'freedom'. What is of more immediate importance to such a subject is its sense of becoming what it 'knows' it is supposed to be: an exerciser of free choice. Within managerial discourse, autonomy is a high status notion and is appropriated into the subject's own governance. The exercise of autonomy centers around the need to continuously choose new constructions of self.

One manifestation of continuous self-construction (i.e., *homo consumptus* in action) is the way in which, under neoliberal reforms, managers of positions in the public service promote their personal careers. Managerialism promotes competition for careers through its assumptions of the subject as a self-interested individualistic, maximizer. Under this ideology, managers employ their current positions to design their curriculum vitae for their next promotion. The curriculum vitae becomes the object for development and their current work-related responsibilities are not necessarily the thing upon which the manager focuses. The self is at the same time a moment of consumption as all energy is devoted by the manager to what he or she might become. In this sense, the subject of managerialism is its own customer. This self-absorbed, privately focused subject seems to be an entity of limited value to be employed in the public service. What is clear is that the managerialist subject serves itself.

The idea of technologies of self enables Foucault (1988a) to elaborate an ethics of self where the subject is situated in the interstices of power relations at the level of individuals' daily practices. Technologies of self show the active engagement of the individual rather than the application of sovereign power. The application of sovereign power has been gruesomely described by Foucault (1979) in *Discipline and Punish*. It belongs to another era of rationality that had the docile body as its object. Neoliberalism, by contrast, demands enterprising subjects who are active in their own governance. Foucault's notion of technology of self is an illustration of his concern for the totalizing and individualizing modes of modern governance. Governing is rational to the extent that individual aspirations and practices conform to those of political government. If governmentality explains the active cooperation of the self in the development of subjectivity, then managerialism (with its severely restricted notion of autonomy) will be illusory as a mode of governance.

In psychologized versions of rationality, the notion of *experience* in the present tense is privileged as authentic and assumed to be able to overcome the sedimented experience of the other. Sedimented experience refers to the idea that a singular unified self is the origin of experience against historical construction and material conditions. There is some basis here for a shallow treatment of the idea of social constructions of reality as presented by Berger and Luckman (1967). The idea of social construction of reality is treated as individuals with independent experiences coming together to reach a consensus. Such a conception of what might be better called *a negotiated order* overlooks the more fundamental issue, that shared meaning arises out of a background set of constitutive practices. In the case of the individual making a choice, the choice is not a real psychological state; but rather, a structuring possibility which precedes the individual. Only on the basis of that structuring possibility can the individual have the experience at all. Because of historical events, ideas, movements and, as it is nowadays, marketing, this structuring possibility is shared and thoroughly social before the individual actualizes it in a particular experience of sharing his or her 'reality'.

Understanding the discourse-saturated nature of the constitution of reality leads us to think of self-identity as both a constituted, and a constituting, subject. Its social origins are of interest. When constitutive acts are separated from the individual and his or her psychological state, a variety of analyses become available. The subject is thus a position, or a positioning in a variety of integrated and conflicting institutional forms in which it appears as an agent. One such position is the neoliberal subject with its particular discourse of rationality as the defining condition of the competitive economy.

Language is one of the self-constituting practices in modern society. It is a major constitutive condition of experience itself, serving as a medium through which other institutions are brought to conception, both in production and in understanding. Berger and Luckman (1967: 69) have argued that language is the "depository of a large aggregate of collective sedimentation which can be acquired as a whole without reconstructing their original process of formation". In this sense, language is deeply political, reproducing both an order and a disguise of that order at the same time. Language constitutes many of the possible ways to engage in the world and produces objects with particular features.

Autonomy is a notion that is dependent on language for both its content and its possibilities. Autonomy is a social production, distinguishing itself from other things. The question is not whether or not autonomy exists, or whether it explains rational behavior, but how it comes to exist, and how it interrelates with the production and reproduction of managerial discourse. The autonomous subject is not fixed through language but is produced out of a set of discourses. The claim of the unitary subject with consistent rational choice making faculties outside discourse, is not so much wrong as merely one description within a limited set of the discourses. The discourse around the notion of autonomy is power laden, and in need of examination if we want to reveal the way in which power operates through the use of such managerial language. Existing representations of, and through, the notion of autonomy may need to be contested.

There are two components to the word autonomous: *autos* and *nomos*. The term *autos* refers to one's self and *nomos* to the law.

> The combination of these two terms into one word implies that 'there must be reference to some law or standards governing significant aspects of one's life, where the law or standards in question are in some important sense one's own, or self imposed (Lankshear, 1982: 97).

There is, according to Lankshear, considerable scope for disagreement about the content of this ideal. The dominant view is that autonomy is a function of the essential rational nature of the self. The development of autonomy in this view would therefore be a matter of developing the faculty of reason. "The *autos* is human reason and the *nomos* set thereby is a rational 'law'" (Lankshear, 1982: 97). Walker (Lankshear, 1982: 97) proposes that personal autonomy be seen essentially in terms of human wants. In other words, autonomy is in some way a function of a person's empirical nature (e.g., wants, desires) rather than reason. This, as Lankshear argues, marks a source of dispute over the very essence of personal autonomy. This analysis suggests that there exists a systematic distortion in the use of the notion of autonomy in managerial discourses.

**The subject of work**

To categorize is to mark off something from everything else. In this way, a category is defined by what it is as much as what it is not. The term *manager* then, in the discourse of managerialism implies that there exists a category called *managers*. This categorization also implies there are categories of other things, say *not managers*, one category of which would be workers. In this discussion, managers are not, by definition, workers—an anomaly that calls into question the assumption that work is central to existence. If, as in the new discourse, work is a defining feature of the subject, then any category such as managers who are defined against workers, is to that extent suspect.

The assumption that the notion of work is the fundamental social fact is seriously questioned on two counts by the neo-Marxist, Offe (1985). Offe's first set of misgivings, regarding the centrality of work, surface as soon as one takes into account the heterogeneous nature of the empirical workplace.

Wage labor, Offe argues, is no longer dependent because of subdivisions in the sphere of work. Symptoms of increasing heterogeneity raise doubts about dependent wage labor as a relevant category for conceptualizing a work society. The second set of misgivings explained by Offe concern the decline in the work ethic. Work has been decentered relative to other spheres of life and in many cases confined to the margins. Offe (1985) divides the labor market into four major segments: the inactive, the unemployed, the self employed and the employed. In this categorization only the employed, a species diminishing in number, are pressured to sell their labor power.

Offe's writing is a counter to the Marxist notion of the worker as an organic class where the "workers are connected in a unity through time as well as geography" (Tucker, 1978: 346). Without work as a defining category, the subject loses the work-related, a priori assumptions about the self which managerialism traditionally required as a mode of governance. Now, self-management becomes the work.

The introduction of managerialism is not seen here as simply another form of domination. What this chapter has suggested is that managerialism is implicated in the demand for a new form of governance which requires the willing cooperation of its subjects. Managerialism has therefore been presented as a neoliberal form of governmentality with unresolved subject positions. Managerialism is similar in many respects to sovereign power, and so is inadequate as an account of governance. As a consequence, its implementation through education is problematic.

# Chapter Eleven: A Poststructuralist Critique of the Subject

Chapter eleven provides a poststructuralist critique of *homo economicus* in order to broaden and validate the thesis beyond Foucault. Apart from his thoughts about the managerial function of the architecture of the panopticon, Foucault did not investigate managerialism by name. Given the problematic nature of managerialism, it is arguable that such (re)search is, itself, a Foucauldian venture. One of the more notable consequences of the introduction of managerialism into education is the inevitability of new explanations for subject positions, and hence, for governance which demands new modalities of self. This demand is necessarily political, although the official discourse may not recognize that this is so.

Adopting a poststructural approach, the chapter firstly investigates the possible changes to the self as a result of the mode of information. Some consideration is given to the way in which the self is constituted under modern electronic technology which has become integral to managerialism. Next, the idea of metaphor as a technology of self is examined as an example of the ways in which self implicates itself. Finally, the chapter examines the social roots of psychoanalytic culture—a culture that allows for the possibility of technologies of self, and considers the existentialist response to social disintegration under neoliberalism, which has shifted the emphasis from the society to individual responsibility. Arguably, a government intent on reforming attitudes, desires, values, expectations and goals must present a well articulated, internally coherent and psychologically plausible metaphor to direct people to the desired end. New thoughts, desires, reasons, attitudes and behaviors, will be required to facilitate change; and new legal, institutional, structural and cultural arrangements will demand new modalities of existence. Within a psychoanalytic cultural context, managerialism is viewed as an element of governmentality.

**Poststructuralism**

Poststructuralism denies any appeal to foundational, transcendental or universal truths or meta-narratives. There is the sense that our current historical situation constitutes a radical break with the period characterized as modernism or the Enlightenment. Above all, there is an attention to language, power, desire and representation as discursive categories. Descombes (1980) locates the emergence of poststructuralism in France in the 1960s as a response to the intellectual scene in Paris. In its very name, poststructuralism reveals its ties to structuralism, and indeed poststructuralism is a response to those theories which purported to discover invariant structures in society, the human psyche, consciousness, history and culture. Poststructuralism, then, is both an attack on elements of structuralism (humanism, phenomenology and existentialism), and an echo of some of themes within structuralism, for instance, the approach to language in terms of discourse or discursive systems.

## The mode of information

*The Foucault Effect* (Burchell et al., 1991: ix) makes "visible, through a particular perspective in the history of the present, of the different ways in which an activity or art called *government* has been made thinkable and practicable". Foucault's own term is governmentality, in which the self participates in its own governance through integration of technologies of domination and technologies of self, within a regime of bio-power (Foucault, 1978).

Governance through the traditional, liberal, professional tradition in education is challenged in the information society, in which experts operate through electronic systems, replacing direct control with distanciated and disembodied notions of the self (Watts, 1994). As language is employed by the (now invisible, disembodied and distanciated) self to constitute and signify its own unstable and digitized representation, there are implications not only for the constitution of the self in this new mode of information, but also for notions of governance under bio-power. The governmental effects of bio-power are conceived as applying to technologies of the body and population (Foucault, 1991b), but according to Marshall (1995b), *bio-power* does not capture the essence of the new subjectivities under the mode of information.

Marshall (1995b) has derived his notion of *busno-power* from bio-power, as a way of understanding governance in education by business interests in the mode of information. Busno-power explains human capital through control over minds. Whereas bio-power controlled the mind through the focus on the body, busno-power must be able to operate without the body in the mode of information with electronic communication. Thus governance in modern information-based societies requires more than a focus on the body—it requires control of the mind in certain ways (Bell, 1976; Lyotard, 1984). Active participation of the desiring self is required as today selves are able to discern different things about their political conditions than they did in the 18$^{th}$ century. They know for example, that they must reinvent themselves continuously in the artificial neoliberal game of entrepreneurial conduct. Through this entrepreneurial self-constituted desire to 'improve' themselves, Foucault (1982: 221) sees the "strategic reversibility of power relations" activated—a correlate of his notion of power. In this way, the self is implicated in its own governance. Neoliberalism however, has no necessary ethic and therefore, apart from becoming enterprising, the self has no other necessary content.

The mode of information involves forms of symbolic exchange which contain internal and external structures, means, and relations of significance. Poster tentatively designates three stages in the mode of information: face to face, orally mediated exchange; written exchanges mediated by print; and electronically mediated exchange. The third stage is characterized by informational simulations where "the self is decentered, dispersed, and multiplied in continuous instability" (Poster, 1990: 6). Although the stages are not real in the sense that they can be discovered empirically, "the current configuration (the third stage) constitutes a necessary totalization of earlier developments: that is one cannot but see earlier developments from the situation of the present" (Poster, 1990: 6).

What is at stake in the mode of information are new language formations that alter significantly the network of social relations and the subjects they constitute. Subjects are constituted in acts and structures of communication. Poster situates the theoretical and social origin of the modes of information within a field of contending discourses. Language as representation recedes in importance as "the referent fades into obscurity, playing less and less of a role in the delicate process of sustaining cultural meanings" (Poster, 1990: 13). In this generalized destabilization, he argues that

> the subject is no longer fixed in an absolute point in time and space where it might enjoy a physical, fixed vantage point from which rationally to calculate its options. ...instead it is ... dissolved and materialized continuously in the electronic transmission of symbols. ... The body then is no longer an effective limit to the subject's position (Poster, 1990: 15).

Through the mode of information which is instantiated with a self-referential linguistic mechanism, Poster has created the possibility of the invisible subject through the introduction of a subject that is dissolved and materialized continuously in the electronic transmission of symbols. This extends Harvey's (1989) idea that disembodiment and distanciation have compressed traditional scientific notions of time and space.

*Managing in the mode of information*
The information society is upon us, and, in essence, information is invisible. The mode of information is already commonplace in the empirical world of work. Touraine (1995) describes this new society as *programmed*:

> The production and distribution of knowledge ... information, and therefore education ... are to the programmed society what metal-working, textiles, chemicals and even the electronic and electronic industries were to industrial society (Touraine, 1995: 244).

Previously the self, in the interests of control, was the subject of brute strength and bodily presences. But in the information society, the body is no longer needed for control and is often not available. On this basis we might have an explanation for the move from the dominance of Taylorist scientific management practices to those of culture management in business as well as education. If Taylorism was traditionally about programming the work situation so that the body would work more efficiently, culture management is about winning the hearts and minds of the workers so that they will control themselves to produce more efficiently within the required busno-power metaphor of quality assurance.

In the mode of information, a quadriplegic for example, with no bodily sensations below the neck, but with an active mind, is an example of an invisible self. To the extent that the body of the quadriplegic is not theorized within the mode of information, it is not within the *gaze* (Foucault, 1975), and cannot be seen.

> We must now describe the concrete exercise of such a perception. ... The observing gaze refrains from intervening: it is silent and gestureless. Observation leaves things as they are; there is nothing hidden to it in what is given. The correlative of observation is never the invisible, but always the immediately visible, once one has removed the obstacles erected to reason by theories and to the senses by imagination (Foucault, 1975:107).

The body of the quadriplegic does not fit current societal norms for a productive unit of human capital, and to that extent becomes invisible. However, it might be argued that the quadriplegic is of more value to busno-power than the fit, 'beautiful' bodies in the gymnasium, because the quadriplegic does not need to spend vast amounts of energy improving a body that has little or no value for busno-power. Since under busno-power, it might be said that the quadriplegic is more adequately theorized for productivity than under a notion of bio-power, it is not at all surprising that many Western governments have enacted legislation to give these differently constructed selves increased rights and protections. The quadriplegic can now access self construction through the new electronic information technologies and, therefore, still be an element of power for the security of the State. One locus of the invisible self can therefore be said to be within the electronic digits. At this point, such a self is effectively decentered. There is still a question here about *digitally challenged* selves (perhaps those who lack finger sensations, or even do not believe in pixels) who are consequently limited in their self-construction.

Notions of disembodiment and distanciation (Watts, 1994) create possibilities for a self that is not necessarily visible. Such notions unsettle Foucault's construct of bio-power with its requirement for control of the body as a means to control the mind. In an electronic culture, the body is not necessarily visible, nor is its visibility required, making *bio-power* less than adequate as an explanation of power relations. The mind is obviously not visible but this is an advantage to busno-power because it is the mind that is interactive with the information. The strategic reversibility of power relations becomes a major problem if the body is still the focus in a disembodied network of power relations which is focused on the mind. This is not to say the body does not exist, merely that it is not required to be visible.

With a decentered self, traditional authority relations become transformed. Internal commitment and motivation replace obedience and hierarchical authority as the primary bond between the self and the task. External supervision is of less value since control of the body is redundant in electronic networks. But there is no escape for the self in this process. Electronic systems can be regarded as information panopticons, operated by reflexive self-constructors, apparently freed from the constraints of space and time. The electronic panopticon does not require the mutual presence of objects for observation, nor even the presence of an observer. We may now portray the subject of busno-power as an invisible, electronic, panoptical, enlightened, reflexive self-improver.

Electronic networks do not require the carceral society. In the modern neoliberal environment, electronic networks are required for the maximization of competitive conduct where, in order to sustain accepted definitions of neoliberalism, there must be instant production, transmission and consumption. The traditional attendance required in disciplinary blocks through the presence of the body, is no longer efficient. The presence of the body in this regime, is simply not required. The individual in the new electronic network need not even be visible. Efficiencies are maximized through instant electronic communication, information retrieval from data bases, and informated work. The new electronic technologies allow a redefinition of the individual as a member of an invisible electronic population, while at the same time, allowing the self to enhance its beliefs about its educational potential in terms of human capital.

Domination rather than power might be exercised by taking the digital subject *off line*, denying that subject any further privilege of access to the network. This does not necessarily stop the self from continuously reconstructing itself by interacting within the digital mode. The off-line self would not, however, be connected to the discourse, and would immediately fail to maximize its utility as the discourse shifted. If the internet is to be an element in busno-power, access to it will need to be free.

## The management of autonomy

Busno-power demands new subjectivities, one of which Marshall (1995b) characterizes as *the autonomous chooser*. The autonomous chooser of the current commodified education discourse presumes new practices of self which can be distinguished from the traditional practices of self available within Enlightenment notions of self. Under busno-power, it is not just that human beings are autonomous, or that their autonomy can be developed:

> Instead there seems to be a constituent faculty of choice which is necessarily continuously exercised on commodities, and which sweeps aside or over-rides the traditional categories and frameworks on human nature of the human sciences (Marshall, 1995b: 13).

Through the rationality of the market, neoliberal doctrine implies for the individual an imperative of continuous choice. Here the chooser must be continually responsive to the environment which at the same time structures and manipulates the choices of the individual. In a discourse of choice, the less visible those manipulations are to the chooser, the more free and responsible the choices will seem.

The so-called freely chosen investments made by the autonomous chooser in developing its human capital for example, are concerned with choice over a selection of "activities that influence future monetary and psychic income" (Becker, 1994: 16) by increasing an individual's personal repertoire of economic productive resources. Any individual security that is available through success in the *game* (in the sense that Lyotard uses this idea) of increasing one's individual human capital, allows the individual to believe in the value of government policy. Even failure in the game is not a failure for governmentality, as the attribution of individual responsibility for success and failure in the education system has a long tradition. Any positive or negative value to the individual in this game simply confirms governmentality.

Since governmentality can be identified with leadership, successive governments in New Zealand since 1984 have attempted to provide a better form of security. Through the promotion of *busno-power*, they have done so by reassessing security in terms of individualism and the neoliberal version of the autonomous chooser in particular. But this individual choice, insofar as it is thought to be an autonomous choice is evidence of busno-power and is largely illusory. It is

> directed not only at individuals to turn them into autonomous choosers and consumers but also at the population as a whole, by a total immersion in the enterprise culture of the social, the economy and the new rationality of state. In the exercise of *busno-power* there can be seen then a merging of the economic, the social and the activity of government (Marshall, 1995b: 6-7).

## Construction of self through language as practice

Managerial language is a significant technology of self. According to Weedon (1987), language is the place where forms of social organization are defined and contested. It is also the place where our sense of ourselves, our subjectivity, is constructed. In other words, subjectivity is not innate, not genetically determined, but socially produced through a whole range of discursive practices and power struggles—economic, social and political.

> Language is not the expression of unique individuality: it constructs the individual's subjectivity in ways which are socially specific ... subjectivity is neither unified nor fixed. Unlike humanism, which implies a conscious knowing, unified, rational subject, postmodernism theories of subjectivity as a site of disunity and conflict, are central to the process of political change and to preserving the status quo (Weedon, 1987: 21).

The subject of managerialism is advanced as the self-managing subject, posing as the sovereign, autonomous individual. Yet, this is a mask for *homo economicus*—the rational, self-interested, utility maximizer, exercising its faculty of choice. In a neoliberal characterization of the world, choice-making must be continuously exercised in order for the subject to be regarded as fully functioning. The subject of managerialism must continuously reconstruct itself, through continuous choice, within a constantly changing environment.

A variety of metaphors for the managerial self are to be found in the literature on the reforms to education. Managerialism for example, presents a view of the subject that is characterized as autonomous, responsible, accountable, enterprising, self disciplined, entrepreneurial, independent and self reliant. These metaphors are mirrored in the language of the underpinning philosophy of the reforms. The State sector structures within which the subject constructs itself are also inextricably intertwined in the development of this subject. These new macro-structures are described as having: "improved accountability mechanisms"; a need to "review the mix of incentives and sanctions for public sector managers", "enhanced adaptability and responsiveness of the public sector", and "de-centralized controls" (Deane, 1986: 15). They are said to have developed "quasi autonomous agencies" (Boston, 1991); "invented real market structures" (State Services Commission 1993); and provided "freedom to manage", "contestability" and "assessment of performance" (Treasury, 1987: 87). More particularly, in education, the Education Amendment Act 1990 has introduced contestability to the provision of education through various funding and accreditation bodies. Accountability and efficiency are held up as model ways of managing in the State sector, and individuals need to take seriously their responsibility for self managing within the space and the model provided by legislation.

The metaphor of self-management explains attempts to secure the willing cooperation of the subject. The term is problematic though, in that it implies a subject free from constraints. Freedom to manage is probably its greatest appeal because ordinary language invests the notion of autonomy with an ideal of unrestrained freedom, despite the evidence to the contrary in the empirical world.

Metaphorical thinking is a technology of self that, among an infinite number and variety of others, constitutes the subject of managerialism. Metaphor allows the subject to "effect certain operations on (its) own thoughts, conduct and way of being" (Foucault, 1982: 18). Lakoff and Johnson argue that human thought processes are largely metaphorical, that the human conceptual system is metaphorically structured and defined, and that, in allowing us to focus on one aspect of a concept, "a metaphorical concept can keep us from focusing on other aspects of the concept that are inconsistent with that metaphor" (Lakoff and Johnson, 1980: 10).

There are many types of metaphor, two of which appear here. Structural metaphors allow for one concept to be structured in terms of another. An example of this type of thinking is where our thinking about the self is structured in terms of metaphors about managerialism. Management is viewed as a personification of managers. A second type are ontological metaphors which serve many purposes and allow us to deal rationally with our experiences. They help us refer to experiences or entities, to quantify and categorize objects, to identify aspects and causes of events, and to set goals and motivate actions (Lakoff and Johnson, 1980).

Metaphors are not mere poetical or rhetorical devices, but are part of everyday speech, affecting how we perceive, think and act. Metaphors are used extensively in poetry, rhetoric and advertizing to provide vivid imagery that transcends day to day reality. Aristotle's argument, that metaphors consist in giving the thing a name that belongs to something else, suggests that the way we think partially defines our world. In this sense, reality itself is defined by metaphor. As metaphors vary from culture to culture, so do the realities they define. Conventional ways of talking about management presuppose a way of thinking that we are hardly ever conscious of.

Metaphors allow us to make sense of non-physical things, using physical imagery. We talk about management as an entity because we conceive of it that way, and we act according to the way we conceive of things. We therefore think of management as something real. The idea that management might be any one of a number of other things independent of our perception ordinarily escapes our attention.

> To admit now that metaphor and story matter also in human reasoning does not entail becoming less rational and less reasonable. On the contrary, as I have said, it entails becoming more rational and more reasonable, because it brings more of what persuades serious people under the scrutiny of reason (McCloskey, 1994: 63–64).

There is already an ample supply of facts. These are interpreted as information translated from statistics and gathered in official sources. Such facts justify efficiencies said to be gained through the introduction of managerialism in the public sector. Explanations of neoliberalism supply the logic for the reforms to the State sector, and yet it is not readily recognized that such explanations can themselves be interpreted as metaphorical. In the interests of manageability, investigation of metaphors here is limited to those concerning the autonomy of the self-managing subject.

Neoliberalism supplies an explanation for the logic of the reforms to the economy with assertions such as, "economics becomes an approach capable of explaining all human behavior" (Gordon, 1991: 43). Economics, in this sense, is a story-telling discipline. In other words, managerialism is an economic story told about the governance of particular forms of social life. The metaphorical thinking of neoliberalism can be seen in the discourse of managerialism which consistently employs such terminology as *individualized remuneration, performance-related, adaptiveness, contestability, responsiveness, incentives, sanctions, authority, accountability* and *responsibility*. These terms are taken as emblematic of the language of managerialism. They are able to be subsumed under a notion of autonomy where the subject has the power to be all of these things. On the surface, the notion of the autonomous subject of managerialism appears to be well articulated, coherent and plausible, because in many social situations it is legitimate to hold someone responsible for his/her actions. Self-government in this small sense is about the normal daily actions that individuals perform as part of the mandate they receive to do so by virtue of their membership or attachment to a group (de Certeau, 1984).

The metaphors of managerialism, however, imply a notion of managerial self-determination in a big sense as the basic structural condition for the provision of neoliberal government. Self-management continues a tradition borrowed from corporate management where individuals are held individually responsible for all their actions and decisions. Individual responsibility is also the juridical notion of responsibility buttressed by neoliberal legislation which underpins managerialism. Such a notion of individualized responsibility might suggest that the subject has an a priori faculty of autonomy. Even though this individualized notion of the autonomous subject is determined by the legally backed sanctions of managerialism, the neoliberal subject is not necessarily an appropriate structural condition for public management.

**Managing oneself**

The acceptance by an individual of any new mode of discipline requires new, maybe even fictitious, technologies of self. Any move from a welfare state involves a major reconstruction of the practices through which dependency is said to have developed. Neoliberalism is one such explanation. Neoliberal metaphors about the *global economy, information superhighway, enterprise culture*, the nation as *community, United Nations, world government*, and so on, function as grand theories. They may even refer to a sense of psychological relief felt by an individual in the process of reconstruction, who thinks that he or she has found the *one true way*. There is an emotional or psychological dimension to having found the answer, related to a feeling of security within the individual. These totalizing, neoliberal metaphors function governmentally to create the illusion of self that must fit in with their defining power. They are within the fabric of the neoliberal reform practices.

Neoliberal practice is one way in which the full emotional life of the individual is engaged in reform and in the development of its rationale. Individuals are to be made aware of their *autonomy* for developing a *sense of responsibility* towards the *enterprise* of their own lives within that reconstructed environment. In this way, the autonomy of the individual and the export-led economic recovery are linked together, constituted with reference to the market. The market thus emerges as a mode of governance as it fulfills the role of a model for self-construction and supplies the reason for intervention through State reform and the inherent requirement for self-management.

It is a contention of this chapter that managerialism is a form of neoliberal governance but it is acknowledged that this is not how management is ordinarily thought of. And, since metaphor is analogous with thinking, the exercise then becomes a genealogical one of investigating the metaphors of managerialism in order to comprehend the discourse that constitutes its definition.

An examination of managerial discourses from 1870 to the present day (see Barley and Kunda, 1992; Pollitt, 1990) shows that language conveys a shifting image of the managerial subject: in bureaucratic theory the subject is a *systems variable*; within administrative management theory the subject is seen as a *cog in a wheel*; within scientific management the subject is the worker as *dumb ox*; within human relations theory the subject *has* a psychological life; within systems rationalism the subject is the *technical expert*; and within culture management the subject is the *worker* in search of an ethic that will help it define its interests in terms of *total commitment to productivity*.

Discursive metaphors for the subject may constitute a belief in certain features of that subject, but do not explain how managerialism discourse functions. The fact that the subject of neoliberal managerial discourse is to be an efficient and productive subject in the interests of a better life through growth in the economy, enlightenment, patriotism, scientific progress or national security, serves to mask the function of neoliberal governance. Individuals are to be disciplined through their own efforts to construct knowledge about themselves from what they are told they necessarily must believe. The fact that individuals believe in the need to be accountable, responsible, efficient, and so on, at the individualized level, is of major importance to governance. For the successful functioning of governance at the subjective level, having the belief and experiencing the need to believe is as important as any claimed objective or contextual content validity of those beliefs. Poststructurally, objective content validity is not available, and contextual validity depends on the ways in which the text is read. Having a belief and a system for acquiring a belief ensures that the subject has hope in an age that is becoming increasingly uncertain or threatening. Belief and belief systems often function as knowledge. A belief can be defined not as the object of believing (as in a dogma), but as "the subject's investment in a proposition, the act of saying it and considering it as 'true'—in other words, a 'modality' of the assertion and not its content" (de Certeau, 1984: 178).

Neoliberalism (and therefore managerialism) institutes practices of management on the basis of the truth of the explanation provided of belief in the subject as a rational, self-interested, utility maximizer. This assertion of belief is up for examination here. It is a rationale that is constructed to enable such assertions to be made and required that must be addressed as well as any value that might attach to the metaphorical contents of those assertions. The discourses of managerialism are deployed in such as way as to have the effect of situating the origins for all social decisions and the fount of all wisdom within the subject. The managerialist subject of neoliberalism assumes an independence free from a critique of the origins or effects of certain ways of speaking. This problem illustrates what Lyotard (de Certeau, 1984: 165) refers to when he says "to arrest the meanings of words once and for all, that is what Terror wants".

An autonomous individual is said to be rational when functioning consistently within the law. Individual responsibility is the fundamental unit of responsibility in Western law. In this view, individuals are expected to make their own decisions, rather than wanting or expecting others to make these for them. They take juridical responsibility for their own lives, so that if things go wrong they do not assume there is always someone to help them. Their activities are oriented towards specific goals or objectives and are concerned to monitor and evaluate their own progress. They are motivated to obtain (and are able to obtain) the necessary resources to acquire whatever skills they might need. Autonomous individuals are able to articulate their progress relative to the goals they set for themselves. Their belief must necessarily be that they are free, otherwise their belief in freedom to choose becomes an absurdity. Without this belief, the illusory nature of the autonomy would be seen and cynicism or rejection might set in.

All of this governmental process could be regarded as tautologous. For this technology of self to function governmentally, it requires the existence of the unexamined belief, and under busnocratic rationality, there must be no space within which to contest either the value of autonomy or the fact that there is no space within which to critique. A pre-condition of autonomy in the busnocratic sense is that it cannot be deconstructed.

A technology of self is required to change perceptions of the self as dependent so that an ethic of autonomy will ensue seemingly from the self-manager's own enterprising thought and practices. An example of efforts towards the embodiment of such an ethic of self is reported from a Japanese management setting where *ethics retreats* are arranged to provide the *self-discipline* needed to enhance the possibility of the adoption of a managerial technology of self.

An example of attempts at developing the disciplined self required for such an ethic of autonomy has been reported, with an account of the technologies of self developed during such ethics retreats for, and on behalf of, the Japanese workplace.

> The ethic's center's ideal self is a *sunao na kokoro*, a gentle, sensitive heart. Responsive to social demands, sensitive to social context, it is a heart capable of appreciating the obligations and joys of living in human society. In order to realize this *sunao na kokoro*, the pedagogies galvanized emotional energies while subjecting the participants to strict systems of disciplines and punishments. It was an exemplary instance of a disciplinary production of subjects (Kondo, 1990: 109).

Kondo acknowledges that since no regime of truth is completely encompassing, resistances and dismissals of the idea can be ascertained by subsequent reactions of the workers and managers. Negative reactions, however, have not dampened the ardor of the self-management movement, in its development of enterprise as a way of being. In this mode, critique has been replaced by sales promotion. Management training of a similar type is common throughout the corporate sector under the rubric of *culture management*.

These issues are important for education in New Zealand since under Human Capital Theory, education is merely an economic device. On this account, it is useful to understand the nature of the workplace modes of governance, and in particular, the technologies used to reconstruct the self for this purpose. In this respect, Donzelot (1991) vividly describes the ideology behind the techniques used in modern management development programs. The aim of these programs is to modify the relation of individuals to their work. Workers are helped to re-conceptualize the idea that work defines them, stamping their place on them like a destiny, robbing them of their identity if they lose their jobs and making change in the place or content of work potentially threatening.

The new approach involves putting the accent on individual autonomy: the capacity to adapt. The individual is invited to become an agent of change in a world of change. Individuals are no longer defined in terms of the work they are assigned to, and productive activity is regarded as the site of deployment of personal skills.

> Whereas the individual freedom previously meant the possibility of either accepting or refusing the assigned status, it is now seen as meaning the possibility of permanently redeploying one's capacities according to the satisfaction one obtains in one's work, one's greater or lesser involvement in it, and its capacity thoroughly to fulfill one's potentialities. Thus we have 'continued retraining' of the whole 'new

psychological culture' (dynamization groups, human potential groups etc)...
(Donzelot, 1991: 252).

In examining the social roots of psychoanalytic culture (a culture that allows for the possibility of the new technologies of self), Turkle (1992) outlines the existentialist response to social disintegration (dislocation in society through the imposition of neoliberal reform) which shifted the emphasis from the society to individual personal responsibility. She sees the psychologization of everyday life, of family life, of urban life, as a step towards a full-blown psychoanalytic culture.

> When individuals lose confidence in their ability to understand the work around them, when they feel split between private and public identities, and when social 'recipes' no longer offer a sense of meaning, they are apt to become anxious consumers of reassurances about their 'authentic' subjectivity, their hidden 'inner life', and their deepest interpersonal experiences (Turkle, 1992: 40).

These practices represent more than the mere imposition of technologies of domination. Love is a common theme in accounts that implicate subjects in governing themselves through the employment of notions of self-management in ways that might otherwise be seen in need of critique. In a very general sense and through ordinary language, the notion of love is often spoken about as a positive emotion that has as one of its effects, a bonding between people which includes the development of a sense of fraternity. In a communitarian sense, the notion of fraternity is the antithesis of extreme individualism, and love is one of the primary values that is accepted as conducive to the development of fraternity.

Although neoliberals write more about economic growth and individual effort than about other values, they claim to consider fraternity (or community, as they usually call it) their primary value (Fowler, 1995: 46). The notion of fraternity in the neoliberal community, however, is not one formed around traditional, sectional, economic, ethnic or religious interests. Rather, community is understood in terms of national community, based on a sense of shared citizenship. The two institutions most important in building a sense of national community are universal military service and the public school, hence the neoliberal focus on education. In neoliberal rhetoric education should be used to develop the economic value system that underpins the neoliberal sense of community.

According to Fowler (1995), neoliberals appropriate the notion of community in the interest of developing a shared value system focused on values of competition and efficiency. *Community* and *fraternity* have traditionally been associated with love or altruism for fellow human beings, without a necessary instrumental purpose. If we extend ordinary language of love and fraternity to the workplace, it functions as a metaphor for the development of altruistic community. Most managerial efforts at the development of community in the workplace, however, are technical in nature, focused primarily on improving self and relationships with others and without asking the political questions about the nature of the practices of self and notions of community being sought. Love and community are therefore employed as technologies of self under a neoliberal regime to 'free' the individual to become self managing, in the interests of a greater instrumental goal of economic growth and State security.

There are questions to be asked about the nature of the community being developed. Descombes (1980) provides a credible account of human relations and love as a technology of self. He refers to Freud's analysis of the Church and the army, in the attribution of individual motivations in dealing with such hardships as discipline, persecution and defeat. Like Freud, Descombes concludes that love is the only force capable of leading an individual to such disdain for his own interests, and that the cohesion of artificial groups must therefore be libidinal. "In such organized communities, orthodoxy is synonymous with a strict observance of forms. It is important to speak in a certain way, to use 'consecrated' words" (Descombes, 1980: 105–106).

Clearly, certain technologies of self are employed by the individual with disregard for its own interests. The acceptance by the subject of the ordinary meanings of the notions of *love, fraternity, care* and *belonging* prevents the subject from critiquing the technology of self inherent in this usage. This explanation discerns the subject as both interpreter and *internaliser* of the discourse. It is difficult, at first glance, to accept that it is a maximization of utility or self-interest to die as a soldier, to sacrifice independence or to submit to humiliating discipline. Yet, through technologies of self inherent in *love, spirituality* or *caring* (Descombes, 1980; Rose, 1993), through permanent redeployment of one's *enterprising abilities* (Donzelot, 1991), and through harnessing 'emotions' (Kondo, 1990), the subject, under certain conditions, clearly develops the requisite attitudes and desires. Not only are such notions made to appear in the subject's best interests, they are also, according to the writers, actually experienced as such.

**Implications for education**

This distanciated, disembodied feature of busno-power, is carried over into educational forms of governmentality. In New Zealand, the invisible population is identifiable through its digital evidence on the NZQA electronic networks. Statistical analysis of the electronic audit trail is regarded nowadays as sufficient evidence of who is identified. The identification of the individual is synonymous with an audit trail of learning which is electronically transferred onto the NZQA national data bases. Data is captured about unit standards and individual records of learning with approved human capital credit values. The unit standards are verbal descriptions of what is to be learned, and the credits are quantified values attributed to that learning. Quantified values are able to be calculated and evaluated statistically so the self is not required, merely the data. Neither the self, nor its quantified evidence, is embodied.

The invisible consumer of education is a self that exercises its choices between various required paths on its journey towards its invisible potential. Through such an invisible process, the self has the illusion of full control over a belief system within which it is implicated in its own construction, and which (de)limits its capacity for its political critique of its own relative position. This level of governmentality, is at the same time, a form of social control which has shaped the subjectivities of autonomous choosers through choices in education, "obscur(ing) the ways in which our notions of ourselves as free and autonomous choosers were themselves social constructions which permitted us to be governed both individually and collectively" (Marshall, 1995a: 24). The Enlightenment ideal of personal autonomy has become the "dehumanized notion of the autonomous chooser imprisoned in the choices offered by the enterprise society" (Peters and Marshall, 1996: 93).

Increasing amounts of human capital, measured through the possession of certificates, are required for the self to gain a place in the current economic regime. And since, under neoliberal discourse, all parts of life are regarded as economic devices, so too is the notion of the invisible self. Higher levels of human capital are required to operate increasingly sophisticated military technology and its *flowdown effects* into industry (Becker, 1994). The invisible self contributes to the OECD (1993; 1994) international tabular comparisons of relative amounts of human capital which signify wealth (Fitzsimons, 1995). Through a perpetual, yet unreachable, quest to fulfill its own invisible self potential, the individual is harnessed to the economy through the stimulation of enterprise activity. The contribution by the self to the economy under these conditions is necessarily continuous. This restlessness of the self can be interpreted as a felt need for continuous change (a position no doubt constructed through sophisticated marketing) and can in turn be regarded as a governmental practice of neoliberalism.

Under the busno-power regime, the educational population is identified as consisting of revenue generating units, who consume the latest self improvement offerings (education modules) purchased from the approved certificate factories (the NZQA accredited education institutions) via the mode of information. NZQA's population is invisible to the extent that in the mode of information, its traditional unit or element—the body—does not need to be present in the educational disciplinary blocks. The parameters of any curriculum in this system are constrained by the discursive practices under which it has been constructed.

NZQA approved accreditation systems demand assessment, moderation and audits. These systems imply certain consumer-oriented notions of educational quality. In the busno-power accreditation system, quality is assured not so much by the content of the matter to be learned, but by the way the system functions. Since the form of assessment is approved within an NZQA accreditation structure prior to the RGU purchasing the module, the required criteria are already known to the RGU. In order to achieve in this commodified version of education, a skilful thinker may merely repeat accurately the approved and pre-purchased assessment words. The final stage in the process is for the NZQA (perhaps through its industry training strategy) to electronically certificate the students (revenue generating units, or RGUs) for their invisible thoughts. Some pixels on screen will be transferred as electronic signals to the screen of the RGU and some electronic digits will be deposited in their record of learning in the NZQA database. Eventually, the RGU will notice a debit in their bank account through the transfer of electronic digits to the NZQA to pay for the uplifting of the qualification.

This system is able to be sustained so long as the RGU can afford to keep funding the certificate factories. These are the educational, industrial and private organizations that supply the new commodified education which itself is represented by certificates themselves indicators of human capital. The role of the government is to provide student loans and transfer the RGU's loan entitlement into its bank account electronically for the RGU to transfer it yet again to the certificate factory of their choice upon their enrolment. So far, in this account, visibility is not required.

The notion of invisibility is problematic for control in a traditional carceral system that focuses on the body in disciplinary blocks but whose target now in the mode of information is the control of the mind. If the neoliberal enterprising self is, by definition, employed in the continuous development of itself, its value will be assessed by its enterprising capacity. This individualizing function of busno-power is totalizing for the self. It is also totalizing for the population as a whole, because increasingly, the new mode of information is an imperative to raise the level of human capital in an international context.

The current emphasis within busno-power is on skills, constituting a de-emphasis on reflexivity and critique. Since it is self-potential (and that is invisible) that is to be achieved, it is difficult for an assessor who is in a position external to the assessee, to evaluate the achievement. Achievement could be measured for example, by an increase in the number of certificates awarded for certain performances, but that is not a measure of potential—it is merely a measure of the number of certificates. And, if as Poster (1990: 15) suggests, "the referent fades into obscurity", then the certificate is merely a signifier.

Poster argues that through electronic writing, the new mode of information invests a new way for the self to know itself, through the interactive effects of the electronic text and the self. Through its interaction with the electronic word, the self can think at will without anyone else knowing what the content of that thinking is. Where the self is writing about itself, in the human sciences or in philosophy, the focus is on the digitized mode. What appears on screen is the self (itself). At any point in the digital construction of the self on screen, the self begins to know itself in ways that are not available within the socially constructed norms of the human sciences. But it is these very discourses through which the self is expected to know itself. It is these discourses that also convey social norms and expectations.

The interpretation of managerialism as governmentality rather than corporate management has implications for the subject. Reform at the structural and institutional levels therefore, must also involve reform of the subject. The subject must be able to be explained more adequately than is currently the case under neoliberalism. A rational explanation must be found to explain the demand for, and the nature of, new subject positions. The object of this chapter then is not managerialism per se, but an examination of possible subject positions available for education. The development of new modes of managerial subjugation suggests that the management of self is an issue for education.

From a neoliberal perspective, the basic unit is the self-managing, autonomous individual, but to be fully human, one must be continuously engaged in the exercise of that autonomy through self-management. To be rational in a neoliberal narrative, the autonomous individual must continuously and actively exercise what Gordon (1991) refers to as a faculty of choice. Since the macro-structural features of a neoliberal condition are continuously changing, there is an inexhaustible range of choices being continuously constructed for the autonomous subject to exercise. There may even be perceived value in new things, since progress and novelty are often conflated in ordinary language. The subject who operates in this rationality will also discern 'evidence' of the need for reform, self-management and the entrepreneurial form.

The term *autonomous* denotes at least some sense of control over a vast array of choices. The technology of self here is the acceptance in ordinary discourse of confusion about what autonomy might signify. The idea that choices are constrained within the political rationality of the market, however, is not ordinarily taken into account. The market is promoted as the *natural* state of affairs: it is spontaneous and is the proper default position. According to Peters (1993), the market does not exhibit Hayek's *spontaneous order*, nor Smith's *invisible hand*; but ironically, the market is highly regulated and controlled through the neoliberal legislation that set it up in the first place and which continues to maintain its structure. Within this current set of governmental practices, *homo economicus* is a construction.

## Chapter Twelve: Futures

This book has drawn upon Foucault's technical notion of governmentality to critique managerialism in education. Governmentality allows for a view of power relations in which the subject is implicated in its own governance through the intersection of technologies of domination and technologies of self. As outlined in chapter seven, the discourses of managerialism promote technologies of domination at the expense of technologies of self (apart from the limited account of self in *homo economicus*). Under governmentality *homo economicus* is not excluded, but is just one of myriad accounts of how people function, based on an a priori, abstract, neoclassical economic theory.

Governmentality admits to the idea of governance on the basis of the actual practices, through which these technologies become integrated into the subject's life experience. Clearly, in order to enjoy life, an individual must do something that integrates the world with his or her self. The book, therefore, has discussed examples of practices of self that implicate the subject in its own governance. This is supported by de Certeau (1984) for example, who argues that in the practice of everyday life, importance must be placed on the very need for belief with its modality of assertion being of as much importance as the actual content of that belief.

Managerialism in chapter seven has been viewed as a disciplinary mode of self governance with its own set of beliefs and practices. Chapter nine showed that governmentality offers a critique of managerialism as an inadequate account of governance. For self-governance under managerial discourse, the self must be the autonomous author of its own decisions. In order for the self to discipline its self under managerialism, then, a sense of agency (illusory or otherwise) is required. In de Certeau's (1984) view, the need for a belief in autonomy is a large element in legitimating such a belief, so is of little importance for managerial discipline whether that autonomy is illusory or not. In fact, as Lankshear (1982) and Marshall (1995b) have argued, the notion of autonomy is ordinarily employed in a simplistic fashion. Therefore, the way in which autonomy is perceived by the subject is of importance if it is to be a credible enough metaphor to function as governmentality. The depiction of autonomy as largely illusory critiques the account of the rational autonomous, self-interested utility maximizer of neoliberal managerialism.

In contrast to the demand from managerialism for a notion of authority based on autonomy, the book has argued at some length that the idea of an essential human nature is false and that the rationally autonomous person of the humanist construction is "already in himself the effect of a subjection much more profound than himself" (Foucault, 1979: 30).

That subjection was brought about through the human sciences. Foucault was interested in how particular kinds of subjects were produced as effects of discursive and power relations. Foucault refused to begin his investigation by taking for granted the idea of a rational, autonomous subject. Instead, his enquiries turned to the historical conditions which made various types of quite specific and differentiated subjects possible in the first place. Foucault did not, according to Althusser (1976), argue the radical structuralist idea that there were no subjects or that the subject could be deleted altogether from philosophical thinking. Foucault argues against the idea that the soul is an illusion, or an ideological effect: "On the contrary, it exists, it has a reality, it is produced permanently around, on, within the body by the functioning of a power" (Foucault, 1979: 29). Foucault also analyzes how these processes of subject production, or subjugation, are effected by modern scientific forms of knowledge.

Foucault's genealogical research suggests that the autonomous rational self free from historical and social contamination, is a fiction. His objection is that

> the self is not an objective reality to be described by our theories but a subjective notion that is actually constituted by them. The self is an abstract construction, one continually being redesigned in an ongoing discourse generated by the imperatives of the policing process (Hutton, 1988:135).

The subject is thus politically dominated.

> I don't think there is actually an autonomous, founding subject, a universal form of subject that one could find everywhere. I am very skeptical and very hostile toward this conception of the subject. I think on the contrary that the subject is constituted through practices of subjection, or, in a more anonymous way, through practices of liberation, of freedom, as in Antiquity, starting, of course, from a certain number of rules, styles and conventions that are found in the culture (Foucault, 1989: 313).

Through his genealogical research then, Foucault has shown that autonomy is largely illusory. Marshall has taken the argument further into education with an attack on the notion of the rational autonomous chooser—a notion that can be deduced from consumerist approaches to education in New Zealand introduced under recent reforms. What this book contributes to this critique is the idea that the illusion of autonomy offered through neoliberal self-management may intersect with other elements that underpin the reforms to education in unpredictable ways. For example, self-management may intersect with the problematic notions of rationality and choice in the spaces opened up by the withdrawal of the State under a neoliberal economy. If managerialism is to control those spaces (as its own discourse suggests it must), it needs more than its own limited account of the self as *homo economicus*. The deconstruction of rationality and choice in chapter ten showed that the autonomous self has been attributed the characteristics of rationality and choice required for autonomous decision making. That attribution, however, may undermine the neoliberal reforms based as they are on a grossly simplified account of the self.

Managerialism, in the guise of self-management in education, can be seen as the means by which the notion of privatization is legitimated. But in the culture management approach, managers attempt to create a particular climate: to encourage identification with corporate goals, to encourage high motivation and to promote the internalization of 'constructive' attitudes. Those who comply with these requirements are often granted individual privileges and increased remuneration through improved individual employment contracts and other inducements. Ultimately, they may even cease to see contradictions or injustices within their employing organizations, to become what might be termed the willing victims of what Lukes (1974) terms the *third dimension* of managerial power.

Alternatively, the self may not be convinced of the value of the new explanations, and increasing surveillance measures is likely to be counterproductive. The self-managing institution requires commitment from the self rather than external surveillance and control. Chapter ten showed governmentality operating through individual commitment to autonomy, rationality and choice. Without such commitment, self-management is likely to be less a matter of conscious choice and more a matter of whether the self is being managed.

An important mechanism of managerialism is to promote and quantify improvements in economic productivity. But given the various technologies of self in play, any improvements in productivity might be located as much in the *imagination* of the subject as in the *actual* rhetoric of managerialism. There is no necessary causal relationship between individuals acting in a certain way and actual changes in the world. Increases in productivity, while real and measurable, may, for example, be attributable to technological invention. Therefore we might say that the mere presence of managers, their practices and their utterances about their practices do not necessarily cause economic productivity. This, of course, is not to deny that there may be some relationship between structure and agency, but to point out that managerialism simply advances its notion of agency, without any critique of how its subject is discourse-bound, as an effect of the human sciences. The book has addressed this issue through a presentation of Foucault's attack on the Enlightenment self.

Managerialism presents itself as technologically determined. It is also possible, and indeed might be desirable, to consider a less technologically determined subjectivity. The self may engage itself in its own construction and may eventually come to think of itself outside of managerial parameters. Under these conditions, a new rationality is required for governance. Marshall has supplied such a model with the notion of busnocratic rationality. Under that rationality, managerialism is exposed as a rhetoric which claims to be self evidently of value and unable to be legitimately questioned. When critique is required, the subject disciplined under managerialism may not have the political will or the critical faculty to carry it out. Education, in the Enlightenment sense, will have failed.

Some modern regimes of power continue to exercise control over the body, even though that is an increasingly redundant form of rationality in the face of new forms of self-knowledge available in an electronic mode of information. This new self is to some extent outside the control of management—that control reliant upon the presence of the body. Postmodern subjectivities are now an effect of unstable electronic pixels on screen and shaped by uncontrollable types and sources of information. In the 1980s, Eastern communist regimes were largely unable to be controlled by governments, and a significant number of selves began to know themselves in a strikingly different manner from the official discourses that relied on surveillance and on control of the body. What followed was a change in reason of state towards a market economy.

Increasingly, the mode of information is an imperative to raise the level of human capital. Higher levels of human capital are required for the knowledge based economy. In a technological world, Becker's account of Human Capital Theory becomes less relevant as it relies on embodied knowledge and skill. Yet resemblances of Becker's assumptions underpin the New Zealand Government's explanation of education.

Chapter eight has described aspects of the New Zealand economy that are infused with neoliberal philosophy where managerialism and human capital theory join hands. Within education, as in many other sectors of society and economy, managerialization of personal identity and personal relations accompanies the capitalization of the meaning of life. Through care of the self, the individual must insure the society against burdens of risks that would otherwise need to be socially indemnified. The subject is required to invest in preventative health care, unemployment insurance, and, more pertinent to the subject of managerialism, to be *upskilled and ready* through education, to choose from a vast array of possibilities presented by an economy focused on an illusory notion of the consumer as sovereign (Abercrombie, et al., 1986). Ironically, choices around education seem to reduce to one thing: education for work.

New expertise and regulatory systems have sought to promote subjectivity rather than oppress it. Miller and Rose (1988) argue that subjectivity should not be regarded as the unchanging basis and standard of evaluation of social interaction; rather, it is the product of definite belief systems and techniques. Abstract doctrines and philosophical reflections upon conduct are linked with the development of precise techniques for the government of self in the minutiae of existence and experience.

In this view, life is to be managed. But under Human Capital Theory, life has capital value. That is the underlying rationale of chapter nine in this volume, *The Management of Human Capital*. Management must capitalize on and increase the value of the human capital, thereby increasing the productivity of the enterprise. Managerialism, in organizational culture, requires commitment from employees who are asked to make no distinction between their own welfare and the welfare of the organization. Unity and loyalty are thought to counteract the unintended consequences of the failings of the rational design of the organization. Within managerialism, commitment is now to quality as, within the previous rhetoric of scientific management, calculation was to efficiency. Production is no longer construed merely as an economic process either for the workers or the management. Production is now characterized as a social process within which both workers and management have a common interest—an interesting idea if we consider that the social nature of production is also a Marxist notion.

Pertinent to the Government's *seamless* education system is its notion of *flexible delivery*. Chapter eight illustrated how knowledge has entered the workplace through (re)training, education, information technology and job redesign, all of which allow for the entry of the expert in the creation and deployment of knowledge. Workplace assessment of learning (or, as Foucault would have it, *the examination*), allows the detailed knowledge about any particular workplace activity to be recorded as performance based documentation, written in competency language, and deposited as a unit standard on the NZQA national qualifications framework to become part of the public domain. This represents a cultural shift from traditional semi-private notions of knowledge under the power of the professional organizations (in earlier times, the Guilds), towards a commodification of knowledge, electronically stored and readily available. Workplace security is enhanced under these conditions, as no one worker or group of workers can block or hold up production through a withdrawal of knowledge. Electronically retrievable and standardized knowledge from the national qualifications frameworks is available to all. Given the right incentives, individual workers can be encouraged by management to step in and provide the knowledge required to drive production.

Parts of the individual's learning history that might previously have been excluded from this process may now be documented under the heading of individual *recognition of prior learning*, for which credit is given towards a public qualification. One's relationship to the work task at hand, to one's fellow employees and to the organization as a whole are no longer private affairs. Employees are now the object of knowledge (*hierarchical observation*) and subject to expert intervention *(correct training)* through a national focus on upskilling, incentivized by individualized employment agreements. The business enterprise itself is thus no longer private but is under a radical redefinition as the subject of economic nationalism. Although power is applied in this redefinition of the worker and the enterprise, it is not power, but the subject, which is the general theme of (this) research into managerialism.

The subject of managerialism contains the elements of autonomy, individualism, rationality and maximization of choice. These elements have been located as emanating from the Enlightenment notions of the universal self. From this truncated set of assumptions, managerial discourse implicates its subject in its ideology. Far reaching and pervasive though managerialism has been, it does not, I have argued, amount to a coherent philosophy. Neoliberal explanations of self are plausible and appealing, although they appeal to a limited notion of individual freedom.

Managerialist rhetoric focuses on a notion of the self as the rational self-interested utility maximizer. Foucault's notion of governmentality suggests that we can no longer view the subject as a symptom of deep essences or even as the owner of a self-assembly identity kit. The subject is now an effect, a force which comes about through being bounded by the categories available in managerial discourse. Other discourses might inscribe the subject differently.

Despite the reforms, there is still a cluster of underlying assumptions and expectations about the nature of education, stemming from scientistic aspirations of the human sciences. The Enlightenment project has been characterized as emblematic of this aspect of scientific excess. Foucault's ideas offer a strong critique of the very basis of Enlightenment notions such as autonomy and knowledge of self arising from the human sciences. This human science search for self knowledge fuels the continual search for enlightenment through improvement of the human condition.

It is this project upon which neoliberal managerialist notions of self-management in education are articulated. Managerialism has been portrayed in the reform literature as a disciplinary technology able to resolve all problems in education. But the problems of education have not been *solved* (if, in fact, that is what we do with them); they have merely been redefined under a banner of (re)form. Education has increasingly become an economic device, a rather limited conception considering the findings of what was arguably the most intensive and large scale democratic investigation into New Zealand society, *The Royal Commission on Social Policy* (1988). The Commission concluded that education is a social good. Chapter eight discussed the limits of human capital as an educational theory.

The effects of the reforms indicate that education is as problematic as ever. When critiqued from a Foucauldian perspective, even the categories and concepts of the reforms are found wanting. As a way of proceeding, it might be a way forward to open up those categories and concepts to critique and a play of differences. This is likely to be difficult given that education is now in the grip of managerialism. Much research in education attempts to address pre-defined problems without asking questions about the basic assumptions upon which those questions are premised. The extent to which the problem is already pre-defined is a problem in itself because the problem of education becomes limited to the problem of managerialism. Clearly the changing social world, and hence education, requires new concepts and categories with which to make sense. We need to deconstruct fundamentally the way we habitually look at education. This means that some basic ideas need to be re-thought, or maybe even discarded.

Education has been captured by neoliberal thought, and redefined in terms of national economic productivity. But the underlying premises of neoliberalism are at best problematic, and in some instances, somewhat incoherent and oppressive. A pragmatic question now is how might we conceptualize education in ways that provide more actual freedom from oppression. Any new approach will not be able to deny the presence of neoliberalism. Nor should it allow education to be captivated solely by an economic vision.

Although Foucault's genealogical approach has been used to deconstruct the application of managerialism in education, genealogy does not provide a blueprint for the future: it illuminates the present. In order to provide an approach to freedom in the present, I will now turn to a poststructuralist view of ethics in education which addresses the heart of education—the pedagogic relation.

**Poststructuralist possibilities**

In a poststructural reading of education, meanings are shifting, receding, fractured, incomplete, dispersed and deferred. Managerialism, on the other hand, is promoted as the antidote to chaos, irrationality, disorder and incompleteness. If only it was a case of never the twain shall meet. However, given the political and commercial arena in which educational values are contested, education is unlikely to suddenly be free of managerialism, and yet in this dichotomy, education is the very antithesis of managerialism.

Following Nietzsche's idea of a truncated dialectic of thesis and antithesis without a synthesis, Foucault argues that there is no necessary progress in history. For Foucault, self-creation and progress are possible, but not inevitable. Since, from Foucault's perspective, there is no meta-narrative of progress, applications of power such as neoliberalism are inadequate to explain the specific cultural adaptations made to that application of power. Managerialism simply cannot predict what the adaptations will be. Progress is not impossible, but nor is it guaranteed.

In the neoliberal account, the self must adapt to demands made on it, including those it has learned to make on itself, by self-managing its *self* in an environment of continuous change. It is important, however, for the functioning of the neoliberal subject to understand its own condition, even though that condition is problematic. It is integral to neoliberalism that the self improves, and to this end the self needs to desire something more adequate than it is at any moment in time. Perpetual restructuring for more productivity may achieve the desired self improvement, but the constant transformation may eventually promote a poststructural play of differences that destroy neoliberal philosophy. Without any guarantee of progress, neoliberalism cannot deliver on its promises of freedom, despite the investment of the self in education.

Managerialism is predicated upon performance as the mode of existence, and education is now under the grip of performativity. Revisiting Lyotard's *The Postmodern Condition* some fifteen years after its publication, Peters (1995) points out that Lyotard's arguments concerning the legitimation of knowledge and education are more relevant today than they were a decade and a half ago, and reason enough to return to Lyotard to re-examine his ideas. Bill Readings isolates two general propositions that structure Lyotard's varying analyses of education. The first proposition is that "it refuses to make the pedagogical relation into an object of knowledge"

(Readings, 1996: 153). The second proposition is that it can never take for granted the nature and function of the institutional forms within and against which teaching takes place" (Readings, 1995: 195–196). Both propositions are intertwined in that we can never imagine that attention to the pedagogic pragmatics can be divorced from attention to institutional forms.

One serious criticism of managerialism is that it renders other possibilities mute. This is particularly serious in education which, contrary to neoliberalism, I take to be a network of ethical obligations derived from the pedagogical relation. The pedagogical relation cannot render opposition mute because of the dialogical nature of its relation with the other. To pay attention to the addressee is not simply to control the conditions of reception of a discourse. We need to write in such a way that respects the space of reading of the other. Ethically, no one can be just, because justice is greater than consciousness. So an addressee, who is hailed to listen but knows not why, illustrates the ethical nature of the pedagogical relation. On this basis, Lyotard maintains a constant alertness to otherness.

In the classroom the *other* has many names: culture, thought, desire, energy, tradition, the event, the immemorial or the sublime. Managerialism seeks to dampen the shock of the other, but does not entirely succeed. Incalculable differences are opened up, the exploration of which is the business of pedagogy. This opening up is not merely a maieutic process of drawing out or *midwifing* the knowledge as if in a Socratic dialogue. Education, for Lyotard, is rather the drawing out of the *otherness* of thought that "undoes the pretension of self-presence (and) that always demands further study. It works over both the student and teachers, though in a dissymmetrical fashion" (Readings, 1995: 198). This is the opposite of the condition where managerialism takes itself to stand at the center of the educational process.

In summary, there are three pitfalls that attend the teaching relation. First is the hierarchy that makes the professor an absolute authority and the students so many receptacles for the transmission of a pre-constituted and unquestionable knowledge. Second is the claim that teaching raises no difference between teachers and students, suggesting that there may be nothing to learn. Third is the reduction of education to the development and training of technocrats, with little or no questioning about the purposes and functions to which that training is dedicated.

> What each of these threats to the pedagogic relation have in common is an orientation toward autonomy, an assertion that knowledge involves the abandonment of a network of ethical relations: to have knowledge is to gain a self-sufficient, monologic voice (Readings, 1995: 199).

In the first pitfall, the authority is secure in the privileged relationship to the meaning of knowledge. This relation is secure against irruption from the addressee. The professor has the relationship with the discourse and this is not affected by the relationship with the addressee. In the second pitfall, "the student's autonomy is a given. With regard to the third pitfall, the autonomy that the students gains through education is the freedom to occupy a place in economy while maintaining the illusion of working for oneself. All three accounts of the function of education feature the student achieving an identity by replication: in the first, replication of the professor; in the second, self replication; and in the third, replication of a place in the system. The achievement of that identity allows an autonomy from any obligated relation to others. Put simply, the student is free. But that freedom, as Foucault reminds us, is an effect of a discourse which denies a deep self-essence. Such a theory of surface inscription of technologies of domination on the subject displaces the phenomenological or essential approaches of managerialism. Hence, the problem of autonomy in self-management is the already preconstituted subject position that is available to the self, even though that subject may believe otherwise.

In education, there is no final position, no absolute efficiency, no freedom from participation. Participation in the form of an ethical relation will sometimes include a critical engagement with the practices of managerialism that sustain the production of human capital. That critical engagement need not fixate on the negative side of the dialectic. Although such engagement is convivial, it must not lose sight of the structures within with pedagogy takes place. This is a very different picture of participation than that proposed under neoliberalism.

This ethical obligation is a "persistent refusal to engage in abstract reflection on pedagogy in isolation from a reflection on the institutions within and against which that teaching takes place" (Readings, 1995: 214). It is also a major reason that managerialism and education are in an uneasy relationship. Electronically mediated technologies have increased the power of managerial practices and are implicated in the exponential improvement of productivity in the commodification of education. Commodification is aided and abetted through standardization, an homogenizing process that systematically reduces the shock of the other. Although it may be experienced as depersonalization, there is nothing personal in the technological pedagogical relation to begin with.

Managerialism, based as it is on notions of autonomy, individualism, rationality, and maximization of choice, is in conflict with ethical relations. To the extent that pedagogy does not appropriate managerialism, it will surrender ethics to profit. To the extent that pedagogy poses a challenge to managerialism, it keeps the question of meaning open, decentering the teacher, the referent, the self and its knowledge. The beginnings of an approach to the appropriation of managerialism for ethics is suggested below.

In education, there is a crisis in the governance of the self because reforms have introduced epistemological shifts from knowledge to information, shifts from content to process, problems of reference of signs in electronic writing, problems of identity and how the self is constituted, and problems relating to authority and governance. Since the managerial self is self-absorbed rather than publicly focused, what is required for governance is an account that will enable practices to be explained accurately at the cultural level. The mere insertion of managerialism into cultural life fails to provide the fine-grained cultural specificity required in an analysis of the problem of provision of tertiary education in New Zealand. And if, as Miller and Rose have argued, continual reform of reform is indicative of governmentality, we might regard the last eleven years of the production and continual (re)constitution of reform initiatives as an indicator that the 'problems' have not been resolved. To this extent, the self is not reformed in any stable or sustainable way, and may be unmanageable for the government. Assuming that managerialism requires stability and order for its functioning, managerialism will have a limited value for governance.

What then will replace managerialism? From the perspective of Foucault's notion of governmentality, it is possible that a pedagogy founded on a network of ethical obligations may be needed to implicate the self in education. This will, of necessity, require the cooperation of the self. The self, as it is now, under legislative duress within the employment relationship, is obviously not a cooperating self. So the interesting question for the future is how to theorize managerialism in the service of education, rather than as it is now with education in the service of managerialism.

Educational discourse needs to be modified to allow for ethical pedagogical relationships that will be able to explore open networks of obligation that decentered the teacher, the referent, and the self and its knowledge. That will allow the other into the pedagogic relation which even from a neoliberal perspective will be better than disruption or withdrawal by the self from the system. The more managerialism defines increasing numbers outside the margins required for production, the more will individuals and groups be disaffected, and the greater will be the cost measured in social terms. This will probably continue because it is an indicator of managerial efficiency to be able to achieve more with less.

Education as production cannot provide for any differences such as feminisms, ecological views, the libidinal economy or cultural differences. Education under busno-power has fallen into Lyotard's third pitfall—that of producing technocrats—and the number of technocrats required to run the increasingly electronically mediated system is getting less and less. What, in time, will we tell the others? It might, therefore, be useful to explore managerialism in a negotiated way that respects the other in the pedagogical relation. Not to do so will invite the defeat of the economic rationalist dream as disruptions begin to occur in protest at the gross inequalities that are emerging under its discourse.

It would also make sense to de-emphasize privatization as an ideology in education policy. Education in a world of continuous change is more or less compulsory until an individual is in his or her early adulthood. *Learning For Life* has been a constant theme in adult education since the 1980s, with individuals needing to upskill as their employment futures become highly unstable. Education is a social good if we look at the external demands being made on societies. The demand comes from the requirements of life-long learning, electronically mediated technologies, and structural adjustments to economies and societies. The notion of the learning workplace under workplace reform requires life-long learning. Knowledge required in the information society is increasingly needed for the economy to function in deregulated markets.

In view of Foucault's characterization of power relations as strategically reversible, we might expect that any challenge to the current managerialization of education will be contested:

> The issue is not of market economy versus government intervention, but one of reactionary intervention versus progressive intervention in which instrumentalities of the state constitute an important arena of conflict and struggle (Jones, 2003: 45).

But the portrayal of such a struggle is itself futile, because both reactionary and progressive interventions are imbued with the Enlightenment spirit. The problem of self-constitution is that it is a problematic for which managerialism cannot adequately account.

# References

Abercrombie, Nicholas, Stephen Hill, and Bryan Turner. 1986. *Sovereign Individuals of Capitalism.* London: Allen & Unwin.
Althusser, Louis. 1976. *Essays in Self Criticism.* London: New Left.
Aucoin, Peter. 1990. Administrative Reform in Public Management: Paradigms, Principles, Paradoxes and Pendulums. *Governance: An International Journal of Policy and Administration,* 3(2):115–137.
Ayer, Alfred. 1980. *Hume.* Oxford: Oxford University Press.
Barley, Stephen, and Gideon Kunda. 1992. Design and Devolution: Surges of Rational and Normative Ideologies of Control in Managerial Discourse. *The Administrative Science Quarterly* 37(3):363-399.
Barnett, Ronald. 1990. *The Idea of Higher Education.* The Society for Research into Higher Education. Buckingham, UK: Open University Press.
Bayliss, Len. 1994. *Prosperity Mislaid: Economic Failure in New Zealand and What Should be Done about it.* Wellington, New Zealand: GP Publications.
Becker, Gary. 1994. *Human Capital: A Theoretical and Empirical Analysis with Special Reference to Education.* 3rd ed. Chicago: The University of Chicago Press.
Bell, Daniel. 1976. *The Coming of the Post-Industrial Society: A Venture in Social Forecasting.* New York: Basic. Original edition, 1973.
Berger, Peter, and Thomas Luckman. 1967. *The Social Construction of Reality.* New York: Doubleday.
Blanchard, Kenneth, and Spencer Johnson. 1983. *The One Minute Manager.* Glasgow: Fontana/Collins.
Blaug, Mark. 1987. *The Economics of Education and the Education of an Economist.* New York: New York University Press.
Boston, Jonathon, John Martin, June Pollot and Pat Walsh. 1996. *Public Management: The New Zealand Model.* Melbourne: Oxford University Press.
Boston, Jonathan. 1991. The Theoretical Underpinnings of Public Sector Restructuring in New Zealand. In *Reshaping the State: New Zealand's Bureaucratic Revolution,* edited by J. Boston, J. Martin, J. Pallot and P. Walsh, 1–26. Auckland: Oxford University Press.
———. 1992. The Funding of Tertiary Education: Rights and Wrongs. In *The Decent Society?: Essays in Response to National's Economic and Social Policies,* edited by J. Boston and P. Dalziel, 186–207. Auckland, Oxford University Press.
Bull, George. 1961. *Niccolo Machiavelli: The Prince.* London: Penguin.
Burchell, Graham, Colin Gordon, and Peter Miller, eds. 1991. *The Foucault Effect: Studies in Governmentality.* Brighton, UK: Harvester Wheatsheaf.
Burchell, Graham. 1993. Liberal Government and Techniques of Self. *Economy and Society* 22 (3):267-282.
Cantor, Barry. 1991. The Aches of Industry. In *Medicine and Charity before the Welfare State,* edited by J. Barry and C. Jones, 207–224. London: Routledge.
Castells, Manuel. 1989. *The Informational City: Information Technology, Economic Restructuring and the Urban-Regional Process.* Oxford: Blackwell.
Chandler, Alfred. 1977. *The Visible Hand: The Managerial Revolution in America.* Cambridge, MA: Harvard Belknap.
Child, John. 1969. *The Business Enterprise in Modern Industrial Society.* London: Collier Macmillan.

Coxon, Eve, Kuni Jenkins, James Marshall, and Lauran Massey, eds. 1994. *The Politics of Learning and Teaching in Aotearoa-New Zealand.* Palmerston North, New Zealand: Dunmore.

Crocombe, Graham, Michael Enright, and Michael Porter. 1991) *Upgrading New Zealand's Competitive Advantage.* Oxford: Oxford University Press.

Dale, Roger. 1994. National Reform, Economic Crisis and "New Right" Theory: A New Zealand Perspective. *Discourse* 14(2), 17–29.

Dandeker, Christopher. 1990. *Surveillance, Power & Modernity: Bureaucracy and Discipline from 1700 to the Present Day.* Oxford: Polity.

de Certeau, Michel. 1984. *The Practice of Everyday Life.* Translated by S. Rendall. Berkeley: University of California Press.

Deane, Roderick. 1986. Public Sector Reform: A Review of the Issues. In *Purpose Performance and Profit: Redefining the Public Sector*, edited by M. Clark and E. Sinclair, 12–24. Wellington: Government Printing Office.

Deleuze, Gilles. 1990. Postscript to the Societies of Control. *October 59.* Cambridge, MA: Massachusetts University Press.

Department of Education. 1989a. *Learning for Life: Two.* Wellington: Government Printer.

———. 1989b. *Learning for Life: Education and Training beyond the Age of Fifteen.* Wellington, New Zealand: Government Printer.

Descombes, Vincent. 1980. *Modern French Philosophy.* Sydney: Cambridge University Press.

Donzelot, Jacques. 1991. Pleasure in Work. In *The Foucault Effect: Studies in Governmentality*, edited by G. Burchell, C. Gordon and P. Miller, 169-180. London: Harvester Wheatsheaf,.

Douglas, Roger. 1993. *Unfinished Business.* Auckland: Random House.

Dreyfus, Hubert, and Paul Rabinow. 1982. *Michel Foucault: Beyond Structuralism and Hermeneutics (Afterword by Michel Foucault).* Chicago: Harvester.

Drucker, Peter. 1974. *Management.* London: Butterworth Heinemann.

———. 1994. *Post Capitalist Society.* Oxford: Butterworth Heinemann.

Economist. 1994. Inequality. In *Economics as a Social Science: Readings in Political Economy*, edited by G. Argyrous and F. Stilwell, 19–23. Sydney: Pluto.

———. 1996. Training and Jobs: What Works? *The Economist*, 6 April, 19–21.

Enteman, Willard. 1993. *Managerialism: The Emergence of a New Ideology.* Madison, WI: The University of Wisconsin Press.

Fitzsimons, Patrick, and Michael Peters. 1994. Human Capital Theory and the Industry Training Strategy in New Zealand. *Journal of Education Policy.* 9(3):245–266.

Fitzsimons, Patrick. 1995. The Management of Tertiary Education in New Zealand. In *Journal of Education Policy.* 10(2):173–187.

Foucault, Michel. 1970. *The Order of Things: An Archaeology of the Human Sciences.* London: Tavistock.

———. 1975. *The Birth of the Clinic: An Archaeology of Medical Perception.* New York: Vintage, Random House.

———. 1976. The Politics of Health in the Eighteenth Century. In *Power/Knowledge: Selected Interviews and Other Writings 1972-1977 by Michel Foucault*, edited by C. Gordon, 166–182. Brighton, UK: Harvester Wheatsheaf.

———. 1977a. Two Lectures. In *Power/Knowledge: Selected Interviews and Other Writings 1972–1977 by Michel Foucault*, edited by C. Gordon, 78–108. Brighton, UK: Harvester Wheatsheaf.

———. 1977b. Truth and Power. In *Power/Knowledge: Selected Interviews and Other Writings 1972–1977 by Michel Foucault*, edited by C. Gordon, 109–133. London: Harvester Wheatsheaf.

———. 1977c. Nietzsche, Genealogy, History. In *Language, Counter-Memory, Practice: Selected Essays and Interviews by Michel Foucault*, edited by D. Bouchard, 139–164. Ithaca, NY: Cornell University Press.

———. 1978. *The History of Sexuality: Vol 1—An Introduction*. London: Penguin.

———. 1979. *Discipline & Punish: The Birth of the Prison*. Translated by A. Sheridan. New York: Vintage.

———. 1980a. Prison Talk. In *Power/Knowledge: Selected Interviews and Other Writings 1972-1977 by Michel Foucault*, edited by C. Gordon, 37-54. Brighton, UK: Harvester Wheatsheaf.

———. 1980b. Introduction. In *Herculine Barbin: Being the Recently Discovered Memoirs of a Nineteenth-Century French Hermaphrodite*. Translated by R. McDougall. New York: Pantheon.

———. 1982. Afterword: The Subject and Power. In H. Dreyfus, and P. Rabinow. *Michel Foucault: Beyond Structuralism and Hermeneutics*. Chicago: Harvester Wheatsheaf.

———. 1984. What Is Enlightenment? In *The Foucault Reader*, edited by P. Rabinow, 32–50. New York: Pantheon.

———. 1988a. The Political Technologies of Individuals. In *Technologies of the Self: A Seminar With Michel Foucault*, edited by L. Martin, H. Gutman and P. Hutton, 145–162. London: Tavistock

———. 1988b. Technologies of the Self. In *Technologies of the Self: A Seminar with Michel Foucault*, edited by L. Martin, H. Gutman and P. Hutton, 16–49. London: Tavistock.

———. 1989. *Foucault Live*, (Interviews, 1966–84). New York: Semiotext(e).

———. 1991a. Questions of Method. In *The Foucault Effect: Studies in Governmentality*, edited by G. Burchell, C. Gordon and P. Miller, 73–86. Brighton, UK: Harvester Wheatsheaf.

———. 1991b. Governmentality. In *The Foucault Effect: Studies in Governmentality*, edited by G. Burchell, C. Gordon and P. Miller, 87-104. Brighton, UK: Harvester Wheatsheaf.

Fowler, Francis. 1995. The Neoliberal Value Shift and its Implications for Federal Education Policy under Clinton. *Educational Administration Quarterly*, 31(1):38–60.

Fraser, Nancy. 1989. *Unruly Practices. Power, Discourse and Gender and Contemporary Social Theory*. Cambridge: Polity.

Gamble, Andrew. 1988. The Thatcher Decade in Perspective. In *Developments in British Politics 3*, edited by P. Dunleavy, A. Gamble and G. Peele, 333–358. London: Macmillan.

Giddens, Anthony. 1995. *A Contemporary Critique of Historical Materialism*. 2nd ed. London: Macmillan.

Gilmour, Ian. 1992. *Dancing with Dogma: Britain under Thatcherism*. London: Simon & Schuster.

Gordon, Colin. 1980. *Michel Foucault: Power/Knowledge: Selected Interviews and Other Writings 1972–1977*. Brighton, UK: Harvester Wheat sheaf.

———. 1991. Governmental Rationality: An Introduction. In *The Foucault Effect: Studies in Governmentality*, edited by G. Burchell, C. Gordon and P. Miller, 1–51. Brighton, UK: Harvester Wheatsheaf.

Gutman, Huck. 1988. Rousseau's Confessions: A Technology of Self. In *Technologies of the Self: A Seminar with Michel Foucault*, edited by L. Martin, H. Gutman and P. Hutton, 99–120. London: Tavistock.
Gutting, Gary. 1989. *Michel Foucault's Archaeology of Scientific Reason*. Cambridge: Cambridge University Press.
Habermas, Jurgen. 1988. *Legitimation Crisis*. Oxford: Polity.
Hacking, Ian. 1986. Self Improvement. In *Foucault: A Critical Reader*, edited by D. Hoy, 235–240. Oxford: Basil Blackwell.
———. 1991. How Should We Do the History of Statistics? In *The Foucault Effect: Studies in Governmentality*, edited by G. Burchell, C. Gordon and P. Miller, 181–196. Brighton, UK: Harvester Wheatsheaf.
———. 1995. *Rewriting the Soul: Multiple Personality and the Sciences of Memory*. Princeton, NJ: Princeton University Press.
Hall, Stuart. 1993. Thatcherism Today. *New Statesman*, 26 November, 14–16.
Hampson, Norman. 1968. *The Enlightenment*. Middlesex, UK: Penguin.
Handy, Charles. 1976. *Understanding Organizations*. Harmondsworth, UK: Penguin.
Harvey, David. 1989. *The condition of postmodernity: An inquiry into the origins of cultural change*. Oxford, UK: Blackwell.
Harvey, Jerry. 1974. *The Abilene Paradox and Other Meditations on Management*. Lexington, MA: Heath.
Haworth, Nigel. 1994. Neo-liberalism and Economic Internationalism. In *Leap into the Dark: The Changing Role of the State in New Zealand Since 1984*, edited by A. Sharp, 19–40. Auckland: Auckland University Press.
Heidegger, Martin. 1962. *Being and Time*. Translated by J. Macquarrie and E. Robinson. Oxford: Basil Blackwell.
Hood, Christopher. 1990. De-Sir Humphreyfying the Westminster Model of Bureaucracy: A New Style of Governance? *Governance: An International Journal of Policy and Administration*, 3(2):205–214.
———. 1991. A Public Management for all Seasons? *Public Administration*, 69(Spring):3–19.
Horne, Donald. 1986. *The Public Culture: An Argument with the Future*. 2nd ed. London: Pluto.
Huczynski, Andrzej. 1993. *Management Gurus: What Makes Them and How to Become One*. New York: Routledge.
Hutton, Patrick. 1988. Foucault, Freud, and the Technologies of the Self. In *Technologies of the Self: A Seminar with Michel Foucault*, edited by L. Martin, H. Gutman and P. Hutton. 121–144. London: Tavistock.
James, Colin. 1992. *New Territory: The Transformation of New Zealand 1984-1992*. Wellington, New Zealand: Bridget William.
Jones, Evan. 2003. Government Intervention. In F. Stilwell and G. Argyrous (Eds.), *Economics as a social science: readings in political economy*, 42-44. 2nd ed. Melbourne: Pluto.
Kant, Immanuel. (1988). *Fundamental Principles of the Metaphysics of Morals*. Translated by T. K. Abbott. New York: Prometheus.
Kaufman, Walter. 1982. *The Portable Nietzsche*. Auckland: Penguin.
Keat, Russell, and Nicholas Abercrombie, eds. 1991. *Enterprise Culture*. The International Library of Sociology. London: Routledge.

Kelsey, Jane. 1993) *Rolling Back the State: Privatization of Power in Aotearoa/New Zealand.* Wellington, New Zealand: Bridget Williams.

———. 1995. *The New Zealand Experiment: A World Model for Structural Adjustment?* Auckland: Auckland University Press with Bridget Williams.

Kieser, Alfred. 1987. From Asceticism to Administration of Wealth. Medieval Monasteries and the Pitfalls of Rationalization. *Organization Studies,* 8(1):103–123.

Kondo, Dorinne. 1990. *Crafting Selves: Power, Gender and Discourses of Identity in a Japanese Workplace.* Chicago: The University of Chicago Press.

Lakoff, George, and Mark Johnson. 1980. *Metaphors We Live By.* Chicago: The University of Chicago Press.

Lankshear, Colin. 1982. *Freedom and Education.* Auckland: Milton Brookes.

Lauder, Hugh. 1990. The New Right Revolution. In *New Zealand Education Policy Today: Critical Perspectives* edited by S. Middleton, J. Codd and A. Jones, 1–26. Wellington, New Zealand: Allen & Unwin.

———. 1991. *The Lauder Report: Tomorrow's Education, Tomorrow's Economy. A Report Commissioned by the Education Sector Standing Committee of the New Zealand Council of Trade Unions.* Wellington, New Zealand: The New Zealand Post Primary Teacher's Association.

Lindsey, Robert. 1987. Gurus Hired to Motivate Workers Are Raising Fears of Mind Control. *The New York Times,* April 6, p. A10.

Lukes, Steven. 1974. *Power. A Radical View.* London. Macmillan.

Lyotard, Jean-Francois. 1984. *The Postmodern Condition: A Report on Knowledge. Theory and History of Literature,* (Vol. 10). Minneapolis, MN: University of Minnesota Press.

Lythe, David. 1995. *Internationalization of Small and Medium Enterprises and Human Resource Development: A Progress Report on the New Zealand Experience.* Wellington, New Zealand: The New Zealand Qualifications Authority.

Marginson, Simon. 1993. *Education and Public Policy in Australia.* Cambridge: Cambridge University Press.

Marshall, James. 1993. Quality and its Applications. Paper read at First Newcastle International conference on Quality and its Applications, 1-3 September 2003, at Newcastle on Tyne.

———. 1995a. Michel Foucault: Governmentality and Liberal Education. *Studies in Philosophy and Education* 14:23–34.

———. 1995b. Foucault and Neoliberalism: Bio-power and Busno-power. In *Philosophy of Education,* edited by A. Neiman, 320–329. Illinois: Philosophy of Education Society.

———. 1996. *Michel Foucault: Personal Autonomy and Education.* Dordrecht: Kluwer.

Mayo, Elton. 2003. The Hawthorne Experiment. In *The Early Sociology of Management and Organizations,* 55-76. New York: Routledge.

McCloskey, Donald. 1994. *Knowledge and Persuasion in Economics.* Cambridge: Cambridge University Press.

Miller, Peter, and Nikolas Rose. 1988. The Tavistock Programme: The Government of Subjectivity and Social Life. *Sociology,* 22(2):171–192.

———. 1993. Governing Economic Life. In *Foucault's New Domains,* edited by M. Gane and T. Johnson, 75–105. London: Routledge.

Ministry of Education. 1989. *Performance Indicators for Tertiary Institutions: Report of the Performance Indicators Task Force.* Wellington, New Zealand.

———. 1991. *Management Control of Student Enrolments.* Wellington, New Zealand.

———. 1993. *Education for the 21st Century.* Wellington, New Zealand.

Mintzberg, Henry. 1974. *The Manager's Work: Folklore or Fact?* Harvard Business Review, Harvard University Press.

O'Brien, Mike, and Chris Wilkes. 1993. *The Tragedy of the Market: A Social Experiment in New Zealand*. Palmerston North, New Zealand: Dunmore.

OECD. 1993. *Economic Surveys 1992-1993: New Zealand.* Paris: OECD.

———. 1994. *Economic Surveys New Zealand*. Paris: OECD.

———. 2007. *Human capital: How what you know shapes your life*. Paris: OECD.

Offe, Claus. 1985. *Disorganized Capitalism: Contemporary Transformation of Work and Politics*. Oxford: Polity.

Olssen, Mark. 1996. Michel Foucault's Historical Materialism. In *Critical Theory, Poststructuralism & the Social Context*, edited by M. Peters, W. Hope, J. Marshall and S. Webster, 82–105. Palmerston North, New Zealand: Dunmore.

Perrow, Charles. 1979. *Complex Organizations: A Critical Essay*. 2nd ed. London: Scott Foresman.

Peters, Michael, and James Marshall. 1996. *Individualism and Community: Education and Social Policy in the Postmodern Condition*. London: Falmer.

Peters, Michael, James Marshall, and Bruce Parr. 1993. *The Marketisation of Tertiary Education in New Zealand: A Comparison with Australia*. Australian Universities Review, 36(2):34–39.

Peters, Michael. 1990. *Performance and Accountability: A Critical Approach to the Issues in New Zealand Higher Education*. An Occasional Research Monograph. Northern Region Tutor Training Center, Auckland Institute of Technology, Auckland, New Zealand.

———. 1991. Handout, Tutorial, Education Department, Auckland University. Paper 14400, p. 58.

———. 1993. Postmodernity and Neoliberalism: Restructuring Education in Aotearoa. *Delta* 47:47–60.

———. 1995. Education and the Postmodern Condition: Revisiting Jean Francois Lyotard. *Journal of Philosophy of Education*. The Journal of the Philosophy of Education Society of Great Britain, 29(3):387–400.

———. 1996. New Zealand: The Failure of Social Policy. In *Economics as a Social Science: Readings in Political Economy*, edited by G. Argyrous and F. Stilwell, 248–250. Sydney: Pluto.

Peters, Tom, and Robert Waterman. 1982. *In search of Excellence: Lessons from America's best-run companies*. New York: Harper & Row.

Pollitt, Christopher. 1990. *Managerialism and the Public Services: The Anglo-American Experience*. Oxford: Basil Blackwell.

Poster, Mark. 1975. *Existential Marxism in Postwar France: From Sartre to Althusser*. Princeton, NJ: Princeton University Press.

———. 1986. Foucault and the Tyranny of Greece. In *Foucault: A Critical Reader*, edited by D. Hoy, 205–220. Oxford: Basil Blackwell.

———. 1990. *The Mode of Information: Poststructuralism and Social Context*. Cambridge, UK: Polity.

———. 1993. Foucault and the Problem of Self Constitution. In *Foucault and the Critique of Institutions*, edited by J. Caputo and M. Yount, 63–80. University Park, Pennsylvania: Pennsylvania University Press.

———. 1994. A Second Media Age? *Arena Journal* 1994 (3):49-91.

Postman, Neil. 1993. *Technopoly: The Surrender of Culture to Technology*. New York: Vintage.

Readings, Bill. 1995. From Emancipation to Obligation: Sketch for a Heteronomous Politics of Education. In *Education and the Postmodern Condition*, edited by M. Peters, 193-208. Westport, CT: Bergin & Garvey.

———. 1996. *The University in Ruins*. Cambridge: Harvard University Press.

Rees, Stuart, and Gordon Rodley, eds. 1995. *The Human Cost of Managerialism: Advocating The Recovery of Humanity*. Sydney: Pluto.

Reich, Robert. 1992. *The Work of Nations: Preparing Ourselves for 21st Century Capitalism*. New York: Vintage.

Romer, Paul. 1990. Endogenous Technological Change. *Journal of Political Economy*, 98(5): S71-S102.

Rose, Nikolas. 1993. Government, Authority and Expertise in Advanced Liberalism. *Economy and Society*, 22(3):283–299.

Rosenberg, Wolfgang. 1993. *New Zealand Can be Different and Better: Why Deregulation Does Not Work*. Christchurch, New Zealand: Monthly Review Society.

Royal Commission on Social Policy. 1988. *The April Report*. Wellington: Author.

Ryle, Gilbert. 1949. *The Concept of Mind*. New York: Barnes & Noble.

Sen, Amartya. 1987. *On Ethics and Economics*. Oxford: Basil Blackwell.

Shapiro, Bernard. 1993. Mass Higher Education: Problems and Challenges. Keynote Address. Joint OECD/Australian Government Conference, *The Transition from Elite to Mass Higher Education*, Sydney 15–18, June.

Sharp, Andrew, ed. 1994. *Leap into the Dark: The Changing Role of the State in New Zealand Since 1984*. Auckland: Auckland University Press.

Shoemaker, Sydney, and Richard Swinburne. 1984. *Personal Identity*. Oxford: Basil Blackwell.

Shoemaker, Sydney. 1963. *Self-Knowledge and Self-Identity*. New York: Cornell University Press.

Smith, Robert. 1993. The Transition from Elite to Mass Tertiary Education Systems: Overview and Current Issues. Keynote address at the joint OECD/Australian Government Conference, *The Transition from Elite to Mass Tertiary Education*, Sydney, 15–18 June.

Snook, Ivan. 1994. Workplace Skills: Whose Responsibility? In K. Secombe *People and Performance: Achieving Success through People*, 2(2):23–26. Wellington, New Zealand.

Solomon, Robert. 1988. *Continental Philosophy Since 1750: The Rise and Fall of the Self*. Oxford: The Oxford University Press.

State Services Commission. 1991. *Review of State Sector Reforms*. Steering Group. Wellington, New Zealand: State Services Commission.

———. 1993. *Briefing Papers for the Minister of State Services*. Wellington, New Zealand: State Services Commission.

Taylor, Charles. 1989. *Sources of the Self: The Making of the Modern Identity*. Victoria: Cambridge University Press.

———. 1991. *The Ethics of Authenticity*. London: Harvard University Press.

Taylor, Frederick Winslow. 1911. *Principles of Scientific Management*. New York: Harper.

Touraine, Alain. 1995. *Critique of Modernity*. Translated by D. Macey. Oxford: Blackwell.

Treasury. 1984. *Economic Management*. Wellington, New Zealand: Government Printer.

———. 1987. *Government Management: Brief to the Incoming Government*. (11), Education Issues. Wellington, New Zealand: Government Printer.

———. 1990. *Briefing to the Incoming Government*. Wellington, New Zealand: Government Printer.

———. 1993. *An Evaluation of the Tertiary System.* Treasury Paper for the Todd Taskforce. Wellington, New Zealand. (Obtained under the Official Information Act).

Tucker, Robert, ed. 1978. *The Marx-Engels Reader.* New York: Norton.

Turkle, Sherry. 1992. *Psychoanalytic Politics: Jacques Lacan and Freud's French Revolution.* 2nd ed. London: Guilford.

Upton, Simon. (1993) 'The Labour Market and the Universities' Presentation to NZCER/AUSNZ Seminar, Wellington. 13 October

Waring, Marilyn. 1988. *Counting for Nothing: What Men Value and What Women Are Worth.* Wellington: Bridget Williams.

Watts, Rob. 1994. Government and Modernity: An essay on Governmentality', *Arena Journal,* New Series, 2/3, February, 1994:105-156.

Weedon, Chris. 1987. *Feminist Practice and Poststructuralist Theory.* London: Blackwell.

# Index

**A**
autonomy · 2, 4, 6-7, 9, 11-13, 32, 36-7, 44, 46, 53, 62, 71-3, 75-7, 80-2, 86, 103-5, 109, 120, 124, 131, 133, 144, 150, 156-8, 160-3, 170-3, 174, 176-7, 180, 182-3, 185-7, 190, 193-4

**B**
bio-power · 64, 95, 99, 125, 129-31, 166, 168-9
busnocratic rationality · 6, 9, 12, 23, 125, 131-5, 138-9, 146, 176, 188
busno-power · 12, 85-6, 102, 125, 131-4, 139, 145-6, 154, 166, 168-9, 170, 171, 179-81, 195

**C**
capitalism · 3, 19, 20-1, 25, 88, 98-9, 107-14, 116, 125-8, 130, 139-41, 144-6, 158, 170, 180, 188, 189
choice · 10, 12, 19, 23, 36, 43, 98-100, 102-4, 109, 119, 121-3, 131, 150, 152-60, 162, 170-1, 181-2, 187, 190, 194
community · 23, 37, 49, 60, 73, 120, 150-1, 156, 174, 178-9
confessional society · 68, 70-1, 75, 77, 83
consumer · 21, 121, 131-2, 157-8, 171, 178
contingency theory · 118-9
criminal · 60-1
culture management · 5, 13, 119, 168, 175, 177

**D**
desire · 6, 10, 36, 38, 67, 78, 95, 116, 149, 165-6, 192, 193
disciplinary blocks · 52, 59, 61-2, 64, 67, 94, 129, 139, 169, 181
disengagement · 33, 79

**E**
education
    participation · 12, 131, 137, 139

Enlightenment · 2, 4-5, 7, 10-14, 24, 29, 31, 43-4, 46-7, 50, 53, 58-9, 72, 78-9, 81-3, 95, 133, 165, 170, 180, 188, 190, 196
enterprise culture · 2, 12, 23, 25, 97, 131-2, 134, 157, 159-60, 171, 174
entrepreneurial · 23
episteme · 53-5
ethics · 1, 5, 16, 73, 76, 81-2, 92, 98, 119, 150, 155-6, 193-5

**G**
genealogy · 2, 7, 11-12, 14-16, 70, 82, 85, 107
governance · 1, 2, 4- 8, 11-17, 19, 24-5, 44, 52, 57, 65, 70, 73, 80-1, 85, 88-91, 95, 100, 102-3, 104, 107, 109, 115-16, 118, 122-3, 125, 133, 144, 158-9, 161, 164-6, 173-5, 177, 185, 188, 195
government · 20, 22, 25-6, 56, 57, 72, 82, 85-98, 100-3, 108, 116, 124-8, 131-2, 135-6, 143, 145-6, 157-8, 160-1, 165-6, 170-1, 173-4, 181, 189, 195-6
    arts of · 11, 85-9, 91
governmentality · 1, 6, 11-13, 15-16, 20, 29, 52-3, 56, 65, 67, 72-3, 85, 88-9, 92, 101-2, 105, 107, 110, 125, 130-4, 139, 143-6, 159, 161, 164-5, 166, 170, 179-80, 182, 185, 187, 190, 195

**H**
Hawthorne studies · 116
*homo consumptus* · 161
*homo economicus* · 4, 6, 11-12, 19, 21, 99, 105, 107, 123, 133, 152, 155, 159, 160, 165, 171, 183, 185, 187
human capital · 3, 6-7, 10, 12, 16, 19, 20-1, 99, 125-6, 127-33, 135, 137-42, 144-6, 166, 168-70, 177, 180-1, 188-9, 191, 194
human resource · 3-4
human sciences · 45, 53-4, 59, 62, 64-5, 69, 71, 73, 75-7, 80-2, 94, 170, 182, 186-7, 190

**I**
identity · 13, 22, 31, 33-4, 38-9, 41-2, 44, 51, 54, 74, 77-8, 81, 119, 144, 162, 177-8, 188, 190, 194-5
information society · 125, 166-8, 196

**L**
liberalism · 5, 12, 24, 29, 85, 93-8, 109

**M**
Machiavelli · 56, 87
managerialism · 1, 2, 4-13, 16, 19, 21, 26, 50, 81-2, 102-5, 107-11, 118, 120-4, 149, 157, 160-1, 163-5, 171-6, 182, 185, 187-96
market · 2-3, 6, 20-1, 25, 94, 96-8, 107-9, 112, 118, 124, 126-7, 133, 135-6, 139-40, 149, 160, 164, 170, 172, 174, 183, 188, 196
marketing · 90, 92, 153-4, 157, 158, 162, 180
Marxism · 14, 94, 114
mercantilism · 91
mode of information · 13-14, 27, 125, 131-3, 165-8, 180-2, 188
monetarism · 19, 21-2, 24, 100
morality · 25, 36-7, 63, 68, 71, 73, 76-7, 80-1, 87, 89, 112, 115

**N**
neoliberalism · 1-6, 10-12, 14, 16-17, 19-21, 23-26, 29, 80, 82, 85, 93, 97-100, 103, 105, 107-9, 123-5, 127-8, 130-1, 133-4, 138, 143, 146, 149-50, 152-54, 156-62, 164-5, 167, 169-71, 173-76, 178-83, 185-86, 188, 190-5, 202
new public management · 8, 107, 131
new right · 3, 19, 99, 100-1, 149, 158
normal · 58, 61-5, 77, 79-82, 100, 173
NZQA · 3, 9, 23, 157, 179-80, 189

**P**
panopticon · 51, 109, 165, 169
pedagogy · 69, 87, 192-6
police · 71-3, 88-9, 95-6
post-capitalism · 123
poststructuralism · 12, 16-7, 29, 165, 191, 192
power
  application · 24, 59-60, 62, 72, 192
  exercise · 15, 52, 56, 80, 86-7, 159
  productive · 15, 17, 52, 109
  regime · 59, 126, 133
  relations · 2, 7, 14-15, 24, 51-2, 61, 64-5, 68, 73, 101, 128-9, 161, 167, 169, 185-6, 196
  sovereign · 11, 15, 20, 51-2, 56-8, 61, 64, 73, 82, 85-7, 89-92, 95-6, 101-2, 104-5, 158, 161, 164
preferences · 65, 121, 150, 152-4, 157
privatization · 8, 22, 99, 100, 187, 196
productivity · 10, 88, 102-3, 114, 122-3, 127-8, 137-9, 142, 144, 146, 157, 159, 168, 175, 187, 189, 191-2, 194
psychiatry · 62-3, 67
public sector · 1, 5, 7-8, 10, 100-1, 123, 131, 172, 173

**R**
rational autonomous chooser · 2, 186
reflexivity · 33, 79, 181
reform · 2-3, 10, 12, 16, 19, 23, 25, 29, 53, 61, 63, 65, 107-8, 113-14, 126, 134, 143, 145-6, 160, 174, 178, 182, 191, 195

**S**
scientific management · 114-15, 117-18, 168, 175, 189
self
  caring · 11, 68-9, 73, 75, 77, 80-2
  conduct · 97
  constitution · 1, 10-11, 14, 76, 123, 133, 166, 196
  construction · 81-2, 161
  examination · 70, 73-4, 86
  experience · 34
  exploration · 33
  interest · 2, 121, 150, 152-7, 179
  knowing · 11, 68-9, 73-4, 80-2
  management · 1-3, 6-8, 10, 12, 85, 102-4, 109, 124, 149, 151, 153, 158, 160, 164, 172, 174, 177-8, 182, 186-7, 194
  metaphysical · 31
  origin · 34
sexuality · 64-5, 70, 77-9, 129
social sciences · 32, 63, 74

State · 1, 3-4, 11-12, 15, 19-22, 24-9, 58, 85-90, 92-7, 99, 100-3, 107-10, 124-5, 131-2, 135, 138, 145-6, 158-9, 160, 171-2, 174, 179, 187
 minimizing the State · 1, 4
 reason of State · 3, 21, 71, 73, 88-9, 96, 124, 146, 188
statistics · 62, 88-91, 117-18, 129, 173
Stoic · 57, 69-70, 74, 80-1
subject · 1-5, 7, 11-12, 14-16, 19-25, 27, 29, 31, 33-5, 40, 44, 46-7, 49, 51-3, 55, 56-7, 60, 63-4, 68, 70, 72-4, 76-7, 81, 86, 90, 94-5, 99, 102-5, 107, 109, 111, 115, 123, 130, 133, 139, 143-6, 149-50, 152-3, 156-65, 167-9, 171-6, 179, 182, 185-8, 190, 192, 194
surveillance · 6, 15, 58, 61, 64, 68-9, 109, 112, 187-8

**T**
technologies of domination · 6, 15-16, 19-20, 22, 24, 29, 51-2, 56, 57, 65, 67, 71, 75, 77, 80, 104, 130-1, 134, 145-6, 159, 166, 178, 185, 194
technologies of self · 6, 11, 13, 15-6, 51-3, 62, 65, 67-8, 71, 75, 77-8, 81, 102, 104, 109, 130-1, 134, 145, 150, 159, 161, 165-6, 174, 176-7, 179, 185, 187
Treasury · 8, 9, 25, 100, 107-8, 172
Treaty of Waitangi · 25

**W**
welfare · 22, 24, 26, 89-90, 93, 96-7, 99, 100-1, 103, 108-9, 112-14, 116, 120, 126, 138, 174, 189